FROM LADIES
TO WOMEN

Recent Titles in
Contributions in Women's Studies

FROM LADIES TO WOMEN

THE ORGANIZED STRUGGLE FOR WOMAN'S RIGHTS IN THE RECONSTRUCTION ERA

ISRAEL KUGLER

CONTRIBUTIONS IN WOMEN'S STUDIES, NUMBER 77

Greenwood Press
New York • Westport, Connecticut • London

Library of Congress Cataloging-in-Publication Data

Kugler, Israel, 1917-
    From ladies to women.

    (Contributions in women's studies, ISSN 0147-104X ;
no. 77)
    Bibliography: p.
    Includes index.
    1. Women's rights—United States—History—19th
century.   2. Women—Suffrage—United States—History—
19th century.   3. Women—United States—History—
19th century.   I. Title.   II. Series.
HQ1236.5.U6K84   1987   305.4'2'0973   86-25759
ISBN 0-313-25239-4 (lib. bdg. : alk. paper)

Library of Congress Catalog Card Number: 86-25759
ISBN: 0-313-25239-4
ISSN: 0147-104X

First published in 1987

Greenwood Press, Inc.
88 Post Road West, Westport, Connecticut 06881

Printed in the United States of America

The paper used in this book complies with the
Permanent Paper Standard issued by the National
Information Standards Organization (Z39.48-1984).

10   9   8   7   6   5   4   3   2   1

To My Wife Helen

A woman who did not counterpose motherhood to the pursuit of professional fulfillment and social activism; a woman who offered encouragement and willingly accepted familial rearrangements, not in the service of a man, but in the recognition of the need for greater understanding of the role of the woman's rights movement in the liberation of all humanity.

The more I advanced in the study of American society, the more I perceived that . . . equality of condition is the fundamental fact from which all others seem to be derived and the central point at which all my observations terminated. . . . The gradual development of the principle of equality is, therefore, a providential fact. It has all the chief characteristics of such a fact: it is universal, it is lasting, it constantly eludes all human interference, and all events as well as all men contribute to its progress. . . . [It is] an irresistible revolution which has advanced for centuries in spite of every obstacle.

Alexis de Tocqueville
Democracy in America

There shall never be another season of silence until women have the same rights men have on this green earth.

Susan B. Anthony

CONTENTS

PREFACE

The struggle for equality is a recurrent theme in the history of America. The country's very origin as an independent nation over 200 years ago was an outcome of a conflict between a dominant mother country and her thirteen colonies for equality of economic status under a mercantilist system. The bondage of this system was broken through political independence.

Yet the yearnings for equality did not stop there, for in the very midst of this titanic effort the poorer yeoman farmers and laborers were making their grievances known. Courageous women were articulating their concerns. The enslavement of black people amidst the rhetoric of democracy and freedom was a monstrous hypocrisy that gave birth to abolitionism and culminated in the bloodshed of the Civil War. Men and women who worked tried to redress an imbalance of power over their wages and working conditions. They formed unions and struggled to overcome the doctrine of conspiracy and the employer domination of the judicial system. Organizations now complemented the formerly isolated woman writers and orators in seeking the right to vote as part of the American fabric of freedom.

There is no end to this urge. Scarcely has one milestone been passed when another appears. Just as one segment of the population achieves a victory, another aggrieved group welds together a social movement to further the quest.

The United States of America, free of the dynasties of monarchy and entrenched economic privilege, blessed with a vast continental expanse, represented a magnificent stage for the drama of equality to be performed. Our focus is on the transformation of American ladies into women increasingly conscious of their inferior status, learning the arts of organization, experiencing the pangs of dissension within their ranks, and experimenting with political strategies. The woman's rights movement, in its various tendencies, militant and conservative, grappled with all issues affecting women, entered into relationships with other reform elements, and dared to storm the citadels of political power.

Woman's rights, as one theme recurring through the composition of American reform, was periodically subdued by other crises and intermingled with erupting social movements. Wars, depressions, child labor, chattel slavery, worker exploitation, environmentalism, consumer advocacy, public education, mental health, prison reform, racial and religious bigotry—each reached a position of dominance in the thought and action of the times relegating the woman's movement to a temporary muted position. There then would be a regrouping of forces, and the issues of woman's rights would come to the fore again. Paradoxically these social convulsions often also accentuated feminist drives.

It took a certain kind of woman to forge the organizations necessary to provide direction for woman's rights. The occasions of discrimination were manifold. They were part of daily life. The personalities had to rise above individual bitterness, avoid retreat into inactive cynicism, be ready to undergo extreme personal sacrifice, involve cadres of women, travel extensively, incur physical hardship, articulate well as speakers and writers, sense opportunities, and exhibit profound courage. They were educated and had to overcome the restrictions of the home, child rearing, and the church. These were no longer ladies, quietly occupying the assigned niche of a male-dominated society. Their movement flowered into expression in the period following the Civil War, especially in what was hailed as the dawn of a new day—Reconstruction. They were a small group of leaders, largely drawn from the middle class, but affected by the deep social and economic changes which permeated all of American society.

After the war against slavery was won, woman leaders hailed the Reconstruction Era as the setting for the establishment of equal rights for all humanity, men and women. The women had taken the places of men in industry and farming; they fabricated medical supplies and ministered to the wounded; they harbored escaped slaves and emancipated freedmen. One can imagine the depths of their bitter disappointment when mores and political pragmatism limited the franchise to men. Their reaction was profound and spurred organizational efforts in diverse directions. Women were thrown upon themselves to ponder anew their status in society. Beyond the franchise, additional considerations emerged—the right to individuality in marriage and property; the causes of prostitution; discrimination at the workplace; entry into skilled trades and professions. They were ready to challenge the privileged sanctuary of men in the church. They beat upon the portals of the major political parties and insisted on being heard.

The defeats that women suffered in the latter part of the nineteenth century were but transient losses in the inexorable struggle. The schism that had enervated them was bridged. The expansion of American industrial might brought more and more women into the workplace, the professions, and the colleges. American efforts had their counterparts in other areas of the world. Here in the United States, some woman's rights were incorporated into law in state after state. Established national labor organizations endorsed their platform. World War I demonstrated their dedication and service. The president, congress and the state legislatures adopted the Nineteenth Amendment, at long last granting women the right to vote.

The gains in occupational entry made during World War I disappeared as the world of work and power reverted back to men. The voting patterns of enfranchised women were no different from those of men. Yet, discernible trends were becoming increasingly manifest. Young college women defied the conventions of dress, grooming, and sexual behavior. Birth control and sex education as social movements sought to emerge from the closet of social convention. The societal reaction to the Great Depression brought about wide-ranging social legislation, which improved the social status of women.

World War II came on the heels of the organization of the mass-production industries. Again women played an indispensable role in war-production industries and in the armed forces. The civil rights struggles for blacks was another illustration of a powerful social movement pressing for justice. Federal antidiscrimination laws were enacted, which went beyond race to include sex. This was no accident, and it represented a radical departure from the times when women were excluded in the Fourteenth and Fifteenth amendments. Women again organized and were encouraged to push ahead with enforcement legislation by forms of affirmative action and a change in the Constitution through the Equal Rights Amendment (ERA).

The alleged dire consequences of woman suffrage predicted by its opponents right up to its passage in 1920 can be arrayed in a deadly parallel with the arguments raised by opposition to ERA. The campaign for ERA was lost. The question arises whether the *full* philosophy of feminism, which extends to a woman's control over her body in the form of the right to abortion and the gaining of full civil rights for lesbians, constitutes a repetition of the side issues that divided the woman's movement and delayed the passage of the Nineteenth Amendment.

Beyond the political battle over the Equal Rights Amendment, one cannot deny the profound social changes that have affected women. Divorce has been so liberalized legally and in practice that well over one in three marriages ends in divorce. Desertions have increased. Couples are living together without the legal or formal sanction of marriage. More and more children are being raised in single-parent families headed overwhelmingly by women. Almost all colleges have become coeducational. More and more occupations once closed to women, in heavy blue-collar trades as well as in the professions, are now open. Indeed, women are virtually in equal numbers to men in the role of indispensable breadwinners. Advertising and all the forms of mass media are increasingly frank with respect to sex. Language itself has been transformed to reflect the egalitarian women's drive. The changes are staggering, bewildering, and the reactions, even in the ranks of the women's movement, chaotic.

Additional questions have arisen, some old, some new, that rack the ranks of women. Is housework to be demeaned? Should it be compensated? Should all women be encouraged to continue working after bearing a child, leaving it to be cared for in a nursery or day-care center? Is the family a social institution of male oppression? Is the sex act a form of male aggression? Has entry of women into the professions and corporate structures been in the form of access to the towers of power or new expressions of tokenism?

There is no final conflict. The struggle for woman's rights is a continuum. Old mores die hard. They persist in a form of cultural inertia. There is no denying the fact of increased consciousness on the part of women, that the survival of the family is rooted more and more in the companionship of equals. These are the trends amidst the swirling forces of societal change.

This study, while focusing on the pioneer efforts of the woman's rights organizations in the post–Civil War period, provides a clarifying perspective on the movement in subsequent periods to the present day. We may then have a better understanding of the transformation of polite, acquiescent, and suffering ladies into women, who seek, search, and struggle for equal rights and status.

Acknowledgments

A passing reference to Susan B. Anthony being a delegate to the 1868 convention of the National Labor Union came to my attention in 1950 and caused me to embark on an investigation of this phenomenon of a middle-class leader of the woman's rights movement associating with organized labor. Over three and a half decades ago there were virtually no scholarly works devoted to the woman's rights movement, a clear reflection of the lack of social recognition and the stagnation of the movement. It is therefore a most gratifying result of the woman's aspect of the civil rights revolution not only to see a rebirth of active feminism, but also to witness the vast amount of scholarly investigation of the woman's rights movement as history and a contemporary complex of societal problems.

In the development of this study there are many who contributed. However, Professor John C. Payne, a distinguished scholar of American history at New York University, played a central role.

Special mention must be made of two women, Alma Lutz, biographer of Elizabeth Cady Stanton, who was associated with the American Historical Association, and Miriam Holden, who provided access to her private library on woman's rights. Bertram Powers, of the International Typographical Union, Local 6, provided important assistance in making available union records and documents.

The librarians of the New York Public Library, the New York Historical Society, the Brooklyn Historical Association, and the Brooklyn Public Library were most helpful. The editors at Greenwood Press were most constructive in helping me bridge the gap of scholarship and perception since the initial investigation over three decades ago.

FROM LADIES
TO WOMEN

PART ONE

SETTING THE STAGE—
THROUGH THE CIVIL WAR

American women who were conscious of their political and economic powerlessness were educated and literate. Ideologists of freedom in Europe affected these women deeply because the very act of revolution and the need for a nation of many different religious believers to exist as a viable new state provided that spark of hope for the relief of women's grievances. American woman speakers, writers, and achievers kept the message alive. Participation by women in the Revolution, the Civil War, and the abolitionist movement developed experience in organization, provided a degree of self-confidence, and created a heightened awareness. Colonial women, who were scarce and valued as coworkers and producers of children, were accorded *de facto* rights beyond those of their European sisters.

Certain patterns emerge. Every national social movement, whether it be the American Revolution, abolitionism, the Civil War, or the two world wars, called upon American women to respond and participate. They demonstrated unquestioned capability only to meet twin setbacks for the cause of woman's rights. Their own movement was relegated to a minor position. Gains that were won in entry into occupations or professions were, in large measure, lost again to men. While women were caught up in these larger social movements, blatant acts of discrimination against them spurred them more and more to rely upon their own effort.

1

PRECURSORS

IDEOLOGISTS FROM ABROAD

Beginnings of the woman's rights movement of America were rooted in the colonial setting. Men and women had come from Europe to settle in the colonies as part of a flight from religious persecution, economic harassment, and incarceration for debt and crime. Mercantile expansion carved out their escape routes and granted the merchant entrepreneurs the opportunity for fortune. In this new world the prospects of immediate extractive wealth, in the form of gold with a quick return to the mother country, vanished as impossible dreams. Reality brought forth pioneers seeking to best a wilderness. Women exercised roles that were vital for survival and tended to give them important status. Yet the colonists brought with them the folkways and mores of the old country, which came into conflict with the social and physical environment of the new world.

The belief that women were inferior to men was grounded in the Judeo-Christian tradition, which was carried to additional areas of conquest by Islam. Thus the Bible held:

Unto the woman God said, I will greatly multiply thy sorrow and thy conception; in sorrow thou shalt bring forth children; and thy desire shall be to thy husband and he shall rule over thee (Gen. 3).

In the New Testament St. Paul builds upon this belief:

For a man . . . is the image and glory of God; but the woman is the glory of the man. For man is not of the woman, but the woman of the man. Neither was the man created for the woman, but the woman for the man (I Cor. 11).

Let the woman learn in silence with all subjection. But I suffer not a woman to teach, nor to usurp authority over the man, but to be in silence (I Tim. 2).

And the Koran, the holy book of Islam: "Men are superior to women on account of the qualities in which God has given them preeminence."

As religious teachings these were articles of faith not to be subjected to rational challenge. They went beyond mere religious practice. Christian power spread throughout Europe, and this patriarchal ideology permeated all social institutions. Having been beguiled and guilty of transgression, women were characterized as weak and prone to emotion. Lacking in intelligence, they were to be silent and could not teach. In all aspects of power—political, social, and economic—women were considered inferior to men. Their role was to produce children, minister to the needs of men, and engage in household tasks.

These beliefs were institutionalized in common law. William Blackstone, whose teachings were embraced by the entire American legal profession, expressly codified this thinking in his *Commentaries on the Laws of England (1759–69)*. He simply stated the common law adage, "The husband and wife are one and that one is the husband."[1] Upon marriage, the wife lost all control over property and was subject to physical abuse. She could not sue in the courts, and if she deserted her husband out of desperation, she could be hunted and reclaimed pretty much as a runaway slave. If she sought divorce on the narrow grounds of male infidelity, her home, property, and children could be lost. Incarceration in an insane asylum could be visited upon her if she were persistent in her claims.

Religious disputation in England went beyond the separation of the Church of England from Roman Catholicism. The Protestant revolt broke the bonds of monolithic faith, and all types of sects emerged, which challenged even the teachings of Martin Luther, John Calvin, and Jan Hus. When religious groups came to America, these conflicts were planted in a frontier soil, fertilized with more freedom than the time-honored conventions of England. Different colonial administrations persecuted minority Catholics, Quakers, Jews, and such outspoken believers in religious freedom as Roger Williams and Anne Hutchinson. Mrs. Hutchinson, an herbal healer and preacher of individual salvation, defied the dictum of St. Paul and insisted upon her right to teach.[2] She was so successful in building a following that she was designated a moral leper and banished. She defied John Knox, who in his *The First Blast Against the Monstrous Regiment of Women*, published in 1558, blared, "Let women keep silence in the congregation, for it is not permitted to them to speak but to be subject as the law sayeth."[3] The unification of the colonies and their independence could only come about on the principle of separation of church and state, and this religious freedom was an important avenue for the expression of woman's rights.

The philosophy of rationalism as opposed to blind faith was ably enunciated by John Milton when he wrote: "Give me the liberty to know, to utter, and to argue freely according to conscience above all other liberties." His advocacy of easy divorce did not spare John Milton from the outspoken wrath of Mary Astell, who wrote that Milton was ready to call upon the people to rise up against a dictatorial king, but not to "cry up liberty to poor *Female Slaves* or plead for the lawfulness of Resisting a private Tyranny."[4]

Her *Some Reflections on Marriage* attacked the widely read work by Lord Halifax, *Advice to a Daughter*. Halifax freely admitted woman's subordinate position, which he claimed was a product of nature. There was nothing that could be done about the fact that men were assigned the preponderance of brainpower, qualifying them to make laws and to supervise women in performing domestic duties. As compensation, nature provided women with sensual beauty and the 'water power' of tears. Mary Astell did not challenge the lower status of women in the holy and permanent marriage bond, but she did set forth a program designed to elevate women. These prescriptions included improved training and schooling for both men and women, so that more intelligent choices could be made in marriage. Men had to respect woman's intellectuality and capability and to use male authority in a consultative fashion rather than in a dictatorial and unilateral manner.

Daniel Defoe's *Essay on Projects*, which was assimilated by Benjamin Franklin, supported the education of women to remove their ignorance and superficiality. Less forthright commentary on women came from the more popular pens of satirist Jonathan Swift and essayist Joseph Addison.[5]

The bombshell that exploded with the most impact on the American scene was Mary Wollstonecraft's *Vindication of the Rights of Women*, published in the United States in 1794. Throughout the entire history of the woman's rights movement this book remained a source of inspiration not only to the leaders of the agitation but also to many educated women in general. Despite the fact that she firmly defended the marriage institution in the book, she was smeared with the radical teachings of the man she married after her book appeared, William Godwin.[6]

Mary Wollstonecraft denied the innate inferiority of women. She emphasized the importance of the environment and held that women's inferior state was a result of inequality of opportunity. She believed that if women had equal education, much of the behavior of subservient quiescence would disappear. Inequality of the sexes in marriage tended to distort the relationship into one of an unstable half-slave and half-free character. Women did not wish to lord it over men; they wanted fulfillment, respect, self-discipline, and control over their own person. Since men could not deny that women had reasoning power, why shouldn't it be exercised? Marriage was meant to be a constructive partnership between equals with standards of ethics and morals applying to both husband and wife.

Marriage based upon economic convenience and satisfaction of the sex urge was little better than prostitution. Fidelity had to be cultivated out of mutual respect. The double standard where men could be free to practice adultery while women were expected to remain chaste and pure was utterly reprehensible to Mary Wollstonecraft. She recognized that the sound basis for a wholesome marriage must be built in childhood. She therefore advocated a public coeducational system of instruction that would militate against the baleful influences of rank, class, and sex dominance.

Her book went into many editions and later was published serially in *Revolution*, the weekly newspaper put out by Susan B. Anthony and Elizabeth Cady Stanton. There is no question but that Mary Wollstonecraft's teachings have represented an important ideological base for the woman's rights movement to the present day.

THE EXPRESSION IN AMERICA

Benjamin Franklin in 1746 wrote *Reflections on Courtship and Marriage*, which rejected marriage based upon sudden passion or economic benefit.[7] He also held that woman's alleged inferiority was imposed by tradition and not by nature. Franklin believed that women were not inferior to men in body or mind, yet inconsistently, he also felt that nature assigned positions of leadership to males.

The Pennsylvania Gazette, supported by Franklin and edited by the revolutionary pamphleteer, Thomas Paine, published three significant essays by Paine commenting on the status of women. In *Reflections on Unhappy Marriages* he rejected marriages based purely on lust, and he characterized those based upon money or economic convenience, as "downright prostitution."[8]

In *Cupid and Hymen* Paine used an allegory against marriages based upon money or power.[9] In the last of the trio of pieces, written in 1775, *Letter on the Female Sex*, Paine described the universal oppression of women and demanded their equality.[10] The philosophy of natural rights, for Paine, held that God created all human beings equal and that He intended that each individual would be able to achieve the full realization of every potentiality.

The thread of woman's rights agitation continued through individual and group actions that served as examples of the capabilities of women. Margaret Brent served as an attorney and was named by Governor Calvert as his executor.[11] This made her eligible to succeed him in the attorneyship of Baltimore. On the grounds of being a property owner as well as the attorney for Baltimore, she sought the right to vote in the House of Burgesses (legislature). When she was denied representation and the franchise, she publicly denounced every act of the legislature as illegal.

Eliza Wilkinson of South Carolina openly expressed her humiliation:

I won't have it thought, that because we are the weaker sex as to *bodily*...we are incapable of nothing more than minding the dairy, visiting the poultry-house, and all such domestic concerns: our thoughts can soar aloft, we can form conceptions of things of a higher nature; and have as just a sense of humor, glory and great actions, as these "Lords of Creation". What contemptible *earth worms* these authors make us! They won't even allow us our liberty of thoughts, and that is what I want.[12]

As the gathering storm of the American Revolution developed, there were no express prohibitions of occupations available to women. They took over businesses from their fathers and husbands. Beyond running farms, they were shopkeepers, teachers, blacksmiths, hunters, lawyers, innkeepers, silversmiths, tinworkers, shoemakers, shipwrights, tanners, gunsmiths, barbers, and butchers. Most babies were delivered by women. In fact, most doctors up to the Revolution were women. Records indicate that eleven women ran printing presses and ten printers' widows published newspapers.[13]

During the Revolution itself the women didn't hide in privileged sanctuaries. They were often in the front lines of the irregular forces. They were nurses and followers of their husbands into the fray loading muskets and cannon, foraging for and cooking food. Some of them, with uncommon boldness, acted as spies. Behind the lines they ran farms, raised money, and made medical supplies. Wartime profiteering met their organized wrath.

Representing the more educated women, Abigail Adams, in correspondence with her husband, articulated the aspirations of women while the Declaration of Independence was contemplated. She wrote,

I long to hear you have declared an independency, and, by the way, in the new code of laws which I suppose it will be necessary for you to make, I desire you would remember the ladies and be more generous and favorable to them than your ancestors. Do not put such unlimited power into the hands of husbands. Remember, all men would be tyrants if they could. If particular care and attention are not paid to the ladies, we are determined to foment a rebellion and will not hold ourselves bound to obey any law in which we have no voice nor representation.[14]

John Adams, while agreeing to the importance of educating women, replied that domination of women by men was more form than substance and went on to write, "We are obliged to go fair and softly, and, in practice, you know we are the subjects. We have only the name of masters, and rather than give up this, which would completely subject us to the despotism of the petticoat, I hope General Washington and all our brave heroes would fight."[15]

In her final reposte to John Adams, Abigail wrote, "I cannot say that I think you are very generous to the ladies, for whilst you are proclaiming peace and goodwill to men, emancipating all nations, you insist upon retaining an absolute power over wives."

Clearly comparing herself to Lysistrata, she wrote, "not withstanding all your wise laws and maxims, we have it in our power, not only to free ourselves, but to subdue our master and without violence, throw both your natural and legal authority at your feet."[16]

Out of sheer necessity, the Revolution propelled women into the political and social birth pangs of the new nation. However, the consolidation of the country under the Constitution, the growth of the economy, and westward expansion enabled the heritage of traditional sex roles to mute the voice of woman's rights.

A new social movement arose within which women sought increased expression—abolitionism. Aware of their own inferior political status, the educated women of the North and South expressed their outrage at the political hypocrisy of the Constitution, the Bill of Rights, and the Declaration of Independence parading as the ideology of a free America while the institution of chattel slavery existed. Economically the merchants and manufacturers of the North resented the expansion of slavery into the western territories as inhibiting the expansion of industry and trade. This provided a friendly climate to the agitators against slavery in the Middle and New England states.

Radical utopians, who questioned the bases of the dominant society of Europe, hoped to find in the relatively free society of America with its abundance of land and lack of a closed hereditary stratification, a receptive atmosphere for their ideas and the establishment of communities that could act as models for a just society. Charles Fourier, Etienne Cabet, and Robert Owen had their followers on the American lecture circuit. Their ideas often embraced antislavery and woman's rights. Among the lecturers was Frances Wright, closely associated with Robert Owen and his son Robert Dale Owen. To her significant following she personified the possibility of woman as articulate and intelligent public speaker. Fanny, as her enemies called her, met her share of ridicule and vegetable missiles of resistance. Her association with the Marquis de Lafayette, Thomas Jefferson, and James Madison, however, established her as a respected, if not respectable, personality in the public mind. Some years later, Ernestine Rose took her place on the lecture platform. Mrs. Rose shed her Orthodox Jewish background of Poland and married a wealthy businessman from London who was attuned to her avant-garde ideas of abolitionism and woman's rights. She participated in developing the woman's rights organizations right through the period following the Civil War. A splendid orator, she attracted large audiences to her lectures in various cities.

The growing abolitionist movement found dramatic support in the persons of Sarah and Angelina Grimké, who had freed the slaves on their southern plantation and joined the forces of abolitionism and woman's rights in the North. The sterling antislavery orator, Frederick Douglass, himself a former slave, was very active on behalf of woman's rights.

He has denied her the facilities for obtaining a thorough education, all colleges being closed against her.

He allows her in church, as well as state, but a subordinate position...

He has created a false public sentiment by giving to the world a different code of morals for men and women...

He has usurped the prerogative of Jehovah himself, claiming it as his right to assign for her a sphere of action, when that belongs to her conscience and to her God.

He has endeavoured, in every way that he could, to destroy her confidence in her own powers, to lessen her self-respect, and to make her willing to lead a dependent and abject life.

Now, in view of this entire disfranchisement of one half the people of this country, their social and religious degradation; in view of the unjust laws above mentioned, and because women do feel themselves aggrieved, oppressed, and fraudulently deprived of their most sacred right, we insist that they have immediate admission to all the rights and privileges which belong to them as citizens of the United States.

We shall employ agents, circulate tracts, petition to the State and National legislatures, and endeavour to enlist the pulpit and press in our behalf. We hope this Convention will be followed by a series of Conventions embracing every part of the country.[22]

Appropriate resolutions were adopted, which positively affirmed the determination to redress these grievances against men. Resolution 9 on suffrage barely passed. It was opposed by Henry Stanton, and Lucretia Mott had serious misgivings about this plank. Two basic concepts were affirmed, which had serious overtones for the future of the woman's rights movement: The male was the oppressor, and women must emancipate themselves.[23]

Two weeks later the convention met again in Rochester, and the declaration was reaffirmed. Significantly, Frederick Douglass was an enthusiastic delegate to that gathering.

In 1852, at a joint convention of the Sons and Daughters of Temperance held in Albany, where "ladies are invited to listen, not to take part in the proceedings," Susan B. Anthony threw the convention into turmoil when she refused to heed this restriction. This was quite in the spirit of Anne Hutchinson, who had expressed a similar defiance 200 years earlier. In protest, a Woman's New York Temperance Society was organized with Elizabeth Cady Stanton as president and Susan B. Anthony as secretary.[24] Thus began an association that lasted for decades in the woman's rights movement.

With the exception of 1857, woman's rights conventions were held annually from 1850 to 1860. During this period signal successes were scored. Some states granted women rights to property and the custody of their children. Increasing numbers of women were admitted to the professions of law and medicine.

The outbreak of the Civil War caused the suspension of the woman's rights movement. Since most of the woman's righters were abolitionists, they threw themselves into the Union's efforts at victory with all the enthusiasm they could command. They were active as nurses with the Sanitary Commission in hospital ships, relief camps, soldiers' lodges, and medical depots. They participated in the Loyal League organizing public sentiment for the Union cause. They urged the Emancipation Proclamation and hailed it after it was established. In all this they retained the vision that they were part of a vast movement for human rights. They looked forward to that day when they would join hands with the freedmen in universal suffrage.

The woman's rights movement, which began as isolated efforts of individuals, took organized form as a result of severe inequities within a movement to raise the blacks to a level of equality with whites. American women had demonstrated in action from colonial times on that they were capable of the most physically trying work in peace and war. They dramatized their organizational abilities in the monumental effort to heal the wounded and sick in that most bloody of American conflicts, the Civil War. They had met and formulated a basic document of principles including suffrage which was to be translated into organization and political action, nationwide.

Lucretia Mott, an older Quaker, was the inspiration. Lucy Stone had already made her mark by insisting that she had an equal right with her husband to a name in marriage, and so she was to be known as Mrs. Lucy Stone married to Henry Blackwell. Elizabeth Cady Stanton, married and the mother of seven children, became the indefatigable writer, agitator, and vanguard feminist. Susan B. Anthony gave up all desire for married life and devoted her entire adult existence with singularity of purpose, bordering on fanaticism, toward organizing for woman's rights. There were many more in this galaxy of leaders in the movement, but these were the bright stars that guided the minions of courageous and forthright women, sometimes in discouraging defeat, loneliness, even in penury; sometimes against each other. The permanent basis for the campaigns, the strategies, the tactics to secure the rights of women was established.

2

CHANGES IN WOMAN'S STATUS

COLONIAL TIMES

The first women in America were, of course, Indians. Their position in tribal society varied. Generally, where the community was engaged in hunting and fishing, the male was dominant. This was modified in the pastoral tribes and changed even more in the tribes with least mobility, those engaged in agriculture. These differing tribal social relations were not pure, but combinations that carried over older traditions. Some tribes were matriarchal. In others governance required consultation between the two gender groups.

The Indians were unassimilable into colonial society as slaves or indentured servants. Expansion pushed them out of their lands, and the emerging economy and polity became the province of the white colonists—peacefully by guile and trade or by force if need be.

Permanent settlements required families as economic units of society. Mating and the legitimization of marriage extended the necessary workforce with women and children. The scarcity of breeders and workers in an economy where labor was already in short supply placed a high value upon women as commodities. Women "voluntarily" left Europe by the "push" of poverty and imprisonment. Others were "shanghaied" and brought over forcibly. The ship owners would hold auctions at debarkation and sell the women to men who would pay their passage. The more fortunate entered into marriage relationships, which grew to have an admixture of love. Others were indentured for a given period of time, often to harsh taskmasters.[1]

A farmer in Illinois frankly articulated the male attitude when he remarked, "I reckon women are like some horses and oxen, the biggest can do the most work, and that's what I want one for."[2] To the asset of work must be added fecundity in producing additional workers—children.

Colonial women were partners in the economic work unit—the family.

Not only did they work in the fields beside men, but they were also engaged in those labors that knew no season—weaving, sewing, making shoes, quilting, carpentry, cooking, baking, preserving, tanning, candle making, washing, dyeing, bearing and rearing children, and tending livestock.

The scarcity of labor created a work ethic given institutional support by the clergy. Idleness was sinfulness. Public workhouses were settings for indigent women and children. The high value placed upon women tended to moderate the harshness of English common law, and women were accorded certain property rights and were given limited access to the courts. This was particularly true for single women and widows. Male primogeniture was the rule, but in the absence of male heirs, women could inherit estates.

Isolated farms soon gave way to villages and towns, which dotted the natural harbors and were also founded inland within fifty miles of the seaboard. The autarchic dependence of the predominantly farm population on the crafts of the individual farmhouse gave way to the growing market and money economy. Enterprising merchants would visit the farmhouses and supply raw materials in what was called a "putting out" system. Above and beyond the needed farm chores, women, children, and the elderly would fabricate various products that were then paid for and taken to the market by this new breed of entrepreneurs. Even after the factory system was entrenched, "putting out" continued with the married women working at home. It was an indelible mark of shame to both the husband and wife for a married woman to labor outside the household. Soon, locations had their production "putting out" specialties—pottery, garments, shoes, and knit goods. These products then went into the village and town general stores or were sold by itinerant peddlers.

The shackles of mercantilism were broken in 1789, when Samuel Slater, by stealth, brought over in his head the plans for the Arkwright spinning machinery. More and more openly, the industrial process was replacing laborious hand labor. The invention of the cotton gin in 1793 vastly expanded the supply of raw cotton for the manufacture of thread and textiles in New England. The South became the supplier of raw materials, not for Great Britain so much as for the industrializing North. The social institution that was the basis for this role was chattel slavery.

To be sure, slavery had already existed for over a hundred years, but "King Cotton" satisfied the thirst for cotton textiles generated by a growing American and European market. Black women who were brought in the slave trade from Africa were prized in much the same way as the original white women—as workers and breeders. Marriage to whites was out of the question for black women, but they were more valued than black men as potential and actual suppliers of labor. White plantation owners did not hesitate to mate forcibly with black women, and the resulting mulatto children were favored as house servants. The upper class of plantation wives swallowed their pride over the immorality of their husbands and relied upon the black women as midwives, wet nurses, cooks, maids, and laundresses.

The black women weren't always docile. They joined their black men in the slave revolts and left when they could on the Underground Railway. The auction block broke up the black families, and this was the historic beginning of the black family headed by a woman. In some of the southern factories slaveowners hired out their slaves to work the machines. The conditions were beyond description and fed the resentment of blacks toward the institution of slavery. During the Civil War some of them spied for the Union forces and greeted the Emancipation Proclamation. Harriet Tubman and Sojourner Truth were but two black women of many who had the organizational, agitational, and oratorical skills to stir the hearts of women, black and white.

In the North, black women found employment largely as domestic servants catering to the needs of a growing class of wealthy women married to merchants, ship owners, manufacturers, and bankers. A few of these white women befriended their black servants and taught them how to read and write. One woman of note, Phyllis Wheatley, became an accomplished poet. With few exceptions, like Frances Ellen Watkins Harper who joined the leadership ranks of the abolitionist and woman's rights movements, the black women played no significant political role.

AFTER THE REVOLUTION

The massive effort that severed the ties of Great Britain to America involved defiance, guerrilla warfare, a public Declaration of Independence, military campaigns, struggles to transform a collection of thirteen ex-colonies into a united nation under the Constitution, and accommodation of disparate elements under the Bill of Rights. It was more than a political change, for it opened up America to independent economic development, which profoundly affected the position of women in society.

The Northwest Ordinance of 1787 made available tracts of public lands. Inland waterways and turnpikes were the pathways of internal migration, which penetrated the area beyond the Appalachian range. At first the wives and children remained behind on the eastern seaboard working at home as carders of wool and cotton as well as in other "putting out" occupations. When the barest structures were completed in the frontier homesteads, the women and children came to complete the hard-laboring family work forces. This westward movement served to stimulate the growth of a factory system for ready-made goods that could satisfy a growing national market. At first the factory towns sprang up along the rapids and falls of New England rivers. The subsequent use of steam to power the machinery allowed flexibility in location, and the mills spread throughout the Middle Atlantic states and into portions of the South.

While the family farm was still predominant and located at some distance from factory towns, the basic factory work force was drawn from these farms in the persons of native-born young women aged from eleven to sixteen. They were considered too frail for the heavy farm chores and could be saved from a life of idleness and temptation by useful labor in the mills. Farms needed cash for goods and could no longer rely on barter or self-sufficiency. Cash was also needed for seed and machinery for planting and harvesting crops. Farmers invested to expand production of agricultural raw materials and food. Farm indebtedness and the desire for cloth and thread in the national market were the compelling forces that encouraged farmers' daughters to go into the mills, leaving behind the wives, very young children, and elderly to work with the farmers and continue with the "putting out" system.

If the farm parents could be assured that the mills would be havens of safety for their daughters from immorality with adequate provisions for education, food, and shelter, they would agree to these new arrangements. The sons had other options. They could remain and inherit the farm, or they could be apprenticed to learn a skilled trade, an avenue that was barred to women.

The young women were attracted by the prospects of escape from the boredom of the isolated farm and had the choice of returning home when they reached a marriageable age. Indeed, should a factory woman become unhappy with mill work, she could always return to the farm. The only possible competing option was teaching school to the nation's growing number of children. Factory work proved more attractive because of higher pay, companionship, and greater independence. The money could be used to amass a dowry or to finance further education, usually for the brothers.

The factory system was a de-skilling process that removed the pride of workmanship associated with fashioning the entire product. It also eased the entry of women into work as job replacements of men who required higher remuneration as breadwinners for urban families. Indeed, the women themselves placed little value on their labor because they had the alternative of returning home. The mechanization lent itself to the destructively competitive piece-work system with the setting of ever-higher standards of quantitative performance.

Francis Cabot Lowell of Waltham's Boston Manufacturing Company was the inventor of the factory community combining work, room and board, school, and church. He had journeyed to Great Britain and was impressed with the operation of the mills in New Lanark, Scotland, run by the utopian socialist Robert Owen. In a number of areas of the United States communal colonies were set up as examples for the beneficent restructuring of society. This idealistic thinking attempted to redirect the business enterprise of weaving of textiles and the manufacture of thread. And so along the Merrimac River, Lowell established his mill community and named it after himself. Visitors who came from Europe were entranced by the landscaping, the literary output, and the seemingly well-run factories.

The truth soon emerged: sleeping rooms were overcrowded, work supervision was rigid, wage cuts were often arbitrary, and "speed-up" on the increase. The original benevolent owners soon became absentees with hired overseers in direct charge of assuring profits from the operations. The regimentation began with the sound of the bell before sunrise. Work continued until after dark by the light of sooty oil lamps. The windows were nailed shut to maintain humidity for the threads. Conversation and singing were frowned upon with heavy punishments for transgressors. Dismissal could be instantaneous with wages withheld for those who left before the expiration of the contract year. Those who departed did not receive their certificates of good conduct, and if they were the agitators who led turnouts, as the strikes were called, they were subjected to the blacklist.

Sarah Bagley, who became a woman's rights leader and exponent of labor reform, was also a talented journalist whose career began as a factory worker in Lowell writing for the *Lowell Offering*, the mill newspaper.[3] When she attempted to describe some deplorable conditions, she was fired, thus revealing the domination of the publication by management. Two newspapers, *The Factory Girl* and *The Voice of Industry*, were founded to articulate the needs of women in industry and agitate for the ten-hour day. Sarah Bagley, Huldah Stone, and Mehitabel Eastman were the outstanding woman writers and agitators, allied with labor reformers Matthew Carey and George Henry Evans.

Evans, in a decided departure from the male worker antagonism to women in industry, wrote that while it was true that women may lower men's wages and swell the labor force and thus cause unemployment, he averred, "But such an assignment ought not to weigh as a feather in the balance. If we are to suffer, let us suffer equally and together."[4]

The Voice of Industry, edited by women, printed contributions from poets James Russell Lowell and John Greenleaf Whittier. The "Female Department" column proclaimed objectives well beyond narrow labor reform, embracing by name "woman's rights" social, moral, and religious concerns affecting women.

In seeking to build up the circulation of this lively paper, which commented forcefully on such topics as slavery, Irish famine relief, capital punishment, temperance, and Fourierist utopianism, Huldah Stone reacted to a man expressing horror at a woman soliciting subscriptions to *The Voice of Industry* as being "out of place."

From my very soul I *pity* such a man...I suppose he is one of those who would wish to have "*the woman*" a domestic animal, that is knowing just enough to cook his victuals, mend his feetings, rock the cradle and keep the house in order; and if she wished for any further information, why she must ask her Lord and Master! An *equal* she must not be.[5]

Sarah Bagley demonstrated her organizing ability when in 1845 she mobilized over 400 women in the Lowell Female Reform Association in a successful campaign to oust a Lowell legislator who was indifferent to the pleas of women workers.

With the devastating potato famine in Ireland in the 1840s, waves of Irish men and women came to the United States. The depression in the previous decade drove many native-born American women out of the factories back to the farms, school teaching, and nursing. The mechanization of the factories made it possible for the impoverished, desperate, and illiterate Irish women to get jobs in the mills. Coming from rural poverty of the worst kind, the Irish were looked upon as pariahs.

This early history of women in industry may then be described as a deep-seated social change which not only brought woman's work out of the home into the factory, but from an economic point of view, replaced unpaid work for direct home consumption with paid labor for manufactured commodities for sale. This transformation widened the range of possible employment and destroyed what was the traditional monopoly of skilled women's work. Whatever individuality their work had possessed at home was destroyed in the process of manufacturing the standardized product.[6]

This fundamental alteration of the position of woman as worker was characterized by frequent changes in employment and places of work, long hours, low wages, unsanitary conditions, overwork together with the lack of skill, training and interest on the part of women in their work. The growth of the factory system, now augmented by the development of the sewing machine, cast women in the roles of underbidders, strikebreakers, and underminers of the male responsibility of the breadwinning head of the family.[7] Men and women shared the ideal of married women staying at home, raising children, and performing household tasks, but the poor, single, and widowed women did not have this choice. The frustration and embitterment of workingmen facing the displacement of human labor by machines, especially in times of industrial depression, made the men resent the growing number of women workers.

The impact on the public was felt as early as 1829 when the *Boston Courier* claimed, "powerful necessity is rapidly breaking down ancient barriers, and woman is fast encroaching, if the assumption of a right be deemed an encroachment upon the exclusive dominion of man."[8]

Men, in efforts to maintain their social status, used the apprenticeship system to train themselves and their sons in the intricacies of the skilled trades. Even when work became mechanized, men jealously guarded their prerogatives and grudgingly and rigidly relegated the simpler tasks to women. Until low wages threatened to undermine male living standards and women could not be barred from employment, men were not particularly concerned that women were paid less for doing similar work.

WOMEN IN TRADE UNIONS

Early unionism among women in the United States may be roughly divided into a formative period between 1825 and 1840, a labor reform era from 1840 to 1860, and a time when the affiliation of women to the male-dominated unions developed from 1860 to 1880.[9]

In the first period the native American daughters of the farmers of New England and the Middle Atlantic states were actively organizing in the cotton textile mills. By 1836 there were 2,500 members of the Factory Girls Association, primarily in New England. They publicly declared, "As our fathers resisted unto blood the lordly avarice of the British ministry, so we, their daughters, never will wear the yoke which has been prepared for us." The young women marched in street parades with placards carrying such slogans as "Liberty for the daughters of the American Revolution."[10]

The sewing trades also organized fairly early. Of a strike these women led in 1835, a newspaper commented, "The late strike and grand public march of the female operatives exhibit the Yankee sex in a new and unexpected light. By and by the governor may have to call out the militia to prevent a gynocracy."[11]

A national industrial congress of male unions held in 1847 invited women to participate. Several women from daughter chapters of the New England Labor Reform Association attended in a period when "even the most advanced reformers were refusing women a part in their deliberations, hooting them off the platform, forcing them to listen to meetings behind screens."[12]

This example of cooperation between men and women in the labor movement was exceptional. The general position remained distrust, hostility, and a desire to exclude women from the male-dominated trades. In 1854 the journeymen printers of the *Philadelphia Daily Register* walked off the job because the publisher employed two women as typesetters. In Ohio men working on *The Lily*, a *women's* magazine, refused to work with a female employee. The men were fired, and four women were hired in their places. Thereafter any newly employed male workers labored in harmony with the women.[13]

In the two decades before the Civil War the character of the female industrial labor force had changed. The native-born white women were increasingly replaced by immigrants—predominantly Irish. Famine, war, and political persecution drove them from Europe. The original women workers returned to the farms to marry; went West in increasing numbers, lured by the added attraction of the discovery of gold; became missionaries; entered schoolteaching; or found employment in retail stores. Their experience in industry yielded a small group of women who became skilled lecturers and organizers in various reform movements—woman's rights, temperance, abolitionism, and labor reform.

The immigrant women workers found the mills and factories to be sweat-shops of the most unsanitary character with wages just above the starvation level. Foremen did not hesitate to engage in sexual harassment. Boarding-houses were now replaced by factory-owned tenements. To avoid eviction, the entire family was compelled to work. Often the wages were paid in company-issued scrip, redeemable only in company stores at high prices. The European tradition of a closed society, as well as language barriers, militated against widespread labor organization. Unions of men were weak and not inclined to organize women. While woman labor unions were shortlived, they were frequent enough in their appearance to provide testimony to the courage and determination the women displayed in the face of blacklisting and other terror tactics employed by factory and mill owners. The modest improvement in some of the wages and working conditions was in great measure the result of the efforts of woman labor reformers.

These labor reform organizations were mainly educational and humanitarian in character. The leaders were native American women, literate and articulate, who led campaigns in the cotton mill centers for shorter hours and protective social legislation. Their tactics included investigation, petition, lobbying, and political action.[14]

During the Civil War and its immediate aftermath, there were thirty national unions organized, but only two admitted women to membership. Organizing efforts among women workers included printers, cigar makers, tailoresses, seamstresses, umbrella sewers, cap makers, textile workers, burnishers, laundresses, and shoe workers.[15]

In printing, the publishers were quick to see that women could be employed at low wages and as strikebreakers. The device used was a training school to teach women the printing craft with promise of employment as strike replacements. Thus in 1864, the Western Publishers Association organized a Typographical Female Seminary in Chicago. There were facilities for forty women to learn how to set type.[16] Within four years the typographical union recognized the threat that unorganized woman printers represented and helped women organize unions within the national organization.

In an interesting turnabout, the woman burnishers union of Brooklyn in 1868 vigorously protested the actions of men attempting to work at lower wages than the union women had demanded.[17]

A memorable union led by Kate Mullaney was organized in Troy, New York, of women laundry workers. The word "laundry" included the manufacture and starching of collars and cuffs as well as the fabrication of shirts and waists. The male unionists of Troy, employed as iron molders in foundries and as bricklayers, were very supportive of the efforts of the women unionists. In 1866 the women's group donated $1,000 to the striking molders. Two years later it contributed $500 to the bricklayers. In 1869 it was a case of reversal of roles. The women went out on strike, and the molders granted the women the sum of $500 weekly. Despite these union solidarity efforts, the strike failed and the union was crushed. The introduction of disposable paper collars and cuffs proved too much of a blow.[18]

The other outstanding example of woman unionism was among the shoe workers—the Daughters of St. Crispin. The Daughters were organized in all the urban shoe manufacturing centers and worked in harmony with the men in the Knights of St. Crispin.[19] The women's union lasted until 1873 when the severe depression wiped it out amidst mounting unemployment.

The Civil War with its gargantuan appetite for goods expanded employment opportunities for women, and their unionization proved to be less and less of a novelty. Women, especially young unmarried women and widows, were now a permanent part of the labor force. Some of the more far-sighted male trade unionists recognized that women would remain a threat to men until they were organized and received equal pay for equal work.

UPPER- AND MIDDLE-CLASS WOMEN

The bulk of literate women who had a significant degree of education were members of the middle and upper social classes. Despite their seminary education, they were trained and constrained to look forward to marriage and the establishment of a home based upon providing comfort and pleasure to their husband and children. Indeed this ideal permeated all society, but working-class women and the poor were unable to realize it for themselves. As children and as single young women they had to go to work. It was a mark of shame for a married woman to work outside the home.

Upper- and middle-class children were in private schools, and young women were discouraged from working. Whatever rudiments of science they had learned were applied to tasks at home—planning menus, making fancy embroidery and needlework, and ministering to the sick. They had household servants, usually white immigrant or native black women, who did the cooking, cleaning, laundering, and the rearing of the young. There was intervisitation among the women engaging in idle chatter about fashion, vacationing, and the stories in the various proper ladies' magazines. The men, as movers and shakers, would retreat into the drawing rooms to smoke cigars, discuss politics, make business deals, and discourse about sports. Women were to be demure and docile; to put off coarseness with the silence and sweetness of exemplary behavior—the "belle-ideal," as one woman historian described them.[20]

Into the homes of these women came periodicals and semireligious tracts—*Ladies' Wreath, Godey's Lady's Book, The Ladies' Pearl and Literary Gleaner,* and *The Young Ladies' Oasis.* When Amelia Bloomer, for reasons of mobility and health, urged the discard of hoopskirts in favor of long pantaloons gathered at the cuff, the propagandists for "true woman-hood" warned that bloomers were "only one of the many manifestations of that wild spirit of socialism and agrarian radicalism which is at present so rife in our land." To this advice offered by a "professor" in this polite publication of 1852, the young lady avers, "If this dress has any connexion with Fourierism or socialism, or fanaticism in any shape whatever, I have no disposition to wear it at all.... no true woman would so far compromise her delicacy as to espouse, however unwittingly, such a cause."

In response to the manifesto of Seneca Falls on woman's rights in 1848, there appeared this bit of instruction:

What Are The Rights of Women?

The right to love whom others scorn,
The right to comfort and to mourn,
The right to shed new joy on earth,
The right to feel the soul's high worth, ...
Such women's rights, and God will bless
And crown their champions with success.[21]

Sarah Josepha Hale, the editor of *Godey's Lady's Book* for many years, occasionally criticized the denial of woman's right to property, but for the most part, *Godey's* would rely on Paris fashions, advice on fresh air and exercise, and pretty stories to maintain its circulation. As one historian of woman's rights put it, "She could no more afford to endorse such women as Susan B. Anthony than the editor of a modern woman's magazine could afford to join a Communist demonstration."[22]

Somewhat more intellectual was a polite woman's press club, Sorosis. It was organized as a result of the exclusion of a woman journalist, Jennie C. Croly, who wrote under the name Jennie June, from a banquet given by the New York Press Club for Charles Dickens.[23] This snub of a woman paralleled the exclusion of woman delegates from the 1840 world antislavery convention in London.

Divorce and marital infidelity never appeared in the pages of books, pamphlets, and periodicals dedicated to "true womanhood." Yet the double standard of morality was very evident. Bishop Matthew Simpson of the Methodist Episcopal Church in 1866 bitterly complained that there were as many prostitutes in New York City as Methodists, placing the number at 20,000.[24] In 1858 Dr. William Sanger estimated that there were as many as 2,000 in New York City jails, victims of such low wages and exploitation as to find the "oldest profession" more lucrative. Sanger estimated that a prostitute had no more than four years of life left after turning to this activity. Syphillis and illegitimacy were widespread. Children of these women had an infant mortality four times the average.[25] The "red light" districts were well protected by the police and operating gangs to ensure anonymity for the men. There is no question but that these conditions were repeated in every large city in America.[26]

The American city was still a walking city with little social residential segregation. Zoning ordinances and exclusive neighborhoods developed later. Poverty and crime existed everywhere, even near the homes of the wealthy. The more educated and socially sensitive women, some of whom had gained organizational experience in the early boardinghouse days of the New England mills, were a distinct minority but became active and broke through the confines of homebound gentility.

They attended annual meetings devoted to prison reform, temperance, woman's rights, mental illness, abolitionism, and factory exploitation. They made up the lecture audiences of Fanny Wright, Ernestine Rose, William Lloyd Garrison, Henry Ward Beecher, Robert Dale Owen, and Wendell Phillips. Networks of consultation took shape as a multitude of women's clubs. It amounted to a rebellion against the ideal of empty idleness for women, which dictated that the less a woman had to do, the higher her social status.

The general emphasis of these clubs was to foster publicity about social conditions. The means employed were firsthand investigations. It was hoped that the powers-that-be in government, business, and industry would correct the most evident terrible situations. Factory owners would be convinced to shorten hours, clean up the workplace, and offer decent compensation. Prisons were to avoid overcrowding, provide good food, and emphasize rehabilitation and training. Store owners were to provide high stools permitting sales clerks to sit instead of standing during the fourteen-hour workday. There was little effort in these associations to organize women into unions or to challenge the dominant political setup by securing voting rights for women. They did offer testimony before legislative bodies, organize petition drives, and lobby in legislative halls. The women got to know one another and became more conscious of their abilities. As one feminist historian put it, "Woman's voluntary associations arose in combined response to personal needs and social demands in growing cities. Through organization, upper and middle class women confronted and evaluated their lives. They created a vibrant feminist ideology, which in turn sparked the demand for woman's rights."[27] These efforts of women gave the lie to the stereotype of women as having no intellect or organizing ability. It flew in the face of the allegations by male professors of anatomy and physiology who found biological structural "evidence" of women having smaller brains, possessing weakness in reasoning power but strength in areas governing emotional propensities.

Above and beyond all causes, abolitionism rivetted the attention of women leaders in the pre–Civil War period. It was the freedom doctrine of a gathering storm, a social movement supported by prominent and respectable ministers, which swept into its ranks the militant and outspoken women.

While submerged in the abolitionist cause, they kept an eye on the miserable conditions of poor women. They hailed every advance of women into the professions. They greeted legislative victories that gave women property rights and the power to vote in school and tax elections. They took ample note of the women of the Far West being granted complete suffrage in a few states and territories—a reflection of the enhanced value of women under conditions of their scarcity and indispensable function.

THE CIVIL WAR

When war broke out, driving men to the front, women replaced them in stores and office work. They were also extensively employed making uniforms and successfully resisted the efforts of private contractors to depress their wages while huge profits were reaped on government contracts. The spread of the public school system, especially in the elementary grades, was based upon an increased need for minimal literacy and arithmetic skills. Women, many with barely an elementary education, made schoolteaching the low-paid female profession.

Wartime inflation spurred white workers in northern cities to organize and strike for higher wages. Employers didn't hesitate to employ blacks as strikebreakers. The whites, many of them of Irish immigrant extraction, were at the bottom of the social ladder, but felt that color elevated them above blacks. The whites feared that the war would engender a migration of blacks to the North, which would threaten their jobs and wages.

In March 1863 Congress enacted the Enrollment and Conscription Act. This law provided that a draftee could purchase a substitute for $300. This piece of class legislation infuriated poor whites, and the scapegoats at which their fury was directed were the blacks. Poor immigrant Irish led massive riots against this law. A black orphan asylum in New York City was burned to the ground. The riots ended only when police were reenforced by soldiers, sailors, and marines. Twelve hundred people had been killed and $2 million worth of property was destroyed. New York City remained under military occupation for a month when the draft was resumed.[28]

In the early days of the Civil War the military brilliance of the Southern leadership caused so many Union casualties that disaffection set in. Northern Democrats, dubbed Copperheads, led by Representative Clement L. Vallandingham of Ohio, found ready support. To heighten the tension, irresponsible journalists publicized stories of blacks raping white women and abolitionists advocating miscegenation.

These events were indelibly printed on the minds of the woman's righters, who had now developed total commitment to the Union cause. With increasing casualties, the women threw themselves into the war effort. They followed Clara Barton into nursing while Dorothea Dix battled the inefficiency of the medical bureaucracy. The Sanitary Commission, largely organized and staffed by women, included 7,000 local societies. They raised and spent $50 million. Aside from being involved in strategy and actual combat, they recruited and trained nurses, made bandages, provided medicines, and distributed diet supplements to combat scurvy. They campaigned for better sanitary conditions in the hospitals, ships, and on the field of battle. They staffed the hospital ships, relief camps, and convalescent homes. The returning wounded seeking reunion with families found ready assistance from commission members.[29]

This passionate attachment to the abolitionist cause impelled a redirection of woman's rights efforts: "The last woman's rights convention before the Civil War was held in Albany in 1861; thereafter all activity for woman's rights ground to a standstill."[30] But the change in the thrust of activity nevertheless found Susan B. Anthony and Elizabeth Cady Stanton as officers of the newly formed National Woman's Loyal League. This organization grew to 5,000 members and amassed nearly 400,000 signatures on petitions for the Thirteenth Amendment abolishing slavery. This monumental effort in and behind the lines of battle gave women self-confidence in their ability to organize and was still further testimony to the utter falsity that a woman's place was in the home, the setting for demure purity. They were forthright in their efforts and hopes that the human rights embedded in the struggle were not to be forgotten in the aftermath of the war. Women had demonstrated their loyalty and service. The articulate women abolitionists looked forward to the postwar Reconstruction as the dawn of a new era of equal rights for all Americans—blacks and whites, women and men.

Part Two

Reconstruction—The Dawn of a New Day?

American women were the industrial and farming shock troops of the Union effort. Years before the war began, the woman's righters were agitating for the end of slavery. They looked forward to the era of peace for the revival of the theme of woman's rights as part of a national transformation ushering in rights for all American humanity—black and white, women and men.

Now the Civil War was over. Men returning to civilian employment recaptured the positions secured by women. The dominant view was that women who sewed blankets and uniforms, tended to the sick and wounded, and taught the children were acting out the roles of "woman's work" of tenderness, ministering to the sick, producing clothing, and similar tasks.

The hope of securing the ballot, the symbol of political power, was dashed by the practical politicos who did not want to endanger the cause of black males' voting rights with the encumbrance of woman's suffrage. The woman leaders, in their travail, went through the trials of splits; expedient moves to gain allies, often from elements opposed to causes they had espoused; overemphasis of woman suffrage as a talisman of power of a panacea for correcting societal ills; swings to complete distrust of men; grappling with side issues of sex, marriage, love, and labor unions; veering from influencing existing major parties toward independent political action.

But what was the national setting? Which were the *dominant* political, social, and economic forces which the woman's rights movement had to contend with to give the thrust of prominence to the cause? In attempting to answer these questions the works of the foremost modern historians specializing in the Reconstruction period were examined. These revisionist historians had overcome the earlier tendentious accounts laced with racism which denigrated the phase of Reconstruction involving the military occupation of the South, the state governments established there which granted suffrage to black males, and the activities of the Freedmen's Bureau.[1]

The respected revisionist historians who had meticulously corrected the record as described by Bowers and Dunning had nothing to write about the woman's rights movement.[2] Even the labor movement, a social force dominated by men, received scant attention. This reflected the lack of specific weight of these social tendencies in the national economy and polity. The view of black inferiority even affected some of the leading cadres of women as they struggled for their own dignity and social status. The task that the woman's rights movement faced was to break through the powerlessness and invisibility by becoming a permanent national force.

The Political and Economic Stakes in the War's Aftermath

POWER POLITICS AND SLAVERY

President Lincoln proclaimed his war aim as limited to preserving the Union. His attitude was free of malice, full of charity toward the conquered Confederacy. He did not regard the *states* as having seceded, just the disloyal *governments* of those states. The Emancipation Proclamation, which freed slaves in the war zone, was a strategic *military* measure that he embraced reluctantly. It did have the effect of disorganizing the military effort of the rebels by destroying the black labor force so important for food, supplies, and labor behind the lines.

Lincoln opposed slavery as a moral evil but did not consider its abolition a war aim. Indeed, until the adoption of the Thirteenth Amendment, slavery continued in the North and border states outside the Confederacy.

Gradual emancipation stretching over fifty years was one of Lincoln's plans for the blacks. Slave owners were to be fully compensated. He opposed blacks as volunteers in the Union army.

As the national leader of the Republican party, Lincoln wanted to bring back the South gently, so that the twenty-two Senators and sixty-three Representatives would go into the Republican column. His plan of Reconstruction started to operate in December 1863. Amnesty was offered to those below the ranks of colonel in the army and lieutenant in the navy who took a loyalty oath. When 10 percent of the oath takers had cast ballots, the state government was admitted back into the Union. Blacks were to be completely excluded from this process.

Congress was furious because of not only the weak specifics of the plan, but also the usurpation of congressional authority. They were irate too

when Lincoln pocket-vetoed the Wade-Davis Bill, which would have sub-
stituted a majority of male citizens for the mere 10 percent.

The day after Lincoln was assassinated, leading Radical Republicans—
Zachariah Chandler, Benjamin F. Wade, and George W. Julian—as members of the Congressional Committee on the Conduct of the War, were
determined that the fruits of victory would not be lost through a soft peace.
As a result of Lincoln's plan Louisiana, Tennessee, and Virginia were reinstated. The group looked favorably upon Lincoln's successor, Andrew Johnson, the Unionist Democrat from Tennessee. A tailor by trade and a
champion of the small farmers and labor, Johnson had opposed secession,
wanted the rebels punished, and was committed to the abolition of slavery
and the dismantling of the huge plantations.

Johnson had no civil rights position for the blacks and looked upon the
yeoman farmers of the South to reconstitute the Democratic party. His
antiwealth position was revealed in his addition to the Lincoln plan of a
$20,000 limitation on the resources of a Confederate who sought reinstate-
ment of his voting power.

He relished the humiliation of the southern wealthy Confederates. Johnson's device was for the former rebels to appeal to him, the president, for
amnesty. Thousands of pardons were issued with great liberality, even for
those who had wealth in excess of the $20,000 limitation. Within a year
after the war was over, Federal troops were withdrawn from the South in
large measure, with only 11,000 black and white civilian volunteers and
54,000 members of the armed forces remaining.

The Freedmen's Bureau, which had been established in March 1865, was
to be extended and enlarged in 1866. Johnson opened his rift with the
Congress by vetoing this measure.

The position of the forthright Radical Republicans became clearly de-
marcated from the Presidential Reconstruction plans. The Radicals felt that
since the Constitution guaranteed every state of the Union a republican form
of government, Congress alone could decide when southern states would
once again be entitled to send Representatives and Senators to Washington.

In overriding the veto, Congress was mindful of the remarkable record
of the Freedmen's Bureau, which was run by the military. White refugees
and black freedmen had received 21 million rations. Forty hospitals were
established, caring for 450,000 cases of illness. Lands that were abandoned
were restored to pardoned rebels. While the Homestead Act of 1866 did
grant land to blacks, for the most part it was inferior and unattractive. No
animals such as mules and cattle were provided. Still the bureau through
courts and boards of mediation helped secure fair conditions for working
blacks. In education more than 250,000 blacks had been enrolled in 4,300
schools at a cost of $5 million. Both attendance and scholarship were good.

Despite Johnson's refusal to enforce measures against racial discrimination, the achievements of the Freedmen's Bureau were outstanding, which

increased congressional anger over Johnson's behavior. The southern rebels went along with Johnson in agreeing to repudiate the Confederate debt, to accept the abolition of slavery, and to cooperate in accepting the loyalty oath. However, Johnson's plea for token voting rights for blacks was flatly rejected. Six Southern states were reinstated under Johnson's plan with provisional governors.

To aid Southern recovery, a moratorium was declared on payment of debts, and imprisonment for debt was suspended. Immigration from Europe was encouraged. Freedom from taxes was granted to entire industries. Mortgage bonds were issued, and massive shipments of food went south. Free public schools were established—for whites only.

In these "redeemed" southern states Black Codes of law were enacted. Slavery-type contracts for black laborers were entered into, with former slave owners being given preference in hiring their ex-slaves as "apprentices." Under vagrancy laws wandering blacks freely seeking work were picked up. The fines imposed were paid by the former slave owners, who now had the right to hire the "vagrants" to work off the fines. Bands of antiblack vigilantes, made up of poor whites, sought to establish their "superiority" and protectiveness of the virtue of white womanhood through force and terror. Any form of black education was bitterly discouraged. This was Reconstruction, Confederate style, while Johnson was in the White House.

Northerners who identified with the Union cause now believed that the Johnsonian state governments in the South were making the bloodiest of all wars to have been fought in vain. They were convinced that the southern agenda was the *de facto* reinstitution of slavery. The abolition of slavery removed in effect that provision in the Constitution that counted slaves as three-fifths of persons in calculating representation in the House of Representatives. With blacks now counted but denied the right to vote, the danger of the legislative branch coming under the control of the former Confederacy loomed ominously.

Led by Thaddeus Stevens in the House and Charles Sumner in the Senate, the Radical Republicans mounted a campaign to ensure that southern restoration would include protection of the freedmen, granting them voting rights, making the rebels pay for the war, and preventing any future secession. Congress then refused to seat the Johnsonian and Lincolnian representatives from the South.

Whatever social legislation of benefit to the southern blacks existed was adopted over Johnson's vetoes. Without black citizenship and the right to vote, the political victory of the North over the South was in danger of becoming pyrrhic. Politically, to give the blacks citizenship and voting rights was as far as the Radical Republicans felt they could go. To extend voting rights to women would be to erect an additional social and political barrier. There was no national consensus that favored this reform.

To be sure, the woman's rights abolitionists in the National Woman's Loyal League, led by Elizabeth Cady Stanton and Susan B. Anthony, railed against the pussy-footing weakness of Lincoln and Johnson on the rights of ex-slaves. They were in for a rude shock, however, on the issue of suffrage. Should it be universal or restricted to males?

Radical Republicans concentrated their efforts on the Fourteenth Amendment, which, in effect, gave blacks citizenship but limited the federal sanction of voting rights to males. To nail down the ballot for black males, the Fifteenth Amendment prohibited any voting restriction based on color, race, or previous condition of servitude, but it did not mention any voting restriction based on sex. The constitutional amendment route of the Republicans would also remove the danger of an adverse Supreme Court decision on legislation that had been enacted over Johnson's veto.

There were riots in the South against black soldiers. Johnson, the commander-in-chief, however, went on the lecture circuit denouncing the Civil Rights Act of 1866 and the proposed Fourteenth Amendment. By 1867 it had nevertheless become part of the Constitution.

In March of that year, the Radical Republicans put their plan into effect. The former Confederacy was divided into five districts under military command. Elections to constitutional conventions were to be held in those areas that were former states. Any adult *male* not disenfranchised because of activity on the side of rebellion could vote.

Johnson's veto of this plan was overridden, and the necessary processes of voter registration, administering of oaths, assembling of conventions, and adoption of state constitutions went on apace under the watchful eye of the military command. Johnson's stubborn defiance, and his constitutionally strategic position as chief executive officer charged with enforcing the law, impelled the Republicans to embark on the impeachment process. Johnson was saved from impeachment by the narrowest of margins—one vote short of the necessary two-thirds vote.

Under the Radicals' plan, now in effect, 700,000 of the 4 million blacks were enfranchised. They were overwhelmingly illiterate, both the ex-slaves and the 200,000 who had been free—the obvious result of being barred from any formal education. Those blacks who assumed positions of leadership were educated in Ohio, Pennsylvania, England, and Canada. A few were self-educated. Most were ministers and school teachers.

While there was some corruption because of a few unscrupulous scalawags and carpetbaggers, it wasn't too widespread. Considering the flagrant abuses in the northern cities, military contracting, and railroad speculation, the cry of corruption in the Reconstruction governments was a transparent effort to downgrade the Radical Republican operation. If added to the exaggeration of malfeasance was the vigilante shriek of danger facing southern white womanhood at the hands of arrogant black males, you have the highly charged emotional ingredients of defense of purity in family life as well as in government. The physical feature of blackness and the recency of low social status of ex-slaves served to mute the feelings of outrage of northern whites against the brutal treatment of the blacks.

As soon as the constitutions were in place and the states restored, most of the troops were withdrawn, leaving minimal garrisons confined to the forts made up of soldiers generally friendly to the whites. The big task facing the new governments was the physical rebuilding of the South, particularly roads and public buildings. There was great interest in constructing a network of railroads to match the ongoing program in the North, where the rails from the west coast would soon be met by those from the northeast. Southerners looked with envy upon the generous land grants that were subsidizing this effort. Revenues for the South were hard to come by. The segregated school system was expensive, and there was no tax base to replace the capital of slaves and plantations.

On the national scene corruption replaced antislavery as the key issue. Liberal Republicans, long associated with the welfare of the blacks, were more agitated by the graft and corruption in the Grant administration. Popular support for the Radical program ebbed quickly and by 1875 had all but vanished. E. L. Godkin, the editor of the liberal *Nation*, became a racist. He personified the fears of the older middle-class whites, who had been imbued with the ideals of public service. This sector was worried that their world was being undermined by the saturnalia of corruption involving mercenary capitalists, city machine politicians—all aided and abetted by enfranchised "inherently inferior" immigrants and blacks. This change in public attitude was not without effect on the leaders of the woman's rights movement, who had seen their hope for enfranchisement dashed in the interests of giving the blacks the vote.

The "scientism" of social Darwinism assigned immigrants and blacks a position of genetic inferiority, making them less fit to function in society. This was the social and "scientific" basis for the vast indifference to the evils of lynching, Jim Crow segregation, and hostility to immigrants. The palpable "facts" feeding this pseudo-scientific approach rested upon physical features and behavioral differences. Biology and criminology in the nineteenth century were based upon classification, using anthropometric measurements including phrenological readings of skulls. Differences in behavior because of grinding poverty and cultural alienation were designated as hereditary in origin. The irony of this is that the same scientists used these procedures to justify the lower status of women.

It is little wonder then that Thaddeus Stevens, the valiant leader of the Radical Republicans and a dedicated believer in equality, was defeated in his effort to confiscate the lands of the rebels and grant these holdings to the impoverished blacks. Even arch-abolitionist crusader William Lloyd Garrison refused to go along with this approach. The Radical program had passed its apogee of achievement and fell apart.

The activity of the Ku Klux Klan (KKK) mounted in intensity. Ex-Con-federates were in control of state governments and asserted their real agenda as the Federal troops were withdrawn. Black schools were set afire. The Union League was driven from the South. Southern white liberals, friendly to the blacks, were victims of social ostracism while the campaign of the hooded night-riders was wrapped in the "moral" cloak of the defense of white womanhood. Blacks and their supporters in the South were soon powerless. Federal laws against the Klan were poorly enforced. Sporadic actions against the KKK only served to stiffen resistance. This activist racism penetrated the national psyche well into the next century.

THE ECONOMICS OF RECONSTRUCTION

Before the Civil War, the South was not a monolithic entity. The Whigs, following the lead of Henry Clay, were most interested in internal improve-ments in roads, railroads, canals, and other infrastructure to aid in the development of Southern business, industry, and commerce. They were not ideologues of slavery and were open to integrating their interests with that of the industrial and financial North. The pro-slavery agrarian, John C. Calhoun, sought to forge an alliance within the Democratic party of slave-owning planters and poor white yeoman farmers. The eruption of the Civil War pushed the Whigs into the Democratic party as loyal supporters of the Confederacy.

With the end of the war, the molecular movement of uniting like interests, North and South, resumed. The Republicans, led first by Lincoln with his soft plan of restoring the South to the Union, were eager to bridge the chasms of war and to get the South to share in the fruits of an expanding national economy. This was not a view born out of altruistic patriotism, but rather out of practical sets of material aspirations. The raw materials of the South and West—animal, plant, and mineral—were to be transported and fed into the maw of the northern industrial machine. The role of gov-ernment in this enterprise was clear, affecting currency, public land policy, banking, taxes, tariff, and railroads. The war had acted as a catalyst speeding up the national industrial and commercial process. This drive continued inexorably despite temporary setbacks of downturns in the business cycle. The people suffered from these declines, but industry and finance had the resources to overcome them.

Northern capital, for reasons of profit, of course, willingly aided the recovery of the war-ravished South. The old exploitative labor agricultural system of chattel slavery was now replaced by tenant farming and share-cropping. With more advanced machinery, the textile industry began to shift to the South, closer to the source of raw material, and was aided by generous subsidies. Beyond cotton were the southern products of tobacco, sugar, nuts, peaches, and turpentine. The returning blacks were the source of the cheapest labor, threatening the jobs of poor whites. The blacks also became domestic servants of the upper- and middle-class whites.

North and South, business, finance, and industry became entranced without restraint in a wild American dream of unlimited prosperity. These were the economic stakes that profoundly affected politics and social relations. The woman's rights movement, despite valiant efforts by legislators such as George Julian, Henry Wilson, and Ben Butler, had to fight for a place in the sun to maintain its presence and organization. It could not play any significant role in this vast game of high economic stakes.

The election of 1872 found the Republicans split. The Liberals led by Horace Greeley and Carl Schurz were so opposed to Grant's corrupt administration that they backed the Democratic ticket. It will be recalled that this was the year which marked the beginning of the end of the Radical phase of Reconstruction. The two national parties were now about equal in strength, poised for the contest over the prize of the presidency in 1876.

The election of 1876 between Republican Rutherford B. Hayes of Ohio and Samuel J. Tilden of New York, Democrat, was inconclusive. The electoral college gave Tilden an undisputed plurality, but not a majority. The electoral votes of southern states were in contention. Congress devised a means of resolving this problem by creating a commission of fifteen—seven Democrats and eight Republicans—to make the decisions. The Republicans voted solidly for Hayes in all contested states. The election of Hayes cemented a relationship in national politics between the Democrats of the "Solid South" and the northern Republicans, which lasted until the New Deal of the 1930s.

This was the broad picture of Reconstruction. The idealism of anti-slavery and equal rights was dissipated in the larger and more powerful quest for national industrial and commercial expansion. The Civil War had assured that growth would be based upon wage labor and private industrial enterprise instead of the plantation system of chattel slavery. The use of the Fourteenth Amendment, which had been adopted to grant the freedmen citizenship, was perverted through litigation and action of the U.S. Supreme Court to affirm the property rights of corporations. It became a *magna carta* for the growth of trusts and monopolies.

Labor's response to unlimited and ruthless exploitation was to form unions by craft, trade, and industry and establish national networks—the National Labor Union in 1866, the Knights of Labor in 1869, and the Federation of Trades and Labor Unions (later the American Federation of Labor) in 1881. Each cyclical recession depleted the ranks of unions through severe unemployment and diverted their direction toward currency reform, establishing producer cooperatives, and embarking on independent political action.

The woman's rights movement became a permanent national institution, testing its strategic aims in legislative activity, before conventions of the major political parties, and the quest for allies. It was beset by a nationwide split in its ranks and was generally barred from the citadels of power. The women, however articulate and militant, were not important in the key battle for commercial and industrial prosperity. The politicians of both the Democratic and Republican parties were content with the dominant "belle-ideal" with the woman's place in the home to attend to the comfort of the husband and the welfare of the children. Indeed almost all women, even the single and widowed who were compelled to work, embraced the concept of escaping to this tender trap of being a housewife.

But there was a gathering storm developing in the beginning of the twentieth century in reaction to the Gilded Age. Corruption, exploitation of women and children, monopoly pricing, contaminated food and drugs all galvanized a Progressive Movement, which passed yet through another bloody titanic conflict, World War I. This was to be the staging ground for a renewal of the woman's rights movement, primarily for suffrage, but also of concern for the welfare of working women and child laborers. The strategic and tactical lessons the woman's righters had absorbed in the Reconstruction Era were brought to bear in another stage of the transformation of ladies into women.

Toward Organizing— The Woman's Rights Convention of 1866

Though the woman's rights movement has been considered to date from the historic Seneca Falls convention of 1848, regular woman's rights conventions did not commence until 1850. They continued until the outbreak of the Civil War, when they were suspended and the entire movement submerged itself in the war effort. In 1866 it rose to the surface again.

The background for this reappearance was the discussion of the proposed Fourteenth Amendment to the Constitution. The Radical Republicans led by Stevens and Sumner, fearful that the Civil Rights Act that had been enacted over Johnson's veto was possibly unconstitutional, proposed to codify its main provisions in a constitutional amendment.[1]

Two powerful currents began to move this proposal forward as early as 1865. One wing of the old abolitionist movement led by Wendell Phillips believed that the struggle had not ended with the Emancipation Proclamation and the passage of the Thirteenth Amendment abolishing slavery. In contrast to William Lloyd Garrison, Phillips was of the opinion that there could not be any real freedom for blacks without giving them the ballot. The control of the Anti-Slavery Society passed into the hands of the Phillips forces, who waged a vigorous campaign in the *Anti-Slavery Standard* to confer upon the freedmen the protection of citizenship and the ballot. "This is the Negro's hour!" was their battle cry.

The second force was the Radical Republicans, who needed black enfranchisement to assure political control of the South in the days when the military occupation would cease. They insisted that no southern state should be permitted to join the Union unless that state voted to ratify the Fourteenth Amendment.

Prior to the publication of the actual text of the proposed Fourteenth

Amendment, much of the talk and agitation was in terms of "universal suffrage." Woman suffragists interpreted these words to include women, and so they participated in campaigns to get signatures on petitions of support. The woman leaders ardently believed that Reconstruction was to be the opportunity to redress all political wrongs.

However, the abolitionists and the Radical Republicans did not want to jeopardize the success of the enfranchisement of blacks with any unpopular impediments such as woman suffrage. For this reason, the proposed Fourteenth Amendment in Section 2 contains three references to males with respect to voting rights and representation. "But when the right to vote... is denied to any of the *male* inhabitants of such State... the basis of representation therein shall be reduced in the proportion which the number of such *male* citizens shall bear to the whole number of *male* citizens... in such State." One historian of woman's rights claims that "Charles Sumner ... covered nineteen pages of foolscap, in his effort so to formulate it as to omit the word 'male' and at the same time secure the ballot for the negro."[2]

In a letter written to Martha G. Wright in late 1865, Elizabeth Cady Stanton wrote: "We have now boosted the negro over our own heads, and we had better begin to remember that self-preservation is the first law of nature.... Some say: 'Be still; wait; this is the negro's hour.' We believe this is the hour for everybody to do the best thing for reconstruction."[3]

An appeal signed by the three outstanding leaders of the woman's movement—Elizabeth Cady Stanton, Susan B. Anthony, and Lucy Stone—was circulated during the same period, echoing this theme. It stated:

As the question of suffrage is now agitating the public mind, it is the hour for woman to make her demands. Propositions already have been made on the floor of Congress to so amend the Constitution as to exclude women from a voice in the government. As this would be to turn the wheels of legislation backward, let the women of the nation unitedly protest against such a desecration of the Constitution, and petition for that right which is the foundation of all government, the right of representation. Send your petition when signed to your representative in Congress, at your earliest convenience.[4]

THE MAY ANNIVERSARIES

The various reform movements of this period had inaugurated a custom known as the May Anniversary Week, held principally in New York City. In the early part of May many of the national societies concerned with woman suffrage, temperance, abolitionism, missionary work, prison reform, and universal peace held their conventions. A call would be issued through newspaper announcements, flyers, and posters; a meeting hall hired; and prominent leaders and speakers engaged to address the audiences. Differences arose now and then, sometimes in heated debate, but the main purpose was to agitate the assemblage and propagandize for the cause. The culmination of these meetings was a host of resolutions, usually adopted in a *viva voce* fashion, and then a collection taken to pay for the necessary expenses.

Formalities of organization for the sponsoring societies were generally not adhered to. The basis for membership was often very loose: attendance at the meeting and a small contribution. The nominal control of the organization between May anniversary meetings was usually vested in an executive committee. The daily affairs and the disbursing of funds were generally handled by an executive secretary, the only full-time functionary.

THE WOMAN'S RIGHTS LEADERSHIP

Leading the Woman's Rights Convention of 1866 were the four individuals who were to dominate the movement throughout the nineteenth century. There were others who played rather prominent roles, but these were the acknowledged leaders. At this convention they were all together. When later the movement split into warring segments, these same women were the key personalities. There was Lucretia Mott, the venerable founder; Elizabeth Cady Stanton, the ideologist and orator; Susan B. Anthony, the indefatigable organizer; and Lucy Stone, a pioneer whose retention of her maiden name after marriage was a symbol of woman's independence.

Before the Woman's Rights Convention opened, the forces that were to be present assembled at a meeting of the Anti-Slavery Society. The differences that were to arise at the woman's rights meeting had their debut at this gathering. Aaron A. Powell, the secretary, moved a resolution that the attention of the people of New York be called to the forthcoming Constitutional Convention of the State of New York and that this convention "would be a proper opportunity to eradicate forever from that constitution the distinction of race in the exercise of suffrage."

Mrs. Stanton offered an amendment to strike out "white" and "male" from the existing constitution. Mrs. Abby Kelly Foster considered it out of place to bring the question of woman suffrage up at the convention. She said, "Suffrage to the negro and woman, although they were one in the broad sense, were separated in the public mind and were best considered separately."[5]

THE ORGANIZATION OF THE WOMAN'S RIGHTS CONVENTION

The *New York World*, a pro-Johnson Democrat newspaper, voiced editorially its hope of driving a wedge between the woman's righters and the Republican-abolitionist coalition. It ran full reports of the proceedings and commented:

In view of the interest attached to the suffrage question, we give *in extenso* the proceedings of the Woman's Rights Convention...It attracted a great crowd of women and the speaking was really very good. Up to this time no considerable number of American men or women ever seriously believed that it would be a desirable thing to invest the gentler sex with the right to vote; but, since the powerful party now in power are earnestly at work to confer suffrage upon huge masses of ignorant degraded blacks, but one short year ago abject slaves, it has become a question with intelligent people why the preference should be given to them over our own sensible and cultivated women. If suffrage is a natural right, then one human being has as much claim to it as another. If a privilege, why should we prefer the African to the members of our own household? And if a trust to be widely used, surely we have more confidence in the judgment of our educated wives, sisters, and mothers, than in that of the besotted freedmen.[6]

The report of the initial meeting of the convention described it as having a "very large attendance" and that "all the anti-slavery people were present."[7] The gathering had been publicized by a widely advertised call signed by Elizabeth Cady Stanton as president and Susan B. Anthony as secretary. The speakers included Ernestine L. Rose, Wendell Phillips, Frances D. Gage, Henry Ward Beecher, Theodore Tilton, Lucretia Mott, Stephen S. and Abby Kelly Foster, Parker Pillsbury, Mrs. Stanton, and Miss Anthony. The available evidence, gleaned from names on a collection list, indicated an overwhelming preponderance of women in attendance.[8]

This extract from the convention call established its *leit-motif.*

The question now is, have we the wisdom and conscience, from the present upheavings of our political system to reconstruct a government on the one enduring basis that has never been tried—'*Equal Rights to All*'....

For, while our representatives in Washington are discussing the right of suffrage for the black man, as the only protection to life, liberty and happiness, they deny that "necessity of citizenship" to woman by proposing to introduce the word "male" into the Federal Constitution. In securing suffrage to but another shade of *man*hood, while we disfranchise fifteen million taxpayers, we come not one line nearer the republican idea.[9]

THE BROADER VISTAS

The dedicated advocates of woman suffrage hardly regarded it as an end unto itself. For most it was an indispensable key to woman's advancement in society. Caroline H. Dall submitted a report of developments in the status of women which reaffirmed the broad objectives. She divided her account into three classifications—education, labor, and law—and justified the division as follows:

A proper education must prepare women for labor, skilled or manual; and the experience of a laborer should introduce her to citizenship, for it provides her with rights to protect, privileges to secure, and property to be taxed. If she is a laborer, she must have interest in the laws which control labor.[10]

Under education, Miss Dall cited the formation of the American Social Science Association with two women on the board of directors, coeducational classes in French, mathematics, and natural sciences as a joint effort of the Lowell Institute and the Massachusetts Institute of Technology, the opening of Baker University in Kansas to women; and the right of women in Algeria and Orenburg, Russia, to attend medical school. The labor section described actual working conditions and implicitly called for a campaign to grant women equal pay for work equal to that of men. Increased employment opportunity for women and the establishment of trade schools to teach skills to women were underscored.[11]

The Dall report further documented the significant increase in women employees in government work since the beginning of the Civil War, the number of instances of women replacing men in the running of farms, and that in the previous year alone, more than 20,000 women had entered printing offices. From official documents of the Massachusetts legislature, she cited specific working conditions: In Boston a glass company paid women from $4 to $8 a week; seamstresses made a dollar a day; makers of fancy goods 40¢ to 50¢ a day. In Chicopee women were paid 90% of men's wages; in Fairhaven, women photographers received one-third of men's pay.[12]

Miss Dall echoed the suspicion that Sarah Bagley had expressed about the authenticity of seemingly favorable conditions reported by factory inspectors. "Lawrence—From the Pacific Mills, that the women are *liberally* paid. We should like to see the figures.... Waltham—Reports the wages of the watch factory are very *remunerative*. In 1860 I reported the factory as paying from $2.50 to $4 a week. Here also we should prefer figures to a general statement."[13]

As to the general state of woman workers, she presented the following analysis:

We are always referred to political economy, when we speak of the low wages of women, but a little investigation will show that other causes cooperate with those, which can be but gradually reached to determine their rates. 1. The willfulness of women themselves, which when I see them in positions I have helped to open to them, fills me with shame and indignation. 2. The unfair competition proceeding from voluntary labor, in mechanical ways, of women well-to-do.[14]

The Dall report was accepted by the convention and incorporated into its official proceedings. Miss Dall failed to comprehend that the movement for the eight-hour day contemplated no reduction in pay because of the reduction in hours and fought any attempt on the part of the government or employers to do this. The sexist advantage taken of young women by un-scrupulous employers in times of severe economic hardship, as reported by Miss Dall, persisted as a stigma attaching immorality to women workers.

After Miss Dall welcomed the support for woman's rights from John Stuart Mill, *The New York Evening Post*, and Theodore Tilton, she casti-gated the daily press for not printing news and letters concerning the move-ment. She suggested the purchase of half a column of space in *The New York Tribune*.[15]

CONVENTION DEBATE

Woman suffrage remained the chief question before the convention with Mrs. Stanton setting forth the major arguments in an eloquent opening address. She felt that in the very chaos of the Reconstruction period was the opportunity "to base our government on the broad principle of equal rights to all."[16]

Mrs. Stanton bitterly criticized those who claimed that the ballot was unnecessary because, as cultured and wealthy women, they already had all the rights they needed. She pointed to the "40,000 women in this city... living at starving prices at the needle.... It is your duty and mine... to open new avenues for work and wages to this class of women; for they are sapping the very foundations of national virtue and strength."[17]

Susan B. Anthony echoed Mrs. Stanton's sentiments: "With you we have passed through the agony of death, the resurrection and triumph of another revolution.... Our demand must ever be: 'No compromise of human rights. No admission into the Constitution of inequality of rights, or disfranchise-ment on account of color or sex.' "[18]

Of the three prominent men who addressed the convention, Theodore Tilton, editor of the influential liberal Protestant religious weekly, *The Independent*; Wendell Phillips, the fiery editor of the abolitionist *Standard*; and Henry Ward Beecher, the outstanding Congregationalist minister, only Beecher came out unequivocally for consideration of the rights of the black and the woman on a coequal basis. Beecher, a master on the lecture platform and the idol of women in and out of the reform movement, claimed if suffrage was acceptable for the black man, the ignorant Irish immigrant, then why not for women?[19]

He directed arguments that are themselves based upon dubious distinc-tions between man and woman against hoary concepts that woman's place was in the home; suffrage would destroy woman's delicacy by her entering the sordid atmosphere of politics; women ought to act through their fathers, husbands, and sons; women are, by nature, excitable creatures who would, by mingling in politics, introduce a vindictive acrimony that would render the practice of politics intolerable and impossible. Beecher, however, characterized women as purifying and idealistic who would change the course of politics—hardly an accurate statement.

Wendell Phillips, aware perhaps of the impending campaign to secure adoption of the Fourteenth and Fifteenth amendments, avoided the issue as to whether or not a vigorous battle should be waged to secure the ballot for women. He claimed that the mere conferring of the ballot was nothing. How suffrage was actually discharged was much more significant. Fashion and custom prevent woman from working and being trained in the professions. Legislation is helpful, but fundamental changes in social values are crucial. He stated:

The sister comes to New York. The prizes of life are before her and her brother wins them—large wages, ample opportunities, breadth for development, every career open. . . . the sister comes to the city; and she finds starvation wages; wages at such a rate that they offer no prospect of any rise even in the future to what her soul aspires to. Vice comes with gilded hand, clad in velvet, attended with luxury, in the chariot of ease and says, "An hour, and all this is yours". Give men honest wages, and ninety-nine out of one hundred will disdain to steal. Give woman what the same labor gives to man, and ninety-nine out of one hundred will disdain to purchase it by vice. (Applause) . . . Let the fifty thousand women that must earn a living have a choice of five hundred occupations, and dictate terms, instead of trembling at the doors and taking work at one-tenth the price of male labor. Then you cure vice, because you withhold the basis upon which it lives.[20]

Phillips then considered efforts toward economic betterment through equal pay for equal work of much greater significance than suffrage agitation. Further, he believed that woman was her own enslaver and could free herself through her own efforts. The ballot for him was only a device that he advocated as a means to differentiate those women who wanted to better their lot from those who were passively captive to traditional mores.[21]

Frances Gage took up the oratorical cudgels against Phillips and replied:

But I was sorry he did not go a little further back and tell us how we came into this position which he described, of being our own bitterest enemies in all the great duties of life. Whence came our frivolousness? How came we wedded to fashion? Why has it not been respectable for women to work? . . .

The wife had no right to her own earnings. The wife had no right to her own property. She could not make a contract and have it legal under the laws of the States. She could not defend her property or reputation. The law-makers of the land, who were men, voted colleges, and schools, and seminaries of learning and kindred institutions for manhood, but denied womanhood the right to set her foot therein. Uneducated, she could not transact business. Without responsibility she could not go to work. . . . She forgot her high duty and there was nobody to tell her—except this: "Stay at home, and wash the dishes and mend the stockings."[22]

It remained for Mrs. F. E. Watkins Harper, a black woman, who encompassed within her the twin aspirations of the blacks and women for equality and civil rights and thus appealed for a broad equal rights movement.

We are all bound up together in one great bundle of humanity and society cannot trample on the weakest and feeblest of its members without receiving the curse in its own soul. You tried that in the case of the negro.

I do not believe that giving the woman the ballot is immediately going to cure all the ills of life. I do not believe that white women are dewdrops just exhaled from the skies. . . .

Talk of giving women the ballot box? Go on. It is a normal school, and the white women of this country need it. While there exists this brutal element in society which tramples upon the feeble and treads down the weak, I tell you that if there is any class of people who need to be lifted out of their airy nothings and selfishness, it is the white women of America.[23]

TOWARD EQUAL RIGHTS FOR ALL

In the hope of developing a strong coalition within the confines of a single organization dedicated to voting rights both for blacks and women, Susan B. Anthony proposed the following resolutions to the convention:

1. Resolved, that Liberty and Equality are the inherent rights of man in civilization, and that no constitution or code should be accepted as law that does not secure them to every citizen. 2. Resolved, that a just government and a true church are alike opposed to class and caste, whether the privileged order be Feudal "Baron", British "Lord", or American "white male citizen". 3. Resolved, that on the threshold of a higher civilization in which ideas are to control nations the time has come for the united action of man and woman—the only union that can ensure the purity, perpetuity, and power of the State. 4. Resolved, that woman demands the ballot— First, because it is the crowning right of citizenship; it is dignity, protection, and power; it is civil and political life. Secondly, the nation needs woman's best thought and action in the State as well as the home. And, thirdly, because woman needs a broader, deeper education, such as a knowledge of science, philosophy, jurisprudence and active cooperation the government alone can give. 5. That it was the duty of Congress in guaranteeing a republican form of government to every State of this union that there be no abridgment of suffrage on account of "color or sex". 6. That the Joint Resolutions of the Committee of Fifteen to introduce the word "male" into the Federal Constitution be condemned. 7. That woman does not desire to be placed above or below man in status but wishes to be placed upon an equal plane. 8. That women be alerted to petition state legislatures removing suffrage restrictions, especially in states holding constitutional conventions.[24]

These resolutions were decisively adopted, and Miss Anthony then introduced yet another resolution specifically setting forth the course of coalition:

Whereas, by the act of the Emancipation Proclamation and the Civil Rights Bill, the negro and woman now hold the same political and civil *status*, alike needing only the ballot; and whereas the same arguments apply equally to both classes, proving all partial legislation fatal to republican institutions, therefore, *Resolved*, That the time has come for an organization that shall demand Universal Suffrage and that hereafter we shall be known as the "American Equal Rights Association."[25]

In support of this resolution, Miss Anthony stated: "As women we can no longer *seem* to claim for ourselves what we do not do for others—nor can we work in two separate movements to get the ballot for two disfranchised classes—the negro and the woman—since to do this must be at double cost of time, energy, and money."[26]

With the forward development of the woman's rights movement deflected by the more forceful currents of abolitionism and the outbreak of the Civil War, the hope of woman's rights focused on the war's aftermath—Reconstruction. The movement had barely surfaced only to confront the dangerous shoals of black male enfranchisement while woman suffrage was to be ignored. In an effort to avoid this split in the ranks of those who truly wanted universal human rights, the leadership of the Woman's Rights Convention transformed the organization into the American Equal Rights Association. The harsh reality of political practicality, backed up by the powerful Radical Republicans and the dedicated abolitionists, interfered with the high-blown plans of Elizabeth Cady Stanton, Susan B. Anthony, and Lucy Stone.

5

The Broadest Platform—The American Equal Rights Association, 1866–1867

FORMATION

With the adoption of a constitution on May 10, 1866, the formal transformation of the Woman's Rights Convention into the American Equal Rights Association took place. This move caused the *New York World* to look upon the movement with hostile ridicule. The newspaper was disappointed over its failure to drive a wedge between the woman's righters and the coalition of abolitionists and Radical Republicans.

"There was established the American Equal Rights Association...having for its object the obtaining of the right of suffrage for all persons 'without regard to complexion, race, or sex' which includes of course, 'Indians not taxed', as well as Chinamen and intelligent ourang-outangs."[1]

Respectable journalism was not evident in that same newspaper's attempt to discuss the personalities of the association.

Elizabeth Cady Stanton is likewise a candidate with considerable strength, favoring as she does, the Copperheads, the Democratic Party, and other dead buried remains of alleged disloyalty. Susan is lean, cadaverous, and intellectual, with the proportion of a file and the voice of a hurdy gurdy. She is the favorite of the convention. Mrs. Stanton is of intellectual stock, impressive in manner and disposed to henpeck the convention which of course calls out resistance and much cackling.... Susan has a controlling advantage over her in the fact that she is unencumbered with a husband....
    Parker Pillsbury, one of the notabilities of the body is a good looking white man naturally, but has a cowed and sneakish expression stealing over him, as though he regretted he had not been born a nigger or one of these females.... Lucy Stone...

is what the law terms a 'Spinster'. She is a sad mild girl, presides with great timidity and hesitation, is wheezy and nasal in her pronunciation and wholly without dignity or command. . . . Mummified and fossilated females, void of domestic duties, habits, and natural affections; crack-brained, rheumatic, dyspeptic, henpecked men, vainly striving to achieve the liberty to open their heads in the presence of their wives; self-educated, oily-faced, insolent, gabbling negroes, and Theodore Tilton, make up less than a hundred members of this caravan, called by themselves the American Equal Rights Association.[2]

STRUCTURE AND OFFICERS

In the exalted prose of a sermon, the preamble to the organization's constitution thundered:

Whereas, by the war, . . . and in the reconstruction of our government we again stand face to face with the broad question of natural rights, all associations based on special claims for special classes are too narrow and partial for the hour. Therefore, from the baptism of this second revolution . . . seeing with a holier vision that the peace, prosperity, and perpetuity rest on EQUAL RIGHTS TO ALL, we, today assembled in our Eleventh National Woman's Rights Convention, bury the woman in the citizen, and our organization in that of the American Equal Rights Association.[3]

In structure the new organization was a carbon copy of the one it supplanted, a membership association holding annual conventions and charging a dollar or more for dues. Lucretia Mott was unanimously elected president. As the most beloved and revered founder of the woman's movement she was an important unifying influence. However, her advanced age and ebbing strength made this title devoid of the power and authority necessary for day-to-day direction. As vice president, Elizabeth Cady Stanton together with Susan B. Anthony, the corresponding secretary, and a coterie on the executive board ran the organization.

Less than a month following the convention, Mrs. Mott was visited by Miss Anthony. There was

a great deal of fault-finding and so we had it. I weary of everlasting complaints, and am glad sometimes that I shall have not much more to do in any of these movements. One thing is certain: that I do not mean to be drawn into any party feeling. I honor S.B.A.————'s and E.C.S.————'s devotion to their great work and try to cooperate as circumstances permit.[4]

While visiting New York later that year, Mrs. Mott wrote to her niece of the hectic pace set by the woman's rights leadership. "Elizabeth was like herself, full of spirit and so pleasant. . . . This Equal Rights movement is no play—but I *cannot* enter into it! Just hearing their talk and the reading makes me ache all over, and glad to come away and lie down on the sofa . . . to rest. . . . I hadn't much rest!"[5]

Other officers completed the *dramatis personae* who were to act prominently in forthcoming actions and disputes. Frederick Douglass and Theodore Tilton as additional vice presidents; Henry B. Blackwell, the husband of Lucy Stone, recording secretary; Parker Pillsbury, Lucy Stone, Antoinette Brown Blackwell, Wendell Phillips, and William Lloyd Garrison were members of the executive board. This composition, including as it did abolitionists, a prominent black, men, and women, symbolized the concept of equal rights for all.

In view of the later schism, the following sections of the constitution are worthy of note: Article III, Membership, provided that any person who consents to the principles of this association and contributes to its treasury may be a member and be entitled to speak and vote in its meetings. Article IV, Officers: Executive Committee membership was to be not less than seven nor more than fifteen. Article V, The Executive Committee had the power to enact their own by-laws, fill any vacancy, determine the pay of agents and corresponding secretaries, direct the treasurer in the application of all funds, and call special meetings. The committee was to make arrangements for all meetings and provide an annual report of the actions of the organization and to submit an accounting of its finances. Article VI, Annual Meeting: The nature of this meeting was to be determined by the committee. Article VIII, Amendments were to be made at regular meetings by a vote of two-thirds of those present. Amendments must be previously submitted in writing to the Executive Committee one month before the meeting takes place.[6]

Constitutional details were rarely honored in a meticulous fashion by the various reform associations including the one devoted to woman's rights. If an internal issue of sufficient gravity arose, then these provisions were appealed to as weapons in a factional struggle.

PROGRAM

Distancing itself from the New York Anti-Slavery Society, the meeting of the Equal Rights Association resolved "that in view of the Constitutional Convention to be held in the State of New York the coming year, it is the duty of this Association to demand such an amendment of the Constitution as shall secure equal rights to all citizens, without distinction of color, sex, or race."[7]

Parker Pillsbury ended the meeting on a buoyant note, sounding again the principal theme: "Even the Anti-Slavery can only demand equality for the *male* half of mankind. And the Woman's Rights Association contemplated only *woman* in its demand. But with us liberty means freedom, equality, and fraternity, irrespective of sex and complexion."[8]

Boston constituted one leg of the geographic triad of organizational activity with Brooklyn Heights, in the then city of Brooklyn, and lower Manhattan representing the other points. Scarcely two weeks after the association was founded, the Boston wing held its first public meeting. While it was of interest that Ira Steward, the leader of the movement for the eight-hour day, addressed the meeting, the speech of Wendell Phillips was far more significant. It ominously raised the question of priority between woman suffrage and voting rights for black males.

Phillips stated:

That the suffrage is the great question of the hour . . . nevertheless, that in view of the peculiar circumstances of the Negro's position, his claims to this right might fairly to be considered to have precedence. . . . This hour, then is preeminently the property of the Negro. Nevertheless, . . . I willingly stand here to plead the woman's cause, because the Republican party are seeking to carry their purpose by newly introducing the word "male" into the Constitution. To prevent such a corruption of the National Constitution as well as for the general welfare of the community, male and female, I wish to excite interest everywhere in the maintenance of woman's right to vote.[9]

Flushed with the success of the Boston meeting, Elizabeth Cady Stanton embarked upon a dramatic move by deciding to run for Congress in the fall elections. Her appeal to voters stated that while she was disenfranchised, nevertheless she was still eligible to seek public office.[10]

The Equal Rights Association in 1867 was to direct its energies toward achieving universal suffrage by restructuring the New York Constitution. Another arena of activity was the state of Kansas where two popular referenda were scheduled on the twin questions of black and woman suffrage.

THE 1867 CONVENTION

When May Anniversary Week rolled around, the American Equal Rights Association held its convention using essentially the same format of its previous, founding session. Its officers were also unchanged except that there was geographical representation from the Midwest and the District of Columbia. Worthy of note was the inclusion of Amelia Bloomer, who had led the revolt against the hoopskirt.[11]

The convention call proclaimed in stentorian tones:

American Democracy has interpreted the Declaration of Independence in the interest of slavery, restricting suffrage and citizenship to a *white male minority*.

The black man is still denied the crowning right of citizenship, even in normally free states. . . .

The black man, even the black soldier is yet but half-emancipated, nor will he be, until full suffrage and citizenship are secured to him in the Federal Constitution. Still more deplorable is the condition of black woman; and legally that of the white woman no better![12]

While the *leit-motif* of equal rights for all was sounded throughout the sessions, the antagonisms inherent in the political reality of black male or woman suffrage priority were muted.

Sparks of progress were brought to the convocation's attention by Susan B. Anthony. In her report she mentioned the efforts of Lucy Stone and Henry Blackwell in stumping Kansas for woman suffrage in the forthcoming referendum.[13]

DEBATE AND RESOLUTIONS

In an obvious attempt to sound the tone against priority for black male suffrage, Mrs. Stanton, in her opening address emphasized the inseparability of rights. "To discuss the question of suffrage for women and negroes, as women and negroes, and not as citizens of a republic implies that there are some reasons for demanding the right for these classes that do not apply to 'white males.' "[14]

These sentiments were echoed in a series of provocative resolutions introduced by Miss Anthony on behalf of the Executive Committee.

Resolved, That as republican institutions are based on individual rights, and not on the rights of races or sexes, the first question for the American people to settle in the reconstruction of government is the *rights* of individuals. *Resolved*, That the present claim for "manhood suffrage" masked with words "equal", "impartial", "universal", is a cruel abandonment of the slave women of the South, a fraud on the tax-paying women of the North, and an insult to the civilization of the 19th century. *Resolved*, That the proposal to reconstruct our government on . . . manhood suffrage, which emanated from the Republican party and has received the sanction of the Anti-Slavery Society, is but a continuation of the old system of class and caste legislation, always cruel and proscriptive in itself and ending in all ages in national degradation and revolution.[15]

Parker Pillsbury, a loyal colleague of Mrs. Stanton and Miss Anthony, led a series of orators against those who wished to place black suffrage above woman's voting privileges. He railed against the Anti-Slavery Society and sectors of the major parties that advocated black suffrage for males as a priority.

And then we impudently assert that "all just governments derive their powers from the consent of the governed". But when was the consent of woman ever asked . . . ?

We talk of trial by "jury of our peers". In this country of ours, women have been fined, imprisoned, scourged, branded with red hot irons and hung: But when or where for what crime or offence, was ever woman tried by a jury of her peers?

And any bill . . . for "manhood suffrage" while it ignores womanhood suffrage . . . should be repudiated as at war with the whole spirit and genius of true Democracy, and a deadly stab in the heart of justice itself.[16]

These shafts of Pillsbury accentuated the divisions within the ranks on
the expansion of suffrage. As Mrs. Stone's daughter put it, these groups
consisted of "(1) Those who thought it unwise to incorporate woman suffrage in it. (2) Those who thought that every effort should be made to
include the women, but if it failed it ought to pass. (3) Those who thought
that if it could not be included then it ought to be defeated."[17]

Ernestine Rose, the queen of the lecture platform castigated the supporters
of universal manhood suffrage:

Just read your public papers and see how our Senators and members of the House
are running through the Southern States to hold meetings and deliver public addresses. To whom? To the freedmen. And why now, and why not ten, fifteen, or
twenty years ago? Why do they get up meetings for the colored men, and call them
fellow-men, brothers and gentlemen? Because the freedman has that talisman in his
hands which the politician is looking after. Don't you perceive then the importance
of the elective franchise?[18]

Frances Gage referred to a highly publicized case of a young woman of
partial black ancestry who was cast out of the Pittsburgh Methodist College
and went on to excoriate the land-grant colleges and other institutions aided
by public funds that denied women entrance as students.[19] She recalled in
her own childhood that she successfully fashioned a barrel, but then was
admonished to go into the house and attend to her knitting. The obvious
generalization was then drawn by her that women were barred from many
avenues of employment simply because they were women.[20]

These sentiments were embodied in a resolution duly adopted:

Resolved, That the ballot alike to women and men, means bread, education, self-
reliance and self-respect; to the wife it means control over her own person, property,
and earnings; to the mother it means the equal guardianship of her children; to the
daughter it means diversified employment and a fair day's wages for a fair day's
work; to all it means free access to skilled labor, to colleges and professions, and
to every avenue of advantage and preferment.[21]

Toward the end of the convention the rumblings of a dispute were heard
that was to become much sharper in the succeeding period. Charles Red-
mond declared, "It might be that colored men would obtain their rights
before women would; but if so, he was confident that they would heartily
acquiesce in admitting woman also to the right of suffrage."[22] However,
Lucretia Mott averred that the addition of so many colored men to the
ranks of the enfranchised male would only make them allies in the fight
against woman suffrage.[23]

George Downing brought the matter to a head by stating that he "wished to know...whether Mrs. Stanton and Mrs. Mott were opposed to the enfranchisement of the colored man unless the ballot should also be accorded to woman at the same time."[24]

Mrs. Stanton answered, "I say no; I would not trust him with all my rights, degraded and oppressed himself, he would be more despotic...than even our Saxon rulers are. I desire that we go into the kingdom together, for individual and national safety demand that not another man be enfranchised without the woman by his side."[25]

The abolitionist, Stephen Foster stated in response, "Even therefore, if the enfranchisement of the colored men would probably retard the enfranchisement of women, we had no right for that reason to deprive him of his right."[26]

Mr. Downing offered a resolution to that effect. "That while we regret that the right sentiment, which would secure to women the ballot, is not as general as we would have it, nevertheless we wish it distinctly understood that we rejoice at the increasing sentiment which favors the enfranchisement of the colored man."[27]

When this resolution went down to defeat, Abby Kelly Foster berated the woman's righters: "Have we any true sense of justice, are we not dead to the sentiment of humanity if we shall wish to postpone his security against present woes and future enslavement till women shall obtain political rights?"[28]

Henry Ward Beecher, the abolitionist preacher, attempted to reconcile the two sides and thus avoided taking a definite stand. "If any man says to me, 'Why will you agitate the woman's question, when it is the hour for the black man?' I answer, it is the hour for every man black or white."[29]

Even though the liberal antislavery press was strangely silent on the woman suffrage question, a resolution was adopted expressing appreciation of the past efforts of Wendell Phillips, Horace Greeley, and Theodore Tilton, perhaps in the hope that *The Tribune, Anti-Slavery Standard,* and *The Independent* would yet come out with strong editorials favoring the franchise for women in the Kansas referendum campaign.[30]

The convention planned to hold a rally in Albany in June pressing the New York State Constitutional Convention to incorporate woman suffrage in the new constitution. Henry Ward Beecher, Frederick Douglass, and Elizabeth Cady Stanton were to represent the view of the American Equal Rights Association.[31]

6

Fissures Over Priorities—The New York Constitutional Convention and the Kansas Suffrage Campaigns, 1867

THE NEW YORK STATE CONSTITUTIONAL CONVENTION

In January 1867 Mrs. Stanton managed to secure a hearing before the Judiciary Committee of the New York State legislature. The chamber was crowded to overflowing with about half the audience composed of women. The appearance itself was a signal achievement.

In her testimony, Mrs. Stanton stated:

We are here to urge the justice of securing to all the people of the State the right to vote for delegates to the coming constitutional convention. As representatives of the people your right to regulate all that pertains to this convention is absolute. In a revision of a constitution, the State for the time being is resolved into its original elements. A state constitution must originate and be assented to by a majority of the people, those whom it disfranchises as well as those whom it invests with the suffrage.[1]

After putting forth this novel idea that the disenfranchised be included in those who are eligible to participate in ratification, she went on to answer the argument that most women did not want the suffrage, by pointing to the suffering of working women:

Remember the gay and fashionable throng who whisper in the ears of statesmen, judges, lawyers, merchants, "*We have all the rights we want*", are but mummies of civilization to be galvanized into life only be earthquakes and revolutions. Would you know what it is in the soul of woman, ask not the wives and daughters of merchant princes, but creators of wealth—those who earn their bread by honest toil—who by a turn of the wheel of fortune, stand face to face with the stern realities of life.[2]

This campaign antagonized Horace Greeley, and the columns of the *New York Tribune* were not as freely available to the woman's suffrage advocates as they once were when Greeley defended the rights of women against James Gordon Bennett's *Herald*. At the constitutional convention, Greeley was the chairperson of the committee "on the right of suffrage and the qualifications for holding office." At a hearing before this committee, George Washington Curtis, the editor of *Harper's Weekly*, and practically the only journalist supporter of woman suffrage, presented a petition favoring the position of woman's right to vote. The very first name on the document was Mrs. Horace Greeley! Horace Greeley fumed at this obvious propaganda ploy and is said to have walked over to Elizabeth Cady Stanton and stormed at her, vowing that the *Tribune* was closed to her and any reference to her in its columns would be to Mrs. Henry B. Stanton.[3]

Greeley's committee report of June 28 stated:

Your Committee does not recommend an extension of the elective franchise to women. However defensible in theory, we are satisfied that public sentiment does not demand and would not sustain any innovation so revolutionary and sweeping, so openly at war with a distribution of duties and functions between the sexes as venerable and pervading as government itself, and involving transformations so radical in social and domestic life.[4]

The convention vote against woman suffrage was overwhelming—19 to 125. Negro suffrage, so ardently advocated by Greeley, also lost. The blame for this debacle was placed on the shoulders of the woman suffrage advocates.[5] Further polarization within the ranks of woman's righters resulted. The hybrid abolitionist–woman's rights wing believed that they should heed the cries of the freedmen and concentrate all effort toward the enfranchisement of the ex-slaves.

A perceptible change was becoming evident in the outlook of Lucy Stone. At an Albany mass meeting her approach was reported as follows:

She declared that it was all right to give negroes the ballot. There was in her opinion, no objection to that, but while the committee proposes to place the male negro on an equal footing with themselves, they propose to place their mothers, sisters, wives in the same category as idiots, lunatics, and criminals. What she wanted is that the extension of suffrage to colored citizens also to females, should be submitted to the people separately.... Neither of these propositions should be mixed up with other provisions of the Constitution.... In this respect Lucy Stone took the opposite ground of that taken by Mrs. Stanton.[6]

It should be recalled that Elizabeth Cady Stanton wanted a suffrage provision to extend to all regardless of sex or race. She was opposed to any possibility that black men might get the ballot and women be deprived of the right to vote.

THE KANSAS CAMPAIGNS

In that same year (1867) Kansas was the arena of a strenuous conflict that was to have far-reaching effects on the woman suffrage movement. The Civil War had weakened the Democratic party to the point of complete ineffectiveness. The Republican party was split into two factions, one, in control, opposed to woman suffrage; the other in favor of woman's vote, a distinct minority.[7]

Two amendments to the Kansas constitution were placed before the voters in the form of separate referenda. One was to decide suffrage for women, the other for black males. While the American Equal Rights Association was meeting in New York in May 1867, Lucy Stone and her husband, Henry Blackwell, were stumping Kansas for woman suffrage. Because of the anti–woman suffrage position of the dominant Kansas Republican party leadership, the only Republican ally who came to side of woman's rights was Sam N. Wood. Lucy Stone and Henry Blackwell would have nothing to do with the Democrats.

Lucy Stone communicated to the Equal Rights Association her strong resentment at the treatment accorded the Kansas campaign by the Eastern liberal press. She wrote:

The Tribune and Independent alone, if they would urge universal suffrage as they do negro suffrage, could carry this whole nation upon the only just plane of equal human rights. What a power to hold and not use!...I trust you will not fail to rebuke the cowardly use of the terms "universal", "impartial", and "equal", applied to hide a dark skin and an unpopular client....I hope not a man will be asked to speak at the convention. If they volunteer, very well, but I have been for the last time on my knees to Phillips, Higginson, or any of them. If they help now, they should ask us, and not we them.[8]

Lucy Stone's desperation increased as she learned that the Kansas Republican party State Central Committee was going to scuttle woman suffrage. With the continued silence of the abolitionist and liberal Republican press, she momentarily burst her traditional political bonds and arrived at the same position of the Anthony-Stanton forces. She wrote in anger against the Kansas Republican leadership: "Till this action is settled we can affirm nothing. Everywhere we go, we have the largest and most enthusiastic meetings and any one of our audiences would give a majority for women; but the negroes are all against us. *These men ought not to be allowed to vote before we do*, because they will be so much more dead weight to lift."[9]

The fierce pleas of Lucy Stone and minority Kansas Republicans fell on deaf ears. The State Committee, meeting in Lawrence on September 5, 1867, passed the following resolution:

Resolved, That we are unqualifiedly opposed to the dogma of "Female Suffrage", and while we do not recognize it as a party question, the attempt of certain persons within the State, and from without it, to enforce it upon the people of the State, demands the unqualified opposition of every citizen who respects the laws of society and the well-being and good name of our young commonwealth.[10]

Lucy Stone's cry for help brought a response from the abolitionist-Liberal Republicans of the East against these resolutions. Henry Ward Beecher, George W. Curtis, William Lloyd Garrison, Wendell Phillips, and Thomas Wentworth Higginson, fearful of driving Lucy Stone and her followers out of their camp, belatedly came through, but the resolutions carried. So blatant was the attack on the part of the Kansas Republican majority that one of the dissidents, R. B. Taylor, urged that certain speakers be stricken from the list of Republican campaigners "For the reason that they have within the last few weeks, in public addresses, public articles, used ungentlemanly, indecent, and infamously defamatory language, when alluding to a large and respectable portion of the women of Kansas or to women now engaged in canvassing the state in favor of impartial suffrage."[11]

Disheartened and discouraged, Lucy Stone and Henry Blackwell returned to the East. The vituperation of the Kansas Republicans together with the ineffectiveness of the eastern Republican establishment seemed to close all doors to success. Their places in the campaign were taken by Susan B. Anthony and Elizabeth Cady Stanton.

ENTER GEORGE FRANCIS TRAIN

Stanton and Anthony believed that the outlook for woman suffrage in Kansas would be dark unless sufficient allies could be recruited among Democrats and dissident Republicans. They were less wedded to the Republican party, and in the past, newspapers did refer to Elizabeth Cady Stanton's leaning toward the Democrats. For purely partisan reasons, the Democrats had pitted woman suffrage against black voting rights in the hope of defeating black suffrage and splitting the Republicans. Mrs. Stanton and Miss Anthony were also mindful of Lucy Stone's outburst opposing the granting of the franchise to the blacks ahead of women. Through the offices of the St. Louis Suffrage Society, they dispatched a telegram to a very popular Democrat, George Francis Train, to lead the fight in Kansas.

Train replied on October 7, 1867, that he would accept and pay his own expenses. All who could be consulted testified to Train's immense eloquence and popularity. In a return wire they wrote, "Come to Kansas and stump the state for equal rights and woman suffrage. The people want you, the women want you." This appeal was signed by Miss Anthony, Mrs. Stanton, and the prominent minority Kansas Republican, Sam N. Wood.[12]

George F. Train entered the campaign with great vigor, drawing huge audiences wherever he spoke. His unrepressed hostility toward and ridicule of recently freed blacks caused vials of wrath to be poured on Susan B. Anthony and Elizabeth Cady Stanton. The Liberal Republican-abolitionist forces were also mindful of Train's association with the Irish, so prominently associated with the draft riots in New York. His advocacy of amnesty for the Confederate soldiers and the end of the Union army occupancy of the South were further reasons for their hatred of Train. As Lucy Stone's daughter put it:

When the Eastern papers announced that this fantastic personage was speaking for woman suffrage in Kansas, Mrs. Stone thought the report was a monstrous hoax. When she found that his meetings were actually advertised as being held under the auspices of the American Equal Rights Association, she felt constrained to publish a card explaining that the Association was not responsible.[13]

The nature of Train's campaigning is revealed in the remarks he made in response to a Republican leader in Kansas who referred to the woman's rights movement as "humbugging" with the most "infernal humbugs" being that woman should receive equal pay for work equal to that of man.

Do you mean to say that the school mistress, who so ably does her duty, should only receive three hundred dollars, while the schoolmaster who performs the same duty gets fifteen hundred?...

Woman first, and negro last is my programme,... disfranchising all of age who cannot read the American Constitution, and the Bible...expresses my views.[14]

Train's support for pay equality for women endeared him to Stanton and Anthony. They weren't too upset by his advocacy of a type of "educated" suffrage, which would in practice eliminate most blacks from the voting population.

The day before the balloting took place, Train sounded forth: "The negro can wait and go to school. And as all are now loyal, the war is over, and no rebels exist, no American in this land must be marked by the stain of attainder or impeachment. No so-called rebel must be disfranchised."[15]

Both the black and woman suffrage proposals lost. The former received approximately 10,000 votes; the latter garnered a bit over 9,000. The defeat of black enfranchisement was blamed on the Anthony-Train campaign.

A contrary view was offered by the prominent woman's righter in the Midwest, Helen Ekin Starett. She wrote:

The work of George Francis Train has been much and variously commented upon. Certainly when he was in Kansas he was at the height of his prosperity and popularity. He was confident he would be the next President. He drew immense and enthusiastic audiences everywhere and was a special favorite with the laboring classes on account of the reforms he promised to bring about when he should be President.[16]

Miss Anthony was bitter about the treatment her phase of the Kansas campaign received and irately expressed her feelings:

So utterly had the women been deserted in the Kansas campaign by those they had the strongest reason to look for help, that at times all effort seemed hopeless. The editors of the New York *Tribune* and the *Independent* can never know how wistfully, from day to day their papers were searched for some inspiring editorials on the woman's amendment, but naught was there.... Yet these two papers, extensively taken all over Kansas, had they been true to woman as to the negro, could have revolutionized the State. But with arms folded, Greeley, Curtis, Tilton, Beecher, Phillips, Garrison, Frederick Douglass, all calmly watched the struggle from afar, and when defeat came to both propositions...the women who spoke in the campaign were reproached for having "killed negro suffrage."[17]

Yet, Mrs. Stanton and Miss Anthony did not regret their course. They believed that it was the only way to press their cause against such combined opposition. It was a belief that the rationale the abolitionists used in justifying criticism of Train could also be applied to the abolitionists. Miss Anthony put it this way:

So long as opposition to slavery is the only test for a free pass and membership of your association and you do not shut out all persons opposed to woman suffrage, why should we not accept all persons in favor of woman suffrage to our platform and association, even though they be rabid pro-slavery Democrats? Your test of faithfulness is the negro, ours is the woman; the broadest platform, to which no party has as yet risen, is humanity.[18]

The assessment of the results of the campaign by Anthony and Stanton was not that the liberal abolitionists were less active out of ignorance of the issue, but that

it was because in their heart of hearts they did not grasp the imperative necessity of woman's demand for that protection which the ballot alone can give; they did not feel for *her* the degradation of disfranchisement.
    ...only from woman's standpoint could the battle be successfully fought and victory secured.[19]

In addition to repeating the omnipotence of the ballot for women, in obvious contradiction of the fact that they embraced Train, a male, they proclaimed that the championing of woman's rights could only be done by women.

Politically, the Kansas campaign had additional meaning for the Anthony-Stanton forces. They estimated that the American Equal Rights Association leaders who were the abolitionists from the old Anti-Slavery Society had so captured the rest of the woman suffrage movement that it "became the toy of the Republican party and has been trifled with ever since."[20] Henceforth Stanton and Anthony would be opportunists seeking whatever political vehicle they could use to carry woman suffrage.

As for Train, he joined Mrs. Stanton and Miss Anthony on a lecture tour for woman's rights on the way back to the East. In a pamphlet which Train subsequently wrote about the Kansas campaign, the following bit of doggerel appeared:

> The Garrisons, Phillipses, Greeleys, and Beechers
> False prophets, false guides, false teachers
>   and preachers
> Left Mrs. Stanton, Miss Anthony, Brown and Stone
> To fight the Kansas battle alone:
> While your Rosses, Pomeroys, and your Clarkes
> Stood on the fence, or basely fled
> While woman was saved by a Copperhead.[21]

The campaigns in the New York Constitutional Convention and in Kansas, where woman suffrage suffered defeats, served to sharpen the differences within the woman's rights movement. Each faction blamed the other for the losses. The entry of George Francis Train into the picture as an antiblack Democrat siding with Mrs. Stanton and Miss Anthony brought charges against these women of being allies of the pro-slavery Democratic party. It was not to be the last time that the militant wing of the woman's rights movement was to embrace a divisive and controversial personage. The rivalry between the Republican-abolitionists and the group around Susan B. Anthony and Elizabeth Cady Stanton went beyond convention polemics to the harsh field of practical politics.

THE STRUGGLE FOR
CONTROL, 1868

THE 1868 CONVENTION

The forthcoming conventions of the various reform organizations during the May Anniversary week provided *Revolution*, the organ of the Anthony-Stanton forces initially financed by George Francis Train, with a broad reading public. The editorials had a dual appeal. On the one hand, the writings appealed for a broad unification where all issues could be discussed. On the other hand, woman suffrage was elevated to being the most important demand of the age.

"E Pluribus Unum"
The Anniversaries

If we examine the creeds of political organizations, church or reform organizations, temperance, peace, prisons, the rights of black men, women, or labor, we find the special pleadings of each and all these platforms resolve themselves at least into the rights of individuals, to be guided in all things by their own reason and conscience; the right to life, liberty, and happiness....

It is the first duty of the American people to vindicate that grand declaration of equality, already twice baptized in blood, and consent to no reconstruction of this nation on any basis but that of equal rights to every citizen of the republic.[1]

This unitary approach is in etched contrast to the sharp tone in an editorial found on the very same page addressed "*To Our Radical Friends*." In striving to justify association with Train, Mrs. Stanton and her collaborators planted the banner of woman suffrage and defied all opponents. This served to forecast some dramatic doings at the American Equal Rights Association convention. Mrs Stanton wrote:

So long as we are enabled to proclaim our principles, it matters not who helps to do it. We regard the enfranchisement of woman as the most important question of the age, and we are determined to keep it before the nation, and to this end we will accept aid from any quarter, affiliate with any man, black or white, Jew or Gentile, saint or sinner, democrat or republican.[2]

Press Ridicule

The following report of the first session of the American Equal Rights Association held on May 14, 1868 is representative of the general public press:

About five hundred persons, chiefly women assembled in the hall of Cooper Institute at the evening session. These were of a decidedly homogeneous class, and were of the gimlet curl, sallow complexioned, short haired, and *pseudo* philosophic stamp, almost every nose bestraddled by a pair of spectacles, a circumstance which had a remarkable effect, as they elevated their chins in order to observe the speakers on the platform, of making them all appear as though they were looking anxiously for something to drop from the ceiling. The bloomer element was also represented... languidly folded its arms and crossed its trousered nether extremities.[3]

Convention Program

Henry B. Blackwell reported on the Kansas campaign and indicated that all went well until at an "inopportune moment, Horace Greeley and others saw fit in the Constitutional Convention to report unfavorably on the proposition to extend suffrage to the women of New York and that influenced Republicans of Kansas."[4]

Mrs. Stone urged support for two petitions to Congress. One was to extend suffrage to women in the District of Columbia and the territories; the other was a Sixteenth Amendment prohibiting the states from disenfranchisement based on sex. Frederick Douglass urged support. Miss Anthony appealed for *Revolution*.[5]

The Open Convention Debates

What appeared so far as an innocuous beginning was transformed dramatically when Olympia Brown engaged in an impassioned debate with Frederick Douglass. The theme was the one of priority given the question of black suffrage.

Brown: Some of our leading reformers work for other objects first: the enfranchisement of the negro, the eight hour law, the temperance cause; and leave the woman suffrage question in the background; but woman will be enfranchised in spite of them. It is no use to tell us to wait until something else is done. *Now* is the accepted time for the enfranchisement of woman.[6]

Douglass: I champion the rights of the negro to vote. It is with us a matter of life and death, and therefore cannot be postponed. I have always championed woman's right to vote; but it will be seen that the present claim for the negro is one of the most urgent necessity. The assertion of the right of woman to vote meets nothing but ridicule: there is no deep-seated malignity in the hearts of people against her; but name the right of the negro to vote, all hell is turned loose and the Ku Klux and the Regulators hunt and slay the offending black man.[7]

Mrs. Stone charged that the Republican party was false to principle unless it protected women as well as colored men in the exercise of their right to vote.[8]

Douglass: The men who stood by Andrew Johnson and opposed impeachment were the men who held the base hell-born sentiment that this was a white man's government.

Mrs. Stanton: Did not the Republican party declare the same?

Douglass: I think there is a difference.

Anthony: ...I say that the Republican party does not demand as a party the white man's government; but it demands a man's government. That is it. And now what is the difference between a man's government and a white man's government? One is a crime against the man of the black race and the other is a crime against seventeen millions of the races white and black.[9]

A journalist commented, "Mr. Douglass laughed, smirked, and seemed a little non-plussed."[10]

Dissension behind the Scenes

At the afternoon business session some expression of the antipathy between the Anthony-Stanton forces and the Boston wing led by Lucy Stone and Henry Blackwell surfaced.

Though this newspaper account has overtones of ridicule, the essential facts are there.

There was no public collision, but at the business meeting of the afternoon the crash came, and a lively time they had of it. The Anti-Train party was headed by Mr. and Mrs. Lucy Stone Blackwell, who formed their attack under the guise of a call for the Treasurer's report, to various items of which they objected. The principally obnoxious item to them was the expenditure of a considerable sum for posters on the occasion of the campaign in Kansas in which Mr. Train took a prominent part.

Miss Anthony came promptly to the response and told them pretty plainly that they never had any treasury;... that she had got the posters for Train and that she considered him a good card; suppose he did spell negro with two "g's", he was in favor of enfranchisement of women and drew crowds to the polls in Kansas, and finally she told them that if they did not choose to pay the bill she would pay it herself.

The anti-Train party squirmed and undertook to talk about orderly methods of doing business, and the inconsistency of affiliating with Democrats, and pitched into the *Revolution* as having very improperly stolen the thunder of the society, and altogether taking too much on itself . . . and rather eclipsing the rest of the party.[11]

This activity of the Republican-abolitionist wing of the Equal Rights Association attempting to censure Mrs. Stanton and Miss Anthony called forth deep resentment. Mrs. Stanton wrote:

Susan and I, though members of the Equal Rights Association, do many things outside that body for which no one is responsible. The idea of starting a paper under its auspices, or as an organ for it, never entered our minds. We went to Kansas as individuals; personal friends outside that association gave us money to go and contributed funds to start a paper. We object to that resolution of censure. . . . The secret of all this furor is Republican spite. They want to stave off our question until after the presidential campaign. They can keep all the women still but Susan and me. They can't control us, therefore the united efforts of Republicans, Abolitionists, and certain women to crush us and our paper.[12]

One can sense a growing disillusionment with the Equal Rights Association as a viable organization for the furtherance of woman suffrage. Organizationally, control passed out of the hands of Mrs. Stanton and Miss Anthony. To be sure, Mrs. Stanton was again vice president and Miss Anthony was on the Executive Committee. However, Miss Anthony was no longer corresponding secretary, and six out of ten members of the Executive Committee were definitely not in sympathy with the collaboration between Train and Mrs. Stanton and Miss Anthony in the Kansas campaign.[13]

Not content with occupying back seats in the Equal Rights Association, the Anthony-Stanton group created a paper organization calling itself the Woman's Suffrage Association of America. It was identical to the editorial offices of *Revolution* and simply expressed the lack of faith behind that paper in the Equal Rights Association. It also represented a center that could focus sentiment and action along the lines of the Anthony-Stanton approach to woman's rights. "It may not be out of place to announce here the organization of a new Woman's Suffrage movement with headquarters at the offices of 'The Revolution', 37 Park Row, with Mrs. Elizabeth Cady Stanton, Mrs. Horace Greeley, Mrs. Abby H. Gibbons, and Miss Susan B. Anthony as the Central Committee and Council."[14]

Confusion reigned in the ranks of the woman's movement, and a week later *Revolution* attempted to clear up the difference between the two organizations.

Some friends write us to know what is the difference is between the "American Equal Rights Association" and the "Woman's Suffrage Association of America". We answer: the former of which Lucretia Mott is President, was organized at the close of the war, before the enfranchisement of the black men of the South, to demand suffrage for women and black men and equal rights for both everywhere, in the church, the state, and the home. During the last year, as Woman's Suffrage Associations have been forming in different parts of the country, for the sole purpose of securing suffrage for women, it was thought advisable to have a central committee of correspondence in New York to plan work, distribute tracts, and petitions and communicate through "The Revolution" with similar Associations throughout the country. The Equal Rights Association speaks through the *Anti-Slavery Standard*, which though not its organ, "hospitably entertains" the question of woman suffrage, while *The Revolution* holding the ground of universal suffrage irrespective of color or sex, is specially the organ of the Woman's Suffrage Association of America.[15]

It was evident from this statement that the Stanton-Anthony group had conceded control of the Equal Rights Association to the Republican-abolitionist combination. The Woman Suffrage Association was described as a correspondence clearing house and not a serious rival organization as yet. The rather benign language was designed to avoid harsh antagonism which might have alienated some Anthony-Stanton supporters, but it soon became clear that it couldn't be contained on that level.

The Rivals—The National Woman Suffrage Association and the American Woman Suffrage Association

THE FIRST WASHINGTON, D.C., WOMAN SUFFRAGE CONVENTION

An annual custom of woman suffragists invading the nation's capital began in January 1869 under the leadership of Miss Anthony and Mrs. Stanton. The structure of this lobbying-convocation combination followed the loose format of the May Anniversaries held in New York. A call went out stating: "A National Woman's Suffrage Convention will be held in . . . Washington, D.C. . . . All associations friendly to Woman's Rights are invited to send delegates from every state. Friends of the cause are invited to attend and take part in the discussions."[1]

By the time of the convention, the Fourteenth Amendment had become part of the Constitution, and the Fifteenth Amendment was pending. There were several suffrage bills before Congress. Lucretia Mott presided and delegates came representing twenty states. Senator Samuel C. Pomeroy, who supported woman suffrage, was the principal speaker.

Susan B. Anthony summed up the significance of the convention:

On the one vital point, that suffrage is the inalienable right of every intelligent citizen who is held amenable to law, and is taxed to support the government, there was no difference expressed. The issue that roused most heated debate was whether the colored man should be kept out of the right of suffrage until woman could also be enfranchised.

The discussion between colored men on the one side and women on the other, as to whether it was the duty of the women of the nation to hold their claims in abeyance, was spicy, able, and effective. . . . When we contrast the condition of the most fortunate at the North, with the living death colored men endure everywhere, there seems to be a selfishness in our present position. But remember we speak not for ourselves alone, but all womankind, in poverty, ignorance, and hopeless dependence, for the women of the oppressed race too, who in slavery, have known a depth of misery and degradation that no man can ever appreciate.[2]

Tone of the Convention

It was quite apparent that the convention was dominated by woman partisans of Mrs. Stanton and Miss Anthony. In this letter it is clearly indicated too that men were not to be trusted.

There was one feature...that we greatly deplore, and that was an impatience, not only with the audience, but with some on the platform whenever any man arose to speak. We must not forget that men have sensibilities as well as women and our strongest hold today on the public mind is the fact that men of eloquence and power on both continents are pleading for our rights.[3]

In her opening speech, Mrs. Stanton set forth the basis for such "impolite" tactics against male speakers.

Compelled to follow our assailants, wherever they go and fight them with their own weapons; when cornered with wit and sarcasm, some cry out, you have no logic on your platform, forgetting that we have no use for logic until they give us logicians at whom to hurl it; and if for the pure love of it, we now and then rehearse the logic that is like a,b,c to all of us, others cry out—the same old speeches we have heard these twenty years.[4]

National Politics and Convention Program

Using every weapon in her oratorical arsenal, Mrs. Stanton went beyond condemnation of the Republican party for passing the Fifteenth Amendment, "securing 'manhood suffrage' and establishing an aristocracy of sex on this continent," by threatening to support the Democrats if the Republicans did not enscribe woman suffrage in their platform.[5]

Advocating the passage of a Sixteenth Amendment, Mrs. Stanton proclaimed three major points:

A government based on the principle of class and caste cannot stand....
    The male element is a destructive force, stern, selfish, aggrandizing, loving war, violence, conquest, acquisition, breeding the material and moral work alike, discord, disorder, disease, and death. See what a record of blood and cruelty the pages of history reveal!...[6]
    If American women find it hard to bear the oppressions of their own Saxon fathers, the best orders of manhood, what may they not be called to endure when all the lower orders of foreigners now crowding their shores legislate for them and their daughters. Think of Patrick and Sambo and Hans and Yung Tung who don't know the difference between a monarchy and a republic; who cannot read the Declaration

of Independence or Webster's Spelling-book, making laws for Lucretia Mott, Ernestine L. Rose, and Anna E. Dickinson.[7]

Not only is the antimale attitude quite evident in her remarks, but also a nativist anti-immigration bias, as well as an antiblack predilection—all subsumed in her advocacy of an "educated suffrage" based upon literacy and education.

Resolutions were adopted without any recording of the votes. One claimed that governments of men had failed because of the record of violence and bloodshed. Another stated that a democracy based upon a republicanism that excluded women and blacks was "a contradiction in terms more offensive and harder to be borne than despotism itself." In the reconstruction of government, suffrage should be "based on loyalty and intelligence and nowhere limited by the odious distinctions on account of color and sex." The delegates were urged to hold state conventions memorializing the state legislatures during their sessions on behalf of impartial suffrage for men and women. The bill that was then pending in Congress to disenfranchise the people of the District of Columbia was roundly denounced. It was further resolved that there was no valid "reason why a colored man should be excluded from a seat in Congress, or any woman either, who possesses suitable capabilities, and has been duly elected." The principles of equal pay for equal work, and freedom of choice in occupations were upheld for both blacks and women.[8]

The Fifteenth Amendment was denounced as creating a worse tyranny than had existed before. "*Resolved*, That a man's government is worse than a white man's government, because in proportion as you increase the tyrants, you make the condition of the disfranchised class more hopeless and degraded."[9]

In a special appeal addressed to the Congressional Committee of the District of Columbia, the convention made note of the power of labor.

If the masses knew their strength, they could turn the whole legislation of this country to their advantage and drive poverty, rags, and ignorance into the Pacific Ocean. If they could learn wisdom in the National Labor Conventions and not sell their votes to political tricksters, a system of Finance, Trade and Commerce, and Cooperation could soon be established that would secure the rights of Labor and put an end to the concentration of wealth in the hands of the few. Labor holds the ballot now; let it learn how to use it. Educated women know how to use it now; let them have it.[10]

This cordial approach to organized labor was no accident. A warm message was received from William H. Sylvis, the president of the National Labor Union, in which he stated: "I am in favor of universal suffrage, universal amnesty, and universal liberty."[11]

AMERICAN EQUAL RIGHTS CONVENTION, 1869

On May 12, 13, and 14 at Steinway Hall in New York City the American Equal Rights Association held its May Anniversary Convention. The atmosphere was extremely charged, and there was a general air of expectancy that dramatic controversy would develop.

Miss Anthony quite frankly conceded that control had firmly passed to the Boston-Republican-abolitionist forces. "Few only were equal to the emergency. Even in the Equal Rights Convention, the slightest opposition to the XIV Amendment called out hisses and denunciation, and all resolutions on that point were promptly voted down."[12]

Convention Debate

Discussion centered on the question as to whether or not the proposed Fifteenth Amendment should be passed without simultaneously passing a Sixteenth Amendment giving the women the right to vote. The debate is given here so that programmatic issues which split the woman's rights movement are clearly set forth.

The President, Mrs. Stanton, argued that not another man should be enfranchised until enough women are admitted to the polls to outweigh those already there. (Applause). She did not believe in allowing ignorant negroes and foreigners to make laws for her to obey. (Applause).[13]

Douglass . . . There is no name greater than that of Elizabeth Cady Stanton in the matter of woman's rights and equal rights, but my sentiments are tinged a little against *The Revolution*. There was in the address to which I allude the employment of certain names, such as "Sambo". I must say that I do not see how anyone can pretend that there is the same urgency in giving the ballot to women as to the negro. With us the matter is a question of life and death, at least in fifteen States of the Union. When women, because they are women are hunted down through the cities of New York and New Orleans; when they are dragged from their houses and hung upon lampposts; when their children are torn from their arms and their brains are dashed out upon the pavement; when they are in danger of having their homes burnt down over their heads; when their children are not allowed to enter schools, then they will have an urgency to obtain the ballot equal to our own. (Great Applause).

A Voice—Is that not all true about black women?

Mr. Douglass—Yes, yes, yes; it is true of the black woman, but not because she is a woman, but because she is black. (Applause). . . . I am in favor of woman's suffrage in order they shall have all the virtue and vice confronted.

Miss Anthony—The old anti-slavery school say women must stand back and wait until the negroes shall be recognized. But we say, if you will not give the whole loaf of suffrage to the entire people, give it to the intelligent first. (Applause) If intelligence, justice, and morality are to have precedence in the Government, let the question of women be brought up first and that of the negro last. (Applause).

Lucy Stone—Mrs. Stanton will, of course, advocate the precedence for her sex, and Mr. Douglass will strive for the first position for his and both are perhaps right. If it be true that the government derives its authority from the consent of the governed, we are safe in trusting that principle to the uttermost. If one has a right to say that you can not read and therefore can not vote, then it may be said you are a woman and can not vote. We are lost if we turn away from the middle principle and argue for one class . . . But I thank God for that XV Amendment, and I hope it will be adopted in every State. I will be thankful in my soul if *any* body can get out of the terrible pit. But I believe that the safety of the Government would be more promoted by the admission of woman as an element of restoration than the negro. I believe that the influence of woman will save the country before every other power. (Applause)[14]

The convention went against Miss Anthony and Mrs. Stanton. Resolutions offered by Henry Blackwell carried:

Resolved, That the extension of suffrage to women is essential to the public safety and to the establishment and permanence of free institutions.

Resolved, That as woman, in private life, in the partnership of marriage is now the conservator of private morals, so woman in public life, in the partnership of a republican state, based upon universal suffrage, will become the conservator of public morals.

Resolved, That while we heartily approve of the Fifteenth Amendment, extending suffrage to men without distinction of race, we nevertheless feel profound regret that Congress has not submitted a parallel amendment for the enfranchisement of women.

Resolved, That any party professing to be democratic in spirit or republican in principle which opposes or ignores the political rights of woman, is false to its professions, shortsighted in its policy, and unworthy of the confidence of the friends of impartial liberty.[15]

The resolution hailing the Fifteenth Amendment was a body blow to the Anthony-Stanton forces, who held out uncompromisingly for universal suffrage. Parker Pillsbury, their spokesperson, complained bitterly:

It is remarkable that, as the worst opposition to the abolitionists twenty and thirty years ago came from the churches and the clergy, so now the most persistent obstruction to the demands of the Equal Rights Association which asks for the ballot for all men *and all women*, are some of the former abolitionists led by tricky, crafty Congressmen, whom none have better understood, or more faithfully exposed in the past years, than these same abolitionists.[16]

In a further attempt to isolate the followers of Anthony and Stanton, open reference was made to Mrs. Stanton's views that morality in marriage only extended to love being an essential ingredient in a marriage relationship; once love ceased to exist between marriage partners, then the marriage itself had no basis. This was interpreted as "free loveism." Thus a resolution that stated that "we abhorrently repudiate Free Loveism as horrible and mischievous to society, and disown any sympathy with it" was defeated on the grounds that the explicit mention of "Free Loveism" was tantamount to a confession that such a doctrine had some supporters in the convention.[17] Nevertheless, Henry Blackwell did introduce a resolution that disclaimed that the supporters of woman suffrage were "seeking to undermine or destroy the sanctity of the marriage relationship." Despite the disclaimer, the very discussion of the issue had a damaging effect.

The last effort to besmirch the reputation of the Anthony forces involved financial integrity. Stephen B. Foster accused Miss Anthony of running the finances of the Equal Rights Association singlehandedly without any financial accountability. She had legitimately been given that authority and, as always, ran up deficits. What really disturbed her opponents was the expenditure of funds on the Kansas campaign involving George Francis Train. The public effort to denigrate Susan B. Anthony was halted after Henry Blackwell divulged that Miss Anthony paid $1,000 to end the dispute. But again the damage to Susan B. Anthony's reputation was there.

Losing out on the issue of the Fifteenth Amendment, smeared with the accusation of "Free Loveism," and having Miss Anthony's financial integrity impugned made it quite evident that the Equal Rights Association was no longer a viable organization for the Anthony-Stanton forces. This situation gave rise to the effort of establishing a new suffrage organization, the National Woman Suffrage Association, dedicated exclusively to voting rights for women.

THE NATIONAL WOMAN SUFFRAGE ASSOCIATION

The National Woman Suffrage Association (N.W.S.A.) was formed during the May Anniversary week of 1869. A simple invitation went out to delegates from various cause organizations, which were meeting at that time in New York City. These invitees were exclusively women, and they came to a reception at the Woman's Bureau, the headquarters where the Anthony-Stanton organ, *Revolution*, was published. Known supporters of Lucy Stone were not invited. Thus, this new organization, which developed a constitution and by-laws, elected officers, and propounded a program, became the province of Elizabeth Cady Stanton and Susan B. Anthony.

The reaction to their isolation and loss of power in the American Equal Rights Association pushed Stanton-Anthony to a position perilously close to female chauvinism. Miss Anthony stated:

There had been so much trouble with men in the Equal Rights Society, that it was thought best to keep absolute control in the hands of women. Sad experience had taught them that in trying emergencies they would be left to fight their own battles, and therefore it was best to fit themselves for their responsibilities by filling the positions of trust exclusively with women.[18]

It was a strange position in view of the fact that they had accepted Train and relied heavily on the loyalty of Parker Pillsbury.

Susan B. Anthony, as the professional functionary of the organization tended to be more practical than her associate, Elizabeth Cady Stanton, and resisted the passage of a resolution opposing the Fifteenth Amendment, preferring that nothing be said about it. To no avail. Mrs. Stanton's ultra position carried the day.[19]

To break out of isolation and garner some financial support, the Anthony-Stanton forces embarked upon a dramatic course, appealing to the wealthiest strata of women in their summer vacation areas—Newport, Rhode Island, and Saratoga Springs, New York. It certainly was a departure from the periodic condemnations that wealthy capitalists received in the columns of *Revolution*. Celia Burleigh wrote amusingly from Saratoga, "Flora Mc-Flimsey has looked into the face of Miss Anthony and has not yet turned into stone."[20] Mrs. Stanton commented on the Newport experience:

So obeying orders, we sailed across the Sound one bright moonlight night with a gay party of the "disenfranchised".... Although trunk after trunk—not of gossamers, laces and flowers, but of suffrage ammunition, speeches, resolutions, petitions, tracts, John Stuart Mills' last work, and folios of The Revolution.[21]

At Newport, a resolution was adopted establishing yet another basis for division and further isolation. This statement of desperation proclaimed:

that the Republican Party, by inserting the word male in the Federal Constitution ...thus establishing an aristocracy of sex; and the Democratic Party, by their general hostility to, and ridicule of Woman Suffrage, are alike undeserving our sympathy, and that we earnestly call upon all true men in both parties to at once organize a new party based upon principle rather than expediency.[22]

Beyond the cadres of activists who knew the inner workings of the woman's rights movement, the circles of sympathetic women were quite naive. The calls of the Anthony-Stanton group had an appealing ring of an all-inclusive national organization dedicated to woman suffrage. The various state organizations, especially in New England and New Jersey, were under the influence of Lucy Stone and her husband, Henry Blackwell. These same forces were tied closely to the Republican-abolitionist coalition. They had wrested control of the American Equal Rights Association from Anthony and Stanton, only to find a new organization championing the ideas of this duo. Organizational measures were soon taken by Mrs. Stone and her followers to reject the opposition to the Fifteenth Amendment, the creation of a new national political party, and the exclusion of men from positions of responsibility in organizations dedicated to woman suffrage.

While this rivalry sharpened between proponents of the enfranchisement of women, an opposition to woman suffrage developed, led by none other than the sister of Henry Ward Beecher, Catherine. The Beecher family was split up, with Henry soon to be the titular head of the organization directed by Lucy Stone and Henry Blackwell and Isabella Beecher Hooker allied with Stanton and Anthony.

Catherine Beecher called a meeting, which adopted resolutions claiming that the chief reason for woman's depressed condition is lack of training in "those branches of industry which are peculiarly appropriate to their sex, such as the educating of childhood, the care of the sick, and domestic avocations generally."[23] It was further agreed that training institutions for these vocations and domestic economy be established as part of common school education. Other "suitable" occupations included horticulture and floriculture, the raising of cotton and silk, and the keeping of bees. Miss Beecher's efforts were aided by the wives of Civil War heroes—General William Sherman and Admiral John A.D. Dahlgren. They repudiated "sympathy with the views and objects of what is popularly known as woman's rights."[24]

THE AMERICAN WOMAN SUFFRAGE ASSOCIATION

Less than three months after the National Woman Suffrage Association was formed, the New England Suffrage Association Executive Committee appointed a Committee of Correspondence, headed by Lucy Stone, to issue a circular letter calling for the establishment of a new national organization to rival National, associated with the Anthony-Stanton group. This call established the myth perpetuated by most secondary histories of the woman suffrage movement, that the basis for the difference between "National" and "American" was that the latter wanted a delegated body based on agitational work in the states and their legislatures, while the former was a nationwide organization dedicated to federal legislative activities on behalf of woman suffrage. Cleveland, Ohio, was the setting for a convention to set up the new organization—The American Woman Suffrage Association (A.W.S.A.)—in late November.

Again, naive supporters of woman suffrage were attracted to the concept of decentralization of activity and representation on a statewide basis. The U.S. Constitution did give the power to the states to set voter qualifications. The leaders of National—Stanton, Anthony, and Pillsbury—knew that this was an attempt to isolate and weaken their organization.

As a safeguard against the possibility of a small clique in a central office controlling the affairs of the association, the American established a provision in their constitution stating that a quorum for a meeting of the Executive Committee would be five, provided a mailing had been sent out to the membership of that committee fifteen days in advance. Furthermore, no action taken by the Executive Committee would be final unless ratified in writing by at least fifteen committee members.[25] This was directed at the manner in which Susan B. Anthony had taken matters into her own hands, such as collaborating with George F. Train in the 1867 Kansas campaign without adequate consultation with other leading figures of the Equal Rights Association.

In the face of clear efforts by Lucy Stone forces to exclude any of the Anthony-Stanton group from the deliberations of the new American Woman Suffrage Association, Miss Anthony journeyed to Cleveland and secured the convention floor. She urged a concerted effort to go to Washington as the route to secure passage of a Sixteenth Amendment as against pursuing suffrage reform in each state. In an impassioned plea she cried out:

So help me, Heaven!...I care not what may come out of this Convention, so this great cause shall go forward to its grand consummation. And though this Convention, by its action shall nullify the National Association of which I am a member, and though it shall tread its heel on *The Revolution*, to carry on which I have struggled as never mortal woman or mortal man struggled for any cause which he or she advocated,...still, if you will do this work in Washington so that this amendment shall be proposed...I will thank God for this convention as long as I have the breath of life. (Applause).[26]

The fiery pleas of Miss Anthony were not successful. There were now two rival woman suffrage organizations which were going to maintain their separate ways for two decades. An amalgam of causes dictated the division: differences over support for the Fifteenth Amendment which guaranteed suffrage to black men; divergent views on the role of males in the leadership of woman suffrage associations; questions over the collaboration with antiblack Copperhead Democrat George Francis Train; odds on the decision-making process within the association; whether a suffrage association should be narrow in purpose or embrace related side issues. Since the American group was willing to make common cause with the Republican-abolitionist tendency, it appeared to be more respectable and conservative. The Anthony-Stanton group was the more militant and radical, ready to embrace new allies and controversial areas of social concern in the pursuit of that single goal—common to both groups—woman suffrage.

The New York Times put it this way:

It is a new organization which includes among its officers and members the soberer and more cultivated friends of the movement and it owes its existence to their desire to get rid of the extravagances and follies that have marked the course of the Association in this city and of its organ, *The Revolution*. Loud talking, gun firing, torchlight processions and brass bands will not do the work.[27]

The titular head of the American Woman Suffrage Association was Henry Ward Beecher, but the real reins of power were firmly in the hands of Lucy Stone as chairperson of the Executive Committee. With her husband, Henry Blackwell, serving as recording secretary there was no danger that matters would get out of hand.

UNITY—THE ATTEMPT AND FAILURE, 1870

THE AGONY OF SCHISM

In the wake of the split between two competing woman suffrage associations, confusion and deep misgivings reigned in the ranks of woman's rights proponents. The ostensible reason for rivalry, namely that the National organization was centered on activities in the national capital, while the American tendency was focused on state legislation, was not accepted as a valid reason for the schism. Even the real underlying causes—the radical exclusionary feminism, suspicious of men; the insistence upon universal suffrage, even at the expense of black enfranchisement; the penchant for becoming involved in side issues such as marriage, divorce, love; the willingness to form coalitions with elements at odds with the basic orientation of the historic woman's rights movement; the abuse of administrative authority within the organization (all considerations associated with the Stanton-Anthony wing)—failed to still the voices urging unification of the two rival groups.

Lucretia Mott, the elder statesperson of the movement, was terribly distraught. She assumed, despite her advanced age, the role of peacemaker and unifier of the movement. Mrs. Mott responded to a resolution urging people to join the American Woman Suffrage Association by stating that Miss Anthony had achieved much good work and "hoped that soon there would be no NWSA or AWSA, that they should know no distinctive societies, but be merged into each other. She felt that they must go on with the cause in harmony and good feeling. We know how easy it is in every organization to disagree and have words."[1]

NATIONAL GOES TO WASHINGTON

In early 1870 the N.W.S.A. held its annual lobbying conference in the national capital. One key demand was the enactment of a Sixteenth Amendment prohibiting the disenfranchisement of any citizens on account of sex. Fostering this proposal was Robert Purvis, a black activist in the ranks of abolitionism. He stated:

Censured as I may be for apparent inconsistency, as a member and an officer of the American Anti-Slavery Society in approving a movement whose leaders are opposed to the passage of the XV Amendment, I must be true to my soul, to my sense of the absolute demands of justice, and hence, I say that . . . I would resist, by every feeling of self-respect and personal dignity, any and every encroachment of power, every act of tyranny (for such they will be) based upon the impious, false, and infamous assumption of superiority of sex.[2]

Other significant positions taken included a proposal to amend the laws affecting federal employment so that women would receive pay equal to that of men for the same work in government employment; an effort to strike the word "male" from the laws governing the District of Columbia; and a plank that focused again on the talismanic power of the ballot, to enfranchise the women of the Utah territory so that the abolition of polygyny may be assured.

Tilton the Unifier

The brilliant editor of *The Independent*, Theodore Tilton, was another influential personality who sought to effectuate unification. The periodical he edited was, in fact, the organ of the group associated with the church headed by Henry Ward Beecher, the Plymouth Church in Brooklyn Heights. Beecher had become the head of the American Woman Suffrage Association controlled by Lucy Stone. Tilton had long associations with leading lights in both wings.

At first, Tilton thought that the very existence of two organizations would generate increased zeal and enthusiasm for the cause of woman suffrage. Referring to the founding convention of the A.W.S.A., he wrote:

Our chief and only solicitude for the convention is that it shall act with sagacity, wisdom, and courage. Let its schedule of officers be confined to no particular wing or party of the one common movement. It is known, for instance, that Mrs. Lucy Stone leads one phalanx and Mrs. Elizabeth Cady Stanton another. Our heart's desire is to see at Cleveland a combination not an unhappy division of these forces.[3]

Tilton now embarked in earnest on his unity campaign. He wrote, reflecting the agony of the movement:

In view of this striking want of cooperation between the two societies—presenting both before the public in a relation difficult to be understood, and delicate to be explained; dividing into rival parties the great body of loyal co-workers in the common cause; creating an embarrassment to hosts of new friends who, flocking to the standard of Woman's Suffrage are perplexed to choose between the two organizations.[4]

In the meantime both organizations issued separate convention calls for the May Anniversary period in New York City. The Anthony-Stanton group urged that "if it would not be better for those Boston ladies to hold theirs at the Hub, and thus agitate two cities at the same time, instead of convulsing one city with two conventions."[5] To no avail, the A.W.S.A. led by Lucy Stone and Henry Blackwell was determined to establish its organization in the very traditional territory of the N.W.S.A. Stanton and Anthony were beginning to feel their growing isolation from the mainstream of woman's righters because of their rift with organized labor, their embrace of such extremists as George F. Train and Victoria Woodhull, and their concern with controversial side issues.

Tilton then issued "A Card Extraordinary": "To the American People, *Greeting*: I am commissioned to procure the name and address of every person in the United States who takes a friendly interest in woman's enfranchisement.... The purpose of this registration is to know to whom to send important documents."[6]

At the same time he wrote an extended essay entitled "The Enfranchisement of Women" setting forth his views and purposes.

The popular interest in the cause of Woman's Suffrage—a sympathy which like a gentle flame is daily spreading to the multitude of new espousers—just now throbs to an unexpected impulse in the hope of a union of the rival organizations which divide the ranks of what ought to be one general army of conquest....

Practically, then, there are two national organizations for woman's suffrage: Mrs. Stanton's and Mr. Beecher's—or to speak more accurately, Miss Anthony's and Mrs. Stone's; two separate rival societies which in our opinion, would quadruple their usefulness if they could be harmoniously combined into one.[7]

Negotiations for Unity

This eloquent appeal of Tilton ended with an invitation for three representatives of National, three from American, and three from the Union Suffrage Society. (The last was a paper organization of Tilton's creation to help effectuate organic unity of all suffrage organizations.) To strengthen his position, Tilton quoted a letter Mrs. Mott wrote to him:

I most willingly have my name attached...I had interviews last Fall with the active workers on both sides, in Boston and New York, and plead with them at the then coming convention in Cleveland they should merge their interests into one common cause and have one universal society. This, however was not done. Still I hope it is not too late for this proposed union to take place.[8]

This appeal had a telling effect and created much sentiment in favor of unification to be aroused within the ranks of both organizations. Henry Blackwell was most eager to disprove Tilton's version of the split. Accordingly, Blackwell took pains to set the record straight as he saw it:

At the annual meeting of the American Equal Rights Association held in New York, last May, persons were present from different parts of the country. After that body had adjourned, and many had left New York, a score of persons more or less, from abroad, from fourteen different states it is claimed, with several times that number in and near the city, convened in the parlors of the "Woman's Bureau", and then and there organized what they called the "National Woman Suffrage Association."... A list of officers, exclusively women, was elected. The control of the Association was vested in an executive committee, resident in New York City.... The result was a close corporation, a local society, national only in name....

The subsequent proceedings of this association, were in accordance with its irregular and irresponsible organ. Weekly meetings were held to discuss a variety of questions, often not germane to the subject of suffrage—such as the causes of the deficiency of offspring, marriage, divorce, the social evil, etc. These transactions were published... as the transactions of the National Woman Suffrage Association. Friends of the cause sent inquiries and remonstrances, which remained unanswered.

At one of these weekly meetings, a resolution was offered by Mrs. Stanton and adopted, repudiating the Fifteenth Amendment; thus committing the movement upon a most important question, in a most unjustifiable manner.[9]

Mrs. Stanton approached this unity conference with a most positive manner. "I will do all I can for union. If I am a stumbling-block I will gladly resign my office. Having fought the world twenty years I do not now wish to turn and fight those who have so long stood together through evil and good report. I should be glad to have all united with Mr. Beecher or Lucretia Mott for our general."[10]

The Failure

With this dispute as a background, the unity conference took place in the Fifth Avenue Hotel. The three delegates from Union were Tilton, Lucretia Mott, and Laura Curtis Bullard; those from American were Lucy Stone, Thomas Wentworth Higginson, and George W. Curtis; the representatives from National were Charlotte Wilbour, Josephine S. Griffing, and Parker Pillsbury. The A.W.S.A. legates let it be known that they were not empowered to act, since they were not elected.[11] This stance was designed to score some points by emphasizing the formal regularity of their association as well as keeping their options open for the future.

Nevertheless, the question was put to the entire assemblage in the form of a resolution: "Are you in favor of a union of the two existing national societies, or is it your judgment that these two associations should continue to exist as separate bodies."[12]

Higginson, Curtis, and Stone voted against unity and urged the other organizations to join the A.W.S.A. All others favored merger. Thus the Union Suffrage Association was projected, with its formal consummation of uniting the pro-merger forces behind Tilton, Mott, Stanton, and Anthony in May.

Higginson challenged the reported version of the meeting, claiming that the proposed constitution offered by Tilton followed "in name and form that of the National Woman Suffrage Association and abandons the plan of a *delegated* society, which is the essential principle."[13]

THE CLEVELAND CLASH

In November 1870 the American held a business convention in Cleveland. Tilton addressed a letter again urging negotiations. The convention rejected unity. An innocuous resolution was adopted urging cooperation with all organizations and individuals desiring woman suffrage, but which would avoid side issues.

Miss Anthony, who attended the convention as an observer, succeeded in gaining the floor and made an impassioned effort to heal the breach.

I do not want to talk blind any longer! Talk plain and say what you mean! If you oppose this union because Mrs. Stanton advocates the right of a woman to free herself from a marriage relation that is worse than slavery, say so.... I want you to come right out and say what you mean by all this discussion. *The Woman's Journal* is the last paper in the world that ought to speak against greater freedom for women in marriage and divorce, for one of its editors, I refer to Mrs. Stone, at her wedding refused to submit to the legal form of marriage, which on her part, was only a conditional one with a solemn protest against the unjust laws bearing upon women in her social relation of wife. How can such a marriage be a legal one? If you are going to keep on hounding Mrs. Stanton I want to know it. There I've had my say! That's my first speech![14]

Higginson, the chairperson of the convention, who had officiated at the wedding of Lucy Stone and Henry Blackwell, charged Miss Anthony with slander. Again Susan B. Anthony took the floor.

Mr. President: I did not intend to insult my friend Mrs. Stone. When she was married she *did* protest against unjust laws, and that was the grandest protest against wrong the world has ever seen. I always honored her for it.... if I said anything against her, I did not mean it. So help me God, I would sooner lose my right hand. Mr. President, I humbly beg the pardon of yourself, of Mrs. Stone, and all of these gentlemen and ladies. (Applause).[15]

This misinterpretation of Miss Anthony's intention reflected the depth of hostile feeling of the Boston group toward the Anthony-Stanton forces.

THE NOSTALGIA OF A UNIFIED PAST

The National Woman Suffrage Association sponsored what was hoped to be a nonpartisan celebration of twenty years of the woman's rights movement. It was a golden occasion for the Anthony-Stanton group, and they made the most of it. The principal feature of the convention was a lengthy historical address by Paulina Wright Davis.

The call itself sounded a nonfactional note.

The movement... in America, may be dated from the first National Convention, held... in October, 1850... In the call for that convention, the following subjects for discussion were presented: Woman's right to *education*, literary, scientific, and artistic; her *avocations*, industrial, commercial, and professional; her *interests*, pecuniary, civil, and political; in a word *her rights* as an individual and *her functions* as a citizen.... As those who inaugurated a reform so momentous and far reaching in its consequences, should hold themselves above all party considerations and personal antagonisms, and as this gathering is in no way to be connected with either of our leading woman suffrage associations, we hope that the friends of real progress everywhere will come together and unitedly celebrate this Twentieth Anniversary of a great National Movement for Freedom.[16]

Mrs. Davis's speech was remarkable in its scope. She marked every milestone on the woman's rights journey and went on to describe that:

women are still frivolous; the slaves of prejudice, passion, folly, fashion, and petty ambitions, and so they will remain till the shackles, both social and political are broken.... Not till then can it be known what untold wealth lies buried in womanhood—"how many mute, inglorious Miltons". Men are still conceited, arrogant, and usurping, dwarfing their own manhood, by a false position toward one half of the human race.[17]

She paid particular attention to the women in the labor movement:

There is another movement that began in the decade now closed upon us, which belongs to its history, viz: that of the Working Women. It has been represented from Boston by Miss Jennie Collins, a slight woman, all brain and soul.... She is the type of a large class that will develop into beautiful symmetrical characters when the shackles are broken and women are free.[18]

Mrs. Davis ended by referring to her objectivity and freedom from bias. "I have endeavored to keep this report free from sectionalism and faction, believing that the *finale* would bring together all parties in one glad day of rejoicing."[19]

Resolutions

The resolutions Miss Anthony presented and the gathering adopted called for the immediate passage of the Sixteenth Amendment giving women voting rights and the support of either major political party that incorporated woman suffrage into its platform.[20] Politically the resolutions spelled out a course of action of being a "third party, or balance of power party, and give their adhesion to Republicanism or to Democracy just as circumstances might warrant with regard to this suffrage question."[21]

A Postscript of Ridicule

The following description of the Twentieth Anniversary Convention cannot be dismissed as mere indulgence in satiric journalism. It appeared in a newspaper that carried on its masthead "organ of the National Labor Union, The Father Matthew and Roman Catholic T.A.B. Societies."

Of course an exasperating amount of hugging was indulged in by the old birds. The young ladies...amused themselves by desperate attempts at flirtation....Lucretia Mott was as pert as a robin, while the Stanton looked as lovely as ever in her silvery locks, Susan B. Anthony had not gained an ounce of flesh since we last saw her, but a skillful dressmaker works wonders....

After a three hour cheerless chat a waiter announced lunch, when there was a fumbling of portmonntaise, a flourish of dollar bills, a rush to the tables, and a race for the championship.[22]

DIMMED HOPES

The attempt at unity engineered by Theodore Tilton failed to bridge the gulf between the N.W.S.A. and the A.W.S.A. The National group's opposition to the Fourteenth and Fifteenth amendments antagonized the Radical Republicans and abolitionists who proclaimed the priority of black male suffrage to secure the South against a restoration of de facto slavery; the association of Anthony and Stanton with George Francis Train, a Copperhead Democrat who was antiblack and an advocate of restrictive "educated suffrage"; the method of running a national organization from the top without adequate consultation with key elements in the leadership; the willingness to consider broader aspects of woman's social positions, which the American group called side issues; the political strategy of focusing on Washington and national legislation as against the state-by-state approach made up the mosaic of differences. The split remained for two decades and further attenuated the vitality and impact of woman's rights on the American scene.

The Side Issues of Contention—Suffrage, Marriage, Divorce, and Sex

Beyond the association of Susan B. Anthony and Elizabeth Cady Stanton with the antiblack, Copperhead Democrat, and "angel" of their organ *Revolution*, George Francis Train, there were divergent perspectives emanating from the American Woman Suffrage Association and the National Woman Suffrage Association. The former veered away from consideration of any demand other than woman suffrage that might antagonize and detach a group from the movement for enfranchisement of women. The National conceived of itself as a broad reform movement primarily interested in votes for women as the key to societal betterment.

This division was not entirely clear-cut. The American group led by Lucy Stone was quite entangled with the abolitionists even to the point of support for the Fourteenth and Fifteenth amendments, which limited enfranchisement to males. Furthermore, Lucy Stone embraced the revolutionary concept of retaining her maiden name as a symbol of equality between husband and wife.

There are parallels to this area of concern in the contemporary woman's rights movement, which go beyond advocacy of the Equal Rights Amendment, equal pay for equal work and for work of comparable worth, and equality of employment and promotion opportunity. Matters such as abortion, gay rights, pornography, and numerical job quotas are akin to side issues that some believe fragment support and militate against the broadest possible consensus of advocacy.

THE PURITANS AND THE ECUMENICALS

Henry Blackwell stated the position of the American organization quite succinctly:

The advocates of woman's political equality differ utterly on every other topic. Some are abolitionists, etc. . . . Unfortunately, many well-meaning people cannot or will not so regard it. They insist upon dragging in their peculiar views upon theology, temperance, marriage, race, dress, finance, labor and capital.[1]

He also opposed having woman suffrage organizations getting involved in dramatic cases illustrating these controversial side issues, such as the Richardson-McFarland love triangle and the Hester Vaughn illegitimate child tragedy. In the Richardson-McFarland situation, McFarland was a drunkard and his wife Abby Sage left him and lived with her lover Albert D. Richardson in a boardinghouse. She divorced McFarland, who then walked into the office of the *New York Tribune*, where Richardson worked, and shot and fatally wounded Richardson. Just before Richardson died, the Rev. Henry Ward Beecher married Abby Sage to Richardson. McFarland was declared insane but given custody of the child born to Abby Sage. Huge protest meetings were held, and Miss Anthony and Mrs. Stanton led a mass of woman's righters in expression of indignation.[2]

Hester Vaughn came from England to Philadelphia to join her husband, who had taken another wife. Hester secured a job as a houseworker and was seduced. A child was born to her in a garret and died. Ms. Vaughn was imprisoned and sentenced to be hanged for murder. A huge protest rally filled the great hall of Cooper Union, addressed by Horace Greeley, Clementine Lozier, and Ernestine Rose. Resolutions were introduced to the meeting by Miss Anthony advocating the presence of women on juries so that a woman could be truly tried by a jury of her peers; urging granting to women a voice in the enactment of laws as well as in their execution; and demanding the abolition of capital punishment.[3]

The attitude of singular purity and concentration exclusively on suffrage was strongly opposed by the Anthony-Stanton group. Mrs. Stanton wrote, "T. W. Higginson, in the *Woman's Journal* agrees that like Paganini, women should play on one string; that from New Year's Morn to Christmas Eve they should sing suffrage songs, and nothing more; no solos on 'side issues' especially on marriage, divorce, or other social oppressions."[4]

Even though married, with a retinue of children, Elizabeth Cady Stanton was rather forthright about her views on marriage. When she was charged as a woman's righter with undermining this "sacred institution," she retorted that under American laws the marriage relationship was a false one, whether happy or unhappy. In most cases marriage was legalized prostitution, a state in which women had no self-respect and men need have no respect for them.[5]

Miss Anthony complemented her colleague's remarks by averring that women would never be able to live honestly until they had the right to vote. Then they wouldn't have to sell themselves for bread, either in or out of marriage. No woman would remain bound to a drunkard or libertine if she could be assured of her subsistence in any other way.[6]

Along with the New York Press Club, the organization of woman writers and journalists, Sorosis, sponsored a public banquet, where Miss Anthony was asked this sardonic question: "Why don't women propose?" Her answer was:

Under present conditions, it would require a good deal of assurance for a woman to say to a man, "Please sir, will you support me for the rest of my life?" When all avocations are open to woman and she has an opportunity to acquire a competence, she will then be in a position where it will not be humiliating for her to ask the man she loves to share her prosperity. Instead of requesting him to provide food, raiment, and shelter for her, she can invite him into her home, contribute her share to the partnership and not be an utter dependent. There will also be another advantage in this arrangement—if he proves unworthy she can ask him to walk out.[7]

Goaded by Mrs. Stanton, *Woman's Journal* of the Lucy Stone wing, did respond but limited its attack on *Revolution's* views on marriage and divorce.

That "woman wants more than suffrage", nobody denies. That she "wants something beyond the ballot and its attendant blessings" is a truth never controverted. The advocate of woman suffrage always asks the ballot as a means to an end....

But what *does* the *Revolution* mean by the following statement? In enumerating woman's wants it states among other things, that one of them is "freedom to marry, and to be a mistress of herself after marriage: *freedom to freely sunder a yoke which she has freely bound, etc.*"

We believe in *marriage for life* and deprecate all this loose pestiferous talk in favor of *easy divorce*.... Our friends who deprecated the formation of "the American Woman Suffrage Society", a year ago, have at last come to see, in the recent utterances of the *Revolution*, a vindication of the wisdom of their course.[8]

Revolution refused to back off and in a riposte to the purist argument stated:

The *Woman's Journal* does not stick to its *own point*. That paper cannot possibly advocate woman suffrage without explaining why woman wants suffrage, namely for the settlement of those identical questions which this sagacious critic forbids a woman's newspaper to discuss....

We value the ballot as precious; we ask for it, and yearn to possess it; ... But we are not dreamers or fanatics: and we know that the ballot, when we get it, will achieve for woman no more than it has achieved for man. And to drop all other demands for the sake of uniting to demand the ballot only, may seem the whole duty of the *Woman's Journal* but it is only a very small part of the mission of *The Revolution*. The ballot touches only interests, either of women or men, which take their root in political questions. But woman's chief discontent is not with her political but with her social, and particularly with her marital bondage.[9]

THE SUPREME SIDE ISSUE—VICTORIA WOODHULL

On January 11, 1871, a "Terrible Siren" appeared on the national scene as an advocate of woman suffrage.[10] Victoria Woodhull addressed a public hearing conducted by the Congressional Joint Judiciary Committee on a memorial that she had supposedly written claiming that under the Fourteenth Amendment, women as citizens of the United States could not have their privileges and immunities abridged by states denying them the right to vote. This was not really a novel conception, for Virginia and Francis Minor had promulgated a similar thesis in October 1869 at a meeting of the National Woman Suffrage Association in St. Louis.

Victoria Woodhull and her younger sister-colleague Tennie C. Claflin were born in abject rural poverty. Their father was a combination of confidence man, buffoon, and politician. The sisters acquired theatrical and oratorical skills from him. Before she was sixteen, Victoria was married to Dr. Canning Woodhull, a medical doctor who was an alcoholic and a notorious roué. Her sister Tennie went on the road selling a quack cancer cure to beguiled open-air audiences.

After giving birth to two children, Victoria divorced Dr. Woodhull, retaining his name, and married Colonel Blood, with all living together in the same household. Blood recognized that his wife Victoria, with her good looks and magnetic platform ability, could be the spokesperson for the causes he espoused: philosophical anarchism, mysticism, spiritualism, free love, and greenbackism.

Mrs. Woodhull did not hesitate to use her wiles to attract and reap benefits from a host of prominent men. Commodore Cornelius Vanderbilt set the sisters up in their own brokerage firm in the Wall Street area. They derived great wealth from stock market tips that Vanderbilt gave them.

Besides Blood, the other great ideological influence on the sisters was the flamboyant Stephen Pearl Andrews, a doctor and lawyer who espoused the doctrines of the Swedish theologian-mystic Emanuel Swedenborg and the French utopian socialist Charles Fourier. Andrews became the editor of their organ *Woodhull and Claflin's Weekly*. He also anticipated Esperanto by advocating a universal language, "Alwato," and a world government, "Pantarchy." This remarkably creative man also devised a system of stenography. The collaboration between Blood and Andrews generated the ideas for the sisters Victoria and Tennie to take to the public.

The memorial to congress that women already had the constitutional right to vote was read by Victoria Woodhull before a Joint Committee on the Judiciary in the hearing room of the House Judiciary Committee. This hearing room had packed with women including Susan B. Anthony and Elizabeth Cady Stanton of the National Woman Suffrage Association. They were very impressed with the Woodhull presentation and sought to bring her into their ranks, particularly since the split in the ranks of woman's righters had reduced their support and influence. They also agreed with the approach that emphasized a national campaign as against the state-by-state strategy for achieving woman suffrage.

In May 1871 Elizabeth Cady Stanton confided to Victoria Woodhull the sordid story of the Rev. Henry Ward Beecher having a love affair complete with sexual trysts with Elizabeth Tilton, the wife of Theodore Tilton. As editor of *The Independent*, Theodore Tilton was closely associated with Beecher's church. Victoria Woodhull kept this information to herself, but when the liberal Protestant establishment kept up a drumfire of criticism of her views on free love and exposed the *ménage à trois* of Dr. Woodhull, Colonel Blood, and Victoria; when the Stanton-Anthony forces resisted her efforts to capture control of the National Woman Suffrage Association convention in May 1872, she blasted what she considered to be the utter hypocrisy of the Beecher entourage. It will be remembered that Beecher was the president of the Stone-Blackwell wing of the woman suffrage movement, the American Woman Suffrage Association.

Woodhull and Claflin's Weekly of November 2, 1872, aired the entire scandal. Interestingly enough, Victoria Woodhull justified Beecher's ama tory adventures by writing: "Every great man of Beecher's type, has had in the past, the need for and the right to, the loving manifestations of many women." It was even bruited about that Beecher had had relations with Woodhull, too. As the news spread of this issue of the Woodhull's weekly, it was snatched up and sold by news-vendor speculators for prices from $40 to $75. Anthony Comstock charged the sisters with sending obscenity through the mails, and Victoria Woodhull was clapped into the Ludlow Street jail where she languished for twenty-eight days without trial.

The free love issue continued to plague the woman's rights movement through the first half of 1875 when the celebrated Tilton-Beecher trial took place. In this proceeding Theodore Tilton charged Beecher with seduction of his wife and the alienation of her affection. The Protestant pillars of society, led by Henry Bowen, the publisher of *The Independent*, secured the best legal talent to defend Beecher. The trial ended with a hung jury, and Beecher was acquitted. However, the entire woman's rights movement had to overcome the obloquy of being associated with free loveism.[11]

Before the trial, Theodore Tilton was given a subsidized prize to buy his silence about the affair involving the Rev. Mr. Beecher and Elizabeth Tilton. The forces around Henry Bowen gave Tilton the opportunity to edit his own publication, to which he gave the name *The Golden Age*. However shortlived, it merits a unique place in the annals of American journalism. Tilton wrote, "One distinctive peculiarity of our journal (and we claim it as a unique merit), will consist in opening its columns to the free entrance of all types of opinion."[12]

There is no question as to where Tilton himself stood in the controversy that permeated the woman's rights movement. He wrote:

The woman's movement originally—as started by Lucretia Mott and Elizabeth Cady Stanton at Seneca Falls, New York in 1848—had more reference to other branches of the general question than to its political.... All those agitators who now limit the question to suffrage have departed from the wise paths of the first (and still surviving) Pilgrim Mothers of the movement.

The majority of women are more interested in their industrial, educational, and social prosperity than they are in political status....

We hope that at the coming anniversaries there will be some courage of speech in regard to these social questions which everybody knows ought to be grappled with, but which almost everybody is afraid to touch.[13]

Tilton delineated three groups dealing with woman's interests. One was interested only with woman suffrage; another was concerned with employment opportunities and increased wages; and the third with adjusting marital relations and getting a uniform divorce law. He deplored the fact that these interests were after each other's throats instead of cooperating and providing a forum for all views. He himself considered the marital question the most important of all.[14]

Until human nature shall lose its present constitution, woman's chief interest in life will be, not her wages, nor her suffrage, but her heart. In conducting the woman's movement, therefore any plan or policy which limits this movement to its industrial or political aspects...is a shallow, evanescent and unphilosophic treatment of the main question.

...The only lady who, above all others has suffered reproach is Mrs. Woodhull; all of whom we make bold to say that she is more honest than nine-tenths of her critics.... We have read several attacks on this woman by persons who persecute *her* for avowing in public, as a matter of theory, what *they* carry on in private, as a matter of practice. There is something in this sort of villification which ought to excite the indignation of all honest minds.[15]

THE GREAT DEBATE—TOPIC: FREE LOVE

The controversy around this phrase affected the entire woman suffrage movement. Charges and countercharges flew back and forth. One of the most remarkable exchanges on this question involved the views of Messrs. Tilton, Greeley, and Blackwell as well as Mrs. Stanton. *The Golden Age* was the arena for this verbal joust.

Theodore Tilton initiated the discussion by castigating his idol Horace Greeley, the editor of the *New York Tribune*, for having the most backward views on all "that pertains to the status of woman.... He holds, for instance, that there ought to be no divorce at all—not for any crime, even the worst.... He holds too, that if a man marries and his wife dies, there should be no second marriage.[16]

Greeley: You are entirely, eminently right, Mr. Editor in asserting my conviction of the proper indissolubility of marriage is the mainspring of my hostility to woman suffrage. In a spirit of hearty hatred for Free Love and all its infernal delusions, I remain yours,

Horace Greeley

Tilton: Mr. Greeley says that his conviction of the indissolubility of marriage is the mainspring of the hostility to Woman Suffrage. How people differ!

Blackwell: On the contrary, as Woman Suffragists, we say that *because* H. Greeley holds these fundamental convictions, all the more logically he is bound to advocate woman suffrage....

Mr. Greeley for the moment forgets that many of the women he loves and honors are Woman Suffragists. In his commendable disgust at the views of social questions expressed by a half a dozen prominent persons, he overlooks that the great body of Woman Suffragists withdrew from all affiliation with these persons two years ago, on account of connecting these views with suffrage. Mr. Greeley ought to know that the AMERICAN WOMAN SUFFRAGE AS-SOCIATION was formed for the very purpose of limiting our demand to WOMAN'S EQUALITY OF RIGHTS in and out of marriage.[17]

Tilton to Greeley: Your letter perforates into a "hearty hatred for free love and all its delusions." What do you mean by free love?... When *I* say (as I do) that I am opposed to free love, I mean by it the promiscuous intercourse of the sexes, in contradistinction to the heart's ideal of monogamic marriage.... But if by free love you imply, as many so-called free lovers do, simply a more human treatment by the civil law of the whole subject of marriage and divorce—then I have no sympathy with your accusation, and hold you to be wrong instead of right.[18]

Blackwell: It is in the multiplication of divorces that Mr. Tilton would find a remedy for that growing mildew of free love "with which", he tells us, "American society is covering itself!"...

We have no words for our feelings of grief and amazement, when one publicly set for... truth and purity becomes an unblushing apologist for "secret sin".[19]

Tilton to Greeley: A just inference... is that I advocate Free Love. On the contrary, I stiffly oppose it. The latest bulletin of Stephen Pearl Andrews castigates me because I hold that the heart's ideal is monogamic marriage—the supreme love of one man for one woman through life and (I hope) beyond death. But this is only my view—I do not judge for others. Furthermore, I hold that love, and love only, constitutes marriage: that marriage makes the bond, not the bond the marriage.[20]

Elizabeth Cady Stanton: Each age has some word of momentous import, with which to hound the lovers of truth and progress.... To say that a man, woman, or book was "romantic" would consign either to speedy oblivion. Then came "blue stocking."... Then came "infidel."... Then came "strong-minded" that sent daughters of Eve scampering in all directions... some new scare must be invented, to keep rebellious womanhood in check, and now comes "free love", most freely used by knaves and libertines, to condemn the virtuous and the brave.[21]

This frank debate not only revealed the intensity with which this issue penetrated the woman's movement, but also exposed the spectrum of views from Woodhull's frank support of the free use of the libidinous sex drive in defiance of convention, to Greeley's puritanical attachment to monogamous marriage brooking no divorce or even remarriage after death of a spouse. The very airing of this matter caused Tilton to be pilloried.

Tilton vainly attempted to lay to rest this mounting criticism against him and his publication, *The Golden Age*. He wrote:

I have an extensive acquaintance among public men and women of our time, including many whom I believe to be uncommonly pure and white in their moral and social character;... the peer of any in all that constitutes purity of life—I place Victoria C. Woodhull.... But I am ashamed of many brethren of the press who, without evidence, without provocation, and without inquiry, have made haste to strike a woman whose private life is a white lily of blamelessness, and who, if altogether a fanatic, is altogether a Christian.

Speaking like a Paris prefect of police, you denounce me as a Communist. Yes *I am*. I accept your indictment as I would a rosette, and wear it in my buttonhole.... The Commune offered to France, what the Republic refused it—namely, local self-government.... It was the Commune, not the Republic that should have triumphed.... But the Commune will yet rise and reign! God speed it.[22]

Woodhull's Decline

Mrs. Woodhull now faced all sorts of privations, and her paper suffered a disastrous decline in circulation. In an effort to raise some funds, she rented a hall and offered a lecture to the public entitled, "Marriage and Divorce, Free Love and Prostitution." With that as a topic she drew an overflow audience. There was, however, no one who would introduce her to the crowd who came to hear her. Henry Ward Beecher was approached, but refused. Courageously, Theodore Tilton accepted the task of chairing the lecture.[23]

Introducing Mrs. Woodhull, Tilton stated:

I came to this meeting, actuated by curiosity to know what my friend would have to say to the great question which has occupied her so many years of her life.... Now as to her character, I know it, and believe in it, and vouch for it. (Applause and a few hisses). It may be that she is a fanatic; it may be that I am a fool; but before high heaven, I would rather be both a fanatic and fool... than to be such a coward as would deny to a woman the sacred right of free speech.[24]

Marriage is not obedience to civil law, Mrs. Woodhull declared, but to the natural law of attraction of opposites. She further stated, "To more specifically define free love I would say that I prefer to use the word love with lust as its antithesis, love representing the spiritual, and lust the animal."[25]

Victoria Woodhull persisted in her various campaigns, which gained her notoriety. Besides forming her own political party and becoming the first woman to run for the presidency of the United States, she headed Section 12 of the American segment of the International Workingman's Association, the First International. Karl Marx and his associate Friedrich Engels, who led the International from London, were appalled at her views because they felt that American women and men workers would be alienated from the cause of socialism. Section 12 was expelled by the American leadership.

Mrs. Woodhull advocated legalized prostitution; favored abortion where the fetus was abnormal; opposed women's fashion which emphasized voluptuousness; supported the making and unmaking of marriage at the will of the individual partner; and believed that poverty was the result of genetic deficiency. Interestingly enough, some of her reform proposals were put into practice in later years—pure food and drug laws, medical care in the public schools, labor arbitration panels to avert strikes, public housing for the poor, and free legal assistance for the needy.

She and her sister Tennie C. Claflin married into respectable wealth in England. Every four years through 1892, Victoria Woodhull would journey to the United States on a lecture tour and proclaim her nomination for the presidency.

Thus, it was that side issues, particularly of love, marriage, and divorce, further widened the gap between the two tendencies of the woman's rights movement. The supreme personification of these issues was Victoria C. Woodhull. Her personal life and her social views on love, marriage, divorce, and prostitution were anathema to the Boston wing, whose president, Henry Ward Beecher, was exposed to the public in *Woodhull and Claflin's Weekly*. The National wing, first attracted to her by the memorial she presented to the Congress on woman suffrage and by her dynamic personality, was barely able to rescue the organization from Woodhull's attempt to take it over. Both sectors of the woman's rights movement were stained by the influence of Woodhull. It would take some time for the movement to divest itself from the effects of the "terrible siren."

POLITICAL ACTION

THE POLITICAL NATURE OF THE STRUGGLE

The woman's rights movement, in essence, is a struggle to create fundamental societal change. It is a challenge to both civil and religious law. The efforts to effect change in property, marriage, child custody, taxation, compensation, employment opportunities are directed at discrimination institutionalized by law.

In a democratic society the voting franchise is the instrument of peaceful political change to place individuals in office, either in a legislative or executive capacity, repeal existing laws, enact new statutes, or begin the necessary process of changing the supreme law of the land through the amendment process.

Women, as voteless citizens, were in the unique position of securing the ballot without a ballot in their hands, a formidable task. Only when men in possession of the elective franchise would consider the granting of suffrage politically worthwhile through conviction, pressure, or the societal needs of the times would it be granted.

The political parties were dominated by men and male officeholders. The basic motivation was power to control the government in the self-interest of various economic and political factions organized as parties. Political power meant patronage in the form of jobs, the letting of contracts, the granting of subsidies, the exercise of the power to tax, the establishment of tariffs, and the inauguration of monetary and fiscal policies. For those who were satisfied with the existing order the goal was to retain power and even increase it by additional supporters in the various legislatures. For those who sought to change things, the effort was to secure power and to pass from minority status to majority control.

The Civil War with its use of military force was an exercise in the supreme form of political power in a brutal contest between two rival economic and social forces—free private enterprise based on wage labor as against the plantation system based upon chattel slavery. It was the aspect of the war directed against the inhumane system of slavery that attracted the woman's rights movement. The woman leaders believed that abolitionism would result in human rights being extended not only to blacks but to women as well.

The proponents of private enterprise centered in the North were represented by the Republican party. When the constraints of peaceful political contest were broken by the dictates of military force, the Republican party was in a fight for political survival. During the course of the war, despite its overwhelming economic superiority, the North had to employ a military-social measure, the Emancipation Proclamation, which freed the slaves in the Confederacy and broke the back of its logistical organism by destroying its labor force.

Following the war, the woman's righters progressed from simple support of the war to exercising their voices toward the hope of their own freedom. The political postwar problem had not been settled by military victory. To assure no return to the antebellum days, the policies of Presidents Lincoln and Johnson had to be overcome by the enactment of the Thirteenth, Fourteenth, and Fifteenth Amendments as well as by a military occupation of the South. This grave situation created the issue of votes for women as against votes for black males.

During the Reconstruction Era the sharp differences over the labor systems and political control became attenuated. Within the Republican party the old divergence between Lincolnian moderates and the Radicals was replaced by a new rift over the conduct of the Grant administration. The Liberal Republicans turned their backs on the blacks and centered their attention on corruption and in 1872 made common cause with the Democrats.

By 1876 the differences between the major parties were devoid of any principled base. The disputed contest over the presidency did not result in any major violent demonstrations or rebellion.

In this Reconstruction period the woman's rights movement became a training ground testing a variety of political efforts that went far beyond the one week of May Anniversaries. They had witnessed women in nascent labor organizations successfully cause the defeat of a legislator who was callously disregarding inhuman conditions in the mills of Massachusetts. They had seen women rise up against the contracting system in the making of army uniforms and succeed in getting the government to resume direct responsibility with resultant restoration of wages.

Thus women recognized the tactics and strategy of politics. Washington, D.C., and the various state capitals were centers for petitioning and lobbying for legislation, even constitutional amendments. Two prominent leaders of the woman's rights movement threw themselves into the political arena, one as a candidate, the other leading a cohort of women to register and vote. Then, too, there was Victoria C. Woodhull forming her own party and running for the presidency.

Woman's righters, being deprived of the franchise and subjected to social and economic discrimination, had less reason to warrant blind adherence to a political party. One wing of the movement, however, remained allied to the Republican party until the passage of the Fifteenth Amendment because of its abolitionist role and the need to help black freedmen.

Both major parties were subjected to visitations by delegations of woman seeking woman suffrage planks in the party platforms, but woman's rights remained in the minor key as far as the Republican and Democratic parties were concerned. Erstwhile supporters of woman suffrage made common cause with anti–woman suffrage elements in the name of combatting corruption.

Efforts at forming third parties of reform occasionally attracted woman's righters, sometimes in the form of threats to major parties, but they proved to be unproductive.

The Reconstruction Era was the training ground for the woman's rights movement in the techniques, strategy, and tactics of politics. National organizations emerged, which eventually overcame schisms, succeeded in having the Nineteenth Amendment become part of the Constitution and in setting the contemporary stage for further gains in the never-ending continuum—the struggle for woman's rights.

CAMPAIGNING FOR WOMAN SUFFRAGE EXPANSION

Despite heroic efforts, there is little in the way of success that can be demonstrated in the growth of the enfranchisement of women during the Reconstruction Era. Only four states—and these in the Far West where the scarcity of women broke the strength of social mores—had universal suffrage. There were certain gains in partial suffrage such as in school board and tax matters. Nineteen states by 1890 granted "school suffrage," and three allowed tax and bond suffrage.[1]

The struggle to achieve universal suffrage in terms of changing the federal Constitution or altering state constitutions was herculean, but meager in results. From the time the Sixteenth Amendment, designed to grant voting rights to woman, was first proposed in 1868 until that right was finally granted as the Nineteenth Amendment in 1920, the woman's rights movement was forced to conduct fifty-six campaigns of referenda to male voters; 480 campaigns to get Legislatures to submit suffrage amendments to voters; 47 campaigns to get State constitutional conventions to write woman suffrage into state constitutions; 277 campaigns to get State party conventions to include woman suffrage planks; 30 campaigns to get presidential party conventions to adopt woman suffrage planks in party platforms, and 19 campaigns with 19 successive Congresses.[2]

Wyoming as a territory had granted woman suffrage in 1869. Its vote for the status of statehood in the Congress in 1890 was positive by a narrow margin. It was the issue of woman suffrage that made this victory a cliffhanger. Indeed the territorial legislature of Wyoming made it clear: "We will remain out of the Union a hundred years rather than come in without the women."[3] Colorado followed in 1893, and Idaho and Utah in 1896.

In January 1871 the N.W.S.A. sponsored a Washington convention that spanned five sessions. It was charged up with the publicity given to the woman suffrage issue by the appearance of Victoria Woodhull before a joint congressional committee where she advanced her memorial that women already had the right to suffrage under the Fourteenth Amendment.

While the convention took place, an amendment was added to a bill dealing with the improvement of the government of Washington, D.C. This proposal, introduced by Representative George W. Julian, aimed to strike the word "male" from the bill. Fifty-five votes were registered in favor with 117 against and 65 not voting, a most encouraging showing despite the defeat.

The glow of achievement surrounding the Woodhull memorial, in spite of its loss, caused Isabella Beecher Hooker to change her political outlook. Since she presided over the convention, her views are significant. She stated: "Thank God! that party is dead; everyone here knows it, feels it, and is waiting to see what will take its place. A great labor and woman suffrage party is ready to spring into life, and a hundred aristocratic Democrats are pledged to the work."[4]

Mrs. Woodhull now became a heroine of the National Woman Suffrage Association. Both Susan B. Anthony and Elizabeth Cady Stanton wrote for *Woodhull and Claflin's Weekly*. They had lost control of *Revolution* to a conservative and staid owner, Mrs. Laura Curtis Bullard. Miss Anthony wrote, "Bravo! My dear Woodhull: Everyone here chimes in with the new conclusion that we are free here already. But how absolutely dead, dead are the Woman's Journal and the Revolution. . . . I am sure you and I and all women who shall wish to vote for somebody, if for Geo. F. Train or Victoria Woodhull."[5]

Mrs. Stanton followed with fulsome praise: "Mrs. Victoria Woodhull: . . . I . . . fully agree with the position you have so eloquently and logically maintained in your demand for a declaratory act."[6] "In view of these monstrous wrongs of our sex, patience and calmness, and a willingness to wait—in those of us that can speak and write are not virtues but crimes."[7]

The shafts of Anthony and Stanton directed against the A.W.S.A. were not quite on target. The Boston wing was also impressed with the memorial, and while they wouldn't quite come out and mention Woodhull directly, they did quote the minority report in favor verbatim in the *Woman's Journal*.[8]

Toward the end of the year, Mrs. Stanton reaffirmed her pride in endorsing Mrs. Woodhull.

When our representatives at Washington granted to Victoria C. Woodhull a hearing before the Judiciary Committee of both houses—an honor conferred on no other woman in the nation before   they recognized Mrs. Woodhull as the leader of the woman suffrage movement in this country. And those of us who were convinced by her unanswerable arguments that her positions were sound, had no choice but to follow.[9]

In the face of this adulation it is noteworthy that presidential elections would be held the following year, in 1872.

At the May 1871 anniversary meeting of the A.W.S.A. resolutions were offered designed to obtain woman suffrage: getting state legislatures to enact laws granting women the right to vote for presidential electors in accordance with Article II, Section 1, of the Constitution; getting the vote by interpreting the Fourteenth and Fifteenth amendments; the passage of a Sixteenth Amendment extending the franchise to women. Henry Blackwell most warmly endorsed the first of these proposals.[10]

Thus it was that all sectors of the woman's rights movement seemed to opt for the assumption that under the Constitution they already had the right to vote. This unity of purpose among woman suffrage proponents caused the opposition to woman suffrage, led by Catherine Beecher, to galvanize its efforts. This group prepared a memorial to Congress setting forth that Holy Scripture dictates for women a "sphere apart from public life"; that women's duties and cares make them unwilling to assume other and "heavier burdens unsuited to our physical organization"; that an extension of "suffrage would be to the interests of the working women"; that these changes "must introduce an element of discord in the existing marriage relation, ... to the infinite detriment of children, and increase the already alarming prevalence of divorce." The anti-woman suffrage group also proposed a Sixteenth Amendment which would outlaw freedom of divorce, allow divorce only in cases involving adultery, and that the adulterer be barred forever from marriage.[11]

DIRECT ACTION

At the convocation sponsored by the National Woman Suffrage Association in January 1872 Mrs. Stanton announced a change of tactics that flowed from the approach of the Woodhull memorial. There would be no vigorous effort on behalf of a Sixteenth Amendment. Rather, "Instead of petitioning Congress for our rights we propose to settle the question before the courts. . . . We have reasoned for twenty-five years, and we now propose to take our rights under the Constitution as it is."[12]

Mrs. Hooker suggested, "Women should attempt to qualify and attempt to vote in every State election. . . . This action not only serves the purpose of agitation of the whole question of suffrage, but it puts upon men, our brothers, the onus of refusing the votes of their fellow citizens, and compels them to show just cause for such proceeding."[13]

Knowing that "illegal" voters were subject to fines as high as $500, sixteen women followed Susan B. Anthony, first to register and then to vote in Rochester, New York. The Republican Grant administration was anxious about this dramatic turn of events and was fearful that unless stopped, it could spread. A new judge, an adherent of the Republican Senator Roscoe Conkling, ordered her to be brought to trial. After Miss Anthony and her associates canvassed all twenty-nine postal districts in Monroe County, the judge ordered a change of venue to a neighboring county. Miss Anthony then traveled over that county to agitate the citizens.

Finally the trial was held, and the judge directed the jury to find her guilty, claiming that Miss Anthony was not protected by the Fourteenth Amendment. She was fined $100 and costs. The judge did permit her to speak on the matter of her sentence. She made a blistering attack on the court's reasoning and stated flatly that she had no intention of paying the fine. Instead of jailing her, which would have given Miss Anthony the right to appeal to the federal courts on the basis of *habeas corpus*, the matter just was allowed to die.[14]

WOOING THE MAJOR PARTIES

Comparing the two wings of the woman's rights movement, the Boston sector led by Lucy Stone remained a steadfast supporter of the Republican party while the Fifteenth Amendment was not yet ratified. It opposed any consideration of independent political action and was firm in remaining in the orbit of the major political parties. When the Republican party split into two wings in 1872, the A.W.S.A. did not hesitate to endorse the candidacy of Grant of the regular Republican wing because of a slim promise of consideration of the needs of women. Lucy Stone broke from the Liberal Republicans led by Greeley, Tilton, and Carl Schurz. Their touting of corruption as the main issue and the merger of the Liberal Republicans with the Democrats were more than enough to end the collaboration of the Stone-Blackwell forces with the former abolitionist wing of the Republican party.

The group around Miss Anthony and Mrs. Stanton remained free of strong ties with either major party. The theme of looking toward independent political action in the form of a national reform party based upon woman suffrage and labor reform was frequently sounded. This tack may have been a scare tactic to frighten the major party into support of woman suffrage or an expression of disgust and frustration with the lack of attention and even ridicule expressed by major parties. The Anthony-Stanton group was not averse to embracing the Democratic party even though that party was opposed to the Fifteenth Amendment. The inclusion of the word "male" in that amendment was enough for that group to break from the Republican party in 1868. It was ready to woo both parties and hold above both the threat of independent political action.

The Republican convention of 1868 met in Chicago six weeks before the Democratic party had its presidential conclave. A special committee consisting of Miss Anthony, Mrs. Stanton, Elizabeth Miller, Mrs. Horace Greeley, and Abby Gibbons "sent a memorial to the Republican National Convention which . . . nominated General Grant, but it never saw light after reaching there."[15]

Parker Pillsbury in an article commented as follows on the Republican Chicago platform:

The laboring, the producing people should spit on all platforms that are not solemnly pledged to overturn this whole system of fraud and cruelty. . . . The Chicago platform really means nothing, more than does the nominations. . . . Now labor is everywhere in chains, and we are fast ripening for Revolution. It may be as we have more than once intimated in the past, another Revolution of blood.[16]

Half-jocularly, Theodore Tilton introduced a resolution at the Equal Rights convention stating:

Miss Susan B. Anthony, . . . had given the world to understand that the hope of the woman's rights cause rests more largely with the Democratic party than with any other portion of the people; therefore she be requested to attend the approaching National Democratic convention in New York for the purpose of fulfilling this cheerful hope by securing in the Democratic platform a recognition of woman's right to the elective franchise.[17]

Miss Anthony accepted, for it was quite in keeping with a resolution passed at the Equal Rights Association convention to the effect "that our State and National Governments are anti-Republican in form, and anti-Democratic in fact; . . . they invite the National conventions of both parties to put a woman suffrage plank in their platforms."[18]

Susan B. Anthony and Elizabeth Cady Stanton then led their coterie, organized as the Woman's Suffrage Association of America, to propose a complete platform to the Democratic convention. "We fear our Democratic brethren will repeat the blunder of Chicago. To save the nation from such a calamity, the Woman's Suffrage Association of America present the following platform."[19]

The platform's plank on suffrage for women was justified on the ground that "wealth, virtue and education" would overcome poverty, ignorance, and crime threatening the nation. Universal amnesty and universal suffrage were counterposed to the occupying army stationed in the South and the continued existence of the Freedman's Bureau. Instead of charity, it called for full employment at a fair day's wages for a fair day's work. Under the heading, "Bread and the Ballot," the proposed platform stated that it was "to the interest of laboring men to extend the right of suffrage to the women of the nation who are now coming fast to compete with them in the world of work." Under "International Rights" it was urged that citizens be protected abroad and that those in British jails be released.[20]

As for monetary policy, the return to specie payments was opposed, the printing of greenbacks advocated, and a radical reduction in military expenditures was favored; instead of the income tax, taxes were to be imposed on all fixed property, all bonds, stocks, and mortgages.[21]

Further analysis of this document reveals that, in deference to the Democratic party, woman suffrage was presented as a counterweight of educated, middle- and upper-class women voting to offset the influx of "pauperism, ignorance and crime" represented by the freed slaves and the waves of immigrants. Universal amnesty would mean the end of the army of occupation of the South. The Freedmen's Bureau was resented by labor as a wasteful expenditure while hundreds of thousands of white male workers were unemployed. The entire proposed platform would distance the Anthony-Stanton forces from the Republican-abolitionist combination.

Much of the document coincided with positions taken by the National Labor Union. The proposal for international rights was clearly an effort to get Train out of a British jail where he was incarcerated for his Irish independence views.

Miss Anthony and her colleagues addressed a letter to the convention. Horatio Seymour, the chairperson, graciously allowed Miss Anthony to be seated and permitted a clerk to read it to the assembled delegates.

I address you by letter to ask the privilege of appearing before you ... to demand the ENFRANCHISEMENT OF THE WOMEN OF AMERICA; the only class of citizens wholly unrepresented in the government; the only class (not guilty of crime) taxed without representation, tried without a jury of their peers, governed without their consent. . . .

We conjure you, then, to turn from the dead questions of the past to the vital issue of the hour. The *brute form* of slavery ended with the war. The black man is a soldier and a citizen. He holds the bullet and the ballot in his own right hand. Consider his case settled. . . .

I desire therefore an opportunity to urge the Convention, the wisdom of basing its platform on *Universal Suffrage* as well as *Universal Amnesty*, from Maine to

California, and thus take the first step toward a peaceful and permanent reconstruction.[22]

There is some dispute as to the nature of the reception this memorial received from the convention delegates. The reports of the press are mixed. One version claimed that the introduction of the statement was met with "laughter, cheers, 'Hear, Hear', and cries of 'Read'."[23] Another declared, "Miss Susan B. Anthony has our sincere pity. She has been an ardent suitor of the democracy, and they received her overtures yesterday with screams of laughter."[24] *The Evening Express* stated that it was received "with great laughter."[25] *The Sun* commented, "Its sharp points excited applause and provoked merriment, though the laughter predominated over the plaudits."[26] *The World* wrote, "When the offertory of the 'Woman of THE REVOLUTION' pleading for the ballot ... was rung forth ... the merriment that obtained was indescribable. Round on round of applause, peal on peal, not of satirical but gentlemanly, good-natured laughter prevailed."[27]

While it is difficult to assess the reasons for the hilarity accorded the memorial to the convention, in decided contrast to the Republican convocation the Democrats did accord Miss Anthony and her colleagues seats on the platform, and her views were given a hearing. This was a substantial achievement. The Democrats would go no further, and the memorial was tabled.

An expression of regret was voiced editorially in *The New York Herald*:

A *Golden Opportunity Lost*—In the tabling of the memorial of Miss Susan B. Anthony....Had the convention boldly taken ground in behalf of suffrage to the intelligent white women of all the United States as against the radical policy of universal suffrage to the ignorant negro men of the South, they might have swept the country....The only alternative left...is an independent Presidential women rights ticket. Let them try it, and they will teach both the republicans and the democrats a lesson to be remembered."[28]

The elements around *Revolution* now embarked upon a campaign for independent political action and repeatedly tore into the major parties. These excerpts establish their position:

If the murmurs of discontent we hear among women, negroes, working men, and the few great souls that feel the mighty sorrow of the masses...are as widespread as they seem, then let the educators of public sentiment...with one simultaneous move galvanize the laboring classes into a new and higher life, teach them what their true interests are, and what laws are needed to secure them food, clothes, and homes, virtue and education, time to read and rest....Why is it that the masses do not rise up in their strength and expel all these corrupt men from office? They have the votes....

To this end, ... let us call a national convention of all those outside party trammels, and make a platform worthy the eventful times in which we live.[29]

Perhaps the most radical statement for political independence of the major parties came in an address of Miss Anthony at the convention of the National Labor Union in September 1868. She stated:

You know that both parties are in the service of capital of this nation, and that they will never propose or bring about any measure for workingmen of real permanent benefit. One party is ruled by Wall Street gamblers and A.T. Stewart, and the other is an outgrowth of a capital monopoly of which Belmont and Co. are the representatives.[30]

As the campaign heated up, the shafts of *Revolution* irked the established press. *The New York Herald*, which had deplored the bad judgment of the Democratic party in not clasping the Anthony-Stanton group to its bosom, burst out in editorial ridicule.

The Women as a Political Element

For some time past, political society, public meetings, and the plans of political pipelayers have been greatly disturbed by the introduction of the female element into politics. Women knock at the gates of political wigwams and demand admission in the name of the sex.... It is the right of suffrage they want and the right to scold everyone according to the "patriotic" inspiration of their temper. Some of them are married and have changed their habiliments—in a metaphorical sense of course—for those of the other sex. Others are unmarried, but are patriotically inspired to get husbands, although perhaps they are not going exactly in the right way to accomplish their ends by attending political meetings and by abandoning the care of kitchen utensils and the darning of their brother's stockings to make speeches at conventions and edit newspapers....

It is astonishing that the class of women who aspire to political influence should find favor with intelligent people or respectable newspapers. They are really becoming...as great a nuisance as the wicked men of Water Street."[31]

The Boston group led by Lucy Stone kept up a drumfire of criticism of the Anthony-Stanton forces as being enamored of the Democrats. Finally *Revolution* set this charge to rest. "It is not true...that 'The Revolution' is favorable to the democratic party and its policy, as at present organized and conducted; but it is true that the malcontents in Boston are strongly committed to the republicans whose claim to the support of honest men and the sympathy of true and progressive women, we do not regard as any better."[32]

The Stanton-Anthony group did not let up on its opposition to the major parties. In 1869 after Grant was ensconced in the presidency, this group sailed into Newport, Rhode Island, the summer watering-pace of the superwealthy, and convened a gathering that adopted a resolution urging "that we earnestly call upon all true men in both parties to at once organize a new party based upon principle rather than expediency."[33]

At the May 1871 anniversary convention, the N.W.S.A. featured a speech by Victoria Woodhull in which she proclaimed her clear intention of forming a new political expression, the Cosmo Political party.[34] Radical as her speech must have sounded then, the reforms proposed are not only relatively mild but anticipated many things in effect today—proportional representation, the United Nations and World Court, marked curtailment of capital punishment. It has even been seriously proposed at various times that ex-presidents be members of the U.S. Senate.

The newspaper most widely read by the working people organized in trade unions in New York City, the *New York Star*, continued in an antagonistic, albeit humorous vein to characterize the woman suffrage movement, in particular, Mrs. Woodhull. "The anniversary of the 'Woodhull' branch of the Woman's Suffrage Convention was the more spicy.... We are sorry... that Mrs. Woodhull-Blood or Blood-Woodhull (her relations toward her two husbands, past and present seem somewhat mixed)."[35]

While the N.W.S.A. was described as attracting "within its circle the out-and-outers upon all social questions" and was antagonistic to both major parties, the A.W.S.A. was characterized as embracing "within its ranks all the conservative adherents of the 'cause'."[36] This group, led by Lucy Stone, remained a steadfast adherent of the Republican party. It remained for the *New York Star* to pour its ridicule upon the A.W.S.A. as it did upon the Anthony-Stanton group: "*Sighings for Suffrage.* The Annual May Wail of the Strong-minded—A High Old Time Among the Petticoated Males and the Pantalooned Females—The Millenium to Dawn with the First Morning's Parade of the Dear Creatures to the Polling Booths—The Bible Dragged In as a Bolster to the Cause—As Clear As Mud."[37]

As the presidential election year of 1872 rolled around, that master of journalistic prose, Theodore Tilton reflected his erratic character by making a 180° turn from radical independent politics in support of woman suffrage and labor reform to joining the Liberal Republican bandwagon led by his idol Horace Greeley with anticorruption directed at the Grant administration as the chief issue.

At first he wrote in September 1871:

now is the opportunity... to found the... party of advanced ideas... the party whose pennon shall be "Equal Rights to All", not meaning half or fraction; the party including Negro Equality, Woman Suffrage, Labor Reform, Anti-Monopoly and every other progressive idea needful to the regeneration of the state and harmony of the world. O for Cromwell to rise again with Milton on one side and Hampden on the other! Come Internationals! Hail Communists! Arise Radicals! Let us have a party of our own, and show (like the other parties) with what little wisdom we too can govern the world![38]

In Cincinnati the Liberal Republicans led by Greeley, Schurz, and Ignatius Donnelly met in convention and nominated Horace Greeley and B. Gratz

Brown as their candidates. The National group sent a delegation of Miss Anthony, Mrs. Isabella Beecher Hooker, and Mrs. Laura de Force Gordon to the conclave and subsequent conventions of the Democrats and the regular Republicans. The Liberal Republicans would not include a woman suffrage plank in the platform. Susan B. Anthony made this interesting commentary: "You see our cause is just where the anti-slavery cause was for a long time. It had plenty of friends and supporters three years out of four, but every fourth year, when a President was to be elected, it was lost sight of; then the nation was to be saved and the slave must be sacrificed. So it is with us women."[39]

The Boston group was just as critical of the Liberal Republicans: "But *because* he hates Woman Suffrage, and as President of the United States would veto a Sixteenth Amendment to the Constitution, every woman suffragist, of whatever party should withhold his vote from Horace Greeley."[40]

Tilton now executed his *volte face*, and at the Cincinnati convention he was among the first to place Greeley's name in nomination with "joy and pride," and he and others "shouted themselves hoarse . . . over Mr. Greeley's nomination."[41]

He admitted that woman suffrage takes "precedence over all other radical issues," but claimed that the right way to push this reform was through newspaper discussion, woman's conventions, public speaking, tracts, and memorials before committees. He held that it was wrong to urge it before national conventions of political parties.

He completed his exercise in casuistry by writing that the argument criticizing the Liberal Republican platform because of the absence of a plank on woman suffrage was "wholly irrelevant and absurd. . . . Such a topic was wholly foreign to it. The call was issued to existing voters. . . . The existing voters in the American republic are men, not women. This is a regretful fact, yet a fact.[42] This line of reasoning would have prevented any major party from coming out for votes for blacks, since they were not voters until the Fourteenth and Fifteenth amendments were added to the Constitution. Tilton is important because he reflected the degree to which the liberals had begun to turn their backs on the plight of the black men and ignore the rights of women to the franchise.

The Democratic party, meeting in Baltimore, merged with the Liberal Republicans with a common platform and endorsed the Greeley-Brown ticket. It was also the last political gasp of the National Labor Union, which had been captured by nonunion politicos, and at a pitiful gathering it also endorsed the ticket.

THE 1872 MAY ANNIVERSARIES

While waiting for the outcome of the Baltimore convention of the Democrats and the convention of the regular Republicans, the usual May Anniversary meetings took place in New York, but with a most unusual result. The increasing organizational influence of Mrs. Woodhull caused some misgivings within the ranks of the National Woman Suffrage Association. Lillie Devereaux Blake, the head of its New York state division, felt that Mrs. Woodhull's views on love, marriage, and divorce were commonly viewed as "free loveism" and damaging to the cause of woman suffrage.[43]

Susan B. Anthony did not participate in the N.W.S.A.'s preparatory efforts for the anniversary meeting. She was on a lecture tour to help pay back some of the debt she had incurred putting out *Revolution* when it was under her control. She wrote to Mrs. Stanton and Mrs. Hooker about her fears, but they were not dissuaded.

Mrs. Woodhull has the advantage of us because she has the newspaper, and she persistently means to run our craft into her port, and none other. If she were influenced by women spirits...I might consent to be a mere sail-hoister for her; but as it is, she is wholly owned and dominated by men spirits and I spurn the control of the whole lot of them.[44]

Apparently Miss Anthony was referring to the widespread view that Victoria Woodhull was the mere mouthpiece for the free love, anarchist, Fourierist views of Colonel Blood and Stephen Pearl Andrews. Susan B. Anthony also felt that to convert the May meeting of the N.W.S.A. into a political convention would be a disaster. "My name must not be used to call any such meeting. I will do all I can to support either of the leading parties which may adopt a woman's suffrage plank or nominee; but no one of them wants to do anything for us, while each would like to use us."[45]

Despite this demurrer from Miss Anthony, the convention call did bear her name. The call read for a *"People's Convention.* We believe the time has come for the formation of a new political party whose principles shall meet the issues of the hour, and represent equal rights for all."[46]

The call went on to declare that a platform would be adopted and candidates for president and vice president of the United States would be chosen. The Republican party was again castigated for barring women from the franchise. The Democratic party was condemned as having attempted to sustain slavery and was politically dead.[47]

Mrs. Stanton was quite enthusiastic about the political direction and hoped that in addition to marshalling articles and arguments for woman suffrage, women would prepare position papers on finance, free trade, land monopoly, protection, prohibition, education, jails, asylums, civil service, and other matters. The purpose was to educate women in these issues and demonstrate to men the capacity of women to grapple with key questions. In this article, which she wrote just prior to the May convention, Elizabeth Cady Stanton seemed to hedge a bit by writing that the convention would consider placing candidates in nomination if there were sufficient numbers and matching enthusiasm at the convention.[48] In a burst of inflammatory rhetoric Mrs. Stanton wrote: "The women who have demanded political equality...have been the target of national ridicule and abuse....

"It may be that this step too in progress is to be achieved not by argument but by blood and that bolder hands shall soon hew straight, short paths to womanhood...to freedom."[49]

Miss Anthony got wind of Mrs. Woodhull's plan to pack and capture the convention. She stopped her lecture tour and came to New York City to salvage the movement, which she felt was in danger of being destroyed by irresponsible reform elements. Indeed in her opening address, Mrs. Stanton, having conferred with Miss Anthony stated that the inauguration of a new party did not necessarily mean fielding candidates. An admission charge of 25¢ was established to limit the number of Woodhull followers.

Miss Anthony made her position quite clear. She said to all assembled that the principle of woman suffrage was foremost and aid should be given to the party supporting that position. The proposed platform of the convention called for equality before the law regardless of nationality, race, color, sex, or religious or political persuasion; maintaining the Union by not reopening the questions settled by the Thirteenth, Fourteenth, and Fifteenth amendments, which freed the slaves and enfranchised all men; universal suffrage and universal amnesty; and planks on tariffs, monetary policy, civil service reform, land to actual settlers, referendum, proportional representation, graduated income tax, quality public education for all, prison reform, a congress of nations to maintain peace, and opening all parties to people regardless of sex, or race.[50]

After the platform was seconded, Miss Anthony proposed a resolution condemning the Liberal Republicans and their candidate, Horace Greeley. The proposal also called for women approaching the major parties that had as yet not met in convention to ascertain their positions on woman suffrage. If these parties did not put woman suffrage into their platform, then and only then would a political nominating convention be called. At this point Mrs. Woodhull announced her intention of calling the convention forthwith to nominate candidates. Miss Anthony replied that this would be imprudent.

A motion was then made to adjourn the N.W.S.A. convention and for the delegates to meet at Apollo Hall, where the Woodhull forces would nominate candidates. Miss Anthony declared the motion out of order, since the present hall had been rented for the next day. Then a voice from the audience called for a vote, and the *viva voce* sentiment seemed to favor Mrs. Woodhull. Miss Anthony then ordered the lights turned off and the meeting broke up in utter confusion.[51]

This development marked the separation of the entire woman suffrage movement from Victoria C. Woodhull. The Boston group in a "I told you so" manner hailed the break by stating: "We congratulate the National Suffrage and Education Committee, and the woman suffragists who prefer to work under their auspices upon having excluded side issues, and thus virtually adopted the platform of the American Society. We hope they have got rid of the 'Free Love' incubus which has done incalculable harm to the cause of woman suffrage."[52]

In June 1872 the regular Republican party met in convention and nominated Ulysses S. Grant for reelection as president. Senator Henry Wilson, a long-time supporter of woman suffrage, was nominated as running mate for the vice presidency. Of significance was the fourteenth plank of the Republican party platform: "The Republican party mindful of its obligation to the loyal women of America expresses gratification that wider avenues of employment have been open to women, and it further declares that her demands for additional rights, should be treated with respectful consideration."

The American Woman Suffrage Association promptly came out in favor of the regular Republican ticket. "Let every State be canvassed by woman speakers and roused by woman's influence. Let the election of Grant and Wilson be a triumph of civilization, a monument of the cordial cooperation of American men and women for the welfare of mankind and the establishment of Equal Rights for All."[53]

Despite Theodore Tilton's ridicule of this plank as "the thinnest piece of pasteboard imaginable and means as much as 'Very truly yours' at the end of a letter,"[54] Miss Anthony resolved to bide her time until the Democratic party completed its convention in Baltimore.

She engaged in a spirited exchange with the *New York World*, the newspaper favorable to the Democrats. The editor asked whether Miss Anthony and her supporters were going to support a party on the sole basis of woman's political equality, irrespective of other issues. She responded: "Yes, Mr. WORLD, put a Woman Suffrage plank and not a Philadelphia splinter in your platform . . . and the best women in the country will work with pen and tongue for the triumph of your party."[55]

The Baltimore convention of the Democratic party accepted, without change, the platform and candidates of the Liberal Republicans. Resolutions for woman suffrage were pigeon-holed. Both woman suffrage wings were now for Grant. The twain had met in this campaign. All the old wounds seemed to have miraculously healed. The American and the National jointly campaigned for the Republican ticket. *Woman's Journal* reported favorably on the activities of Susan B. Anthony and Elizabeth Cady Stanton.

RUNNING FOR OFFICE WITHOUT VOTES

After a public meeting of the American Equal Rights Association in Boston in May 1866 Mrs. Stanton, flushed with the success of the rally, decided to run for a seat in the House of Representatives in the fall elections. She appealed to the voters that while she was disenfranchised, she was still eligible to run for public office. Her creed was free speech, free press, free men, and free trade. She opposed the Republican party for including the word "male" in the Constitution and because it was protectionist. She berated the Democrats because of their support of caste and class privileges.[56]

She made no campaign at all in the form of flyers, canvassing, or public meetings. Twenty-four votes were cast in her favor against 13,816 and 8,210 for her opponents.[57] A journalist reported this exchange at the Radical Republican headquarters on election night: "A Voice—'Mrs. Stanton elected over Brooks' (Loud laughter and cries of 'How are you Katie', and 'Who'll mind the baby.')"[58]

Six years later in the 1872 presidential campaign, Mrs. Woodhull, having been shut out of the N.W.S.A. convention, gathered her forces in Apollo Hall on May 10 under the banner of the Cosmo Political party. There were over 200 delegates in attendance according to newspaper accounts, but the party officials claimed 620 delegates from over twenty states. The hall was festooned with banners and posters:

> GOVERNMENT PROTECTION AND PROVISION FROM THE
> CRADLE TO THE GRAVE
> PUBLIC EMPLOYMENT, THE REMEDY FOR STRIKES
> INTEREST ON MONEY IS A DIRECT TAX ON LABOR TO SUP-
> PORT WEALTHY PAUPERS
> NATIONALIZATION OF LAND, LABOR, EDUCATION, AND
> INSURANCE
> THE UNEMPLOYED DEMAND WORK OF THE GOVERNMENT
> THE WORLD IS OUR COUNTRY; TO DO GOOD OUR
> RELIGION
> I.W.A. AND THEY HAD ALL THINGS IN COMMON
> THE PRODUCTS OF THE PAST SHOULD BE THE EQUAL IN-
> HERITANCE OF THE LIVING GENERATION
> THE LAWS MUST BE SUBMITTED TO THE PEOPLE
> EQUAL RIGHTS, PEACE AND COMPENSATION
> WHAT LACK I YET
>   JESUS SAID TO HIM: GO SELL ALL THOU HAST AND GIVE
>   TO THE POOR (MATTHEW XIX:21,22)
> NEITHER SAID ANY THAT WHAT HE POSSESSED WAS HIS
> OWN;
>   BUT THEY HAD ALL THINGS IN COMMON (ACTS V:32)[59]

These slogans were also reflected in the platform of the party. Additional points included constitutional revision; proportional representation; referendum; abolition of monopoly; graduated income tax; abolition of capital punishment; international arbitration to abolish war; universal suffrage.[60]

All the possible varieties of radical reform were represented, and the convention was a gathering point for all those who felt that the traditional major political parties were devoid of principle and offered little hope of solving basic social problems. Mrs. Woodhull was the personality that welded this diverse group together. It also was a classic expression of the political role of radicalism advancing programmatic planks which later were incorporated into law or given wide consideration. It was also a gathering with a vision of establishing a cooperative commonwealth generated by humanistic values.

The delegates were eager to get to the choice of candidates. While there was no contest for the presidential nomination, Mrs. Woodhull receiving unanimous approbation, there were various names presented for the vice presidential choice. Frederick Douglass, without being present or having accepted, was the vice presidential nominee.[61]

The convention then broke up after a collection was taken to pay for the expenses. No campaign of any kind was mounted. Apparently, Mrs. Woodhull was hard-pressed to keep her periodical, *Woodhull and Claflin's Weekly*, alive. She faced constant ridicule and abuse over her views, which were characterized as "free loveism." The effort, however shortlived, represented a first—a woman running for the highest elective post in the land.

POLITICAL DOLDRUMS

The split in the woman's rights movement continued and served to ennervate it. The A.W.S.A. tried to concentrate on state referenda, while the N.W.S.A. worked on securing a woman suffrage amendment. Such a measure was first introduced in 1868, but then superseded by the concept that under the existing Constitution women already had the right to vote. Eloquent and logical support for such a position by the Minor resolutions and the Woodhull memorial generated sporadic efforts, which were struck down by the courts. In 1878 Senator A. A. Sargent of California, who was associated with the efforts of Susan B. Anthony, introduced a measure that without a change of wording was finally adopted in 1920. It was known as the "Anthony Amendment" and read: "The right of citizens of the United States to vote shall not be denied or abridged by the United States or by any state on account of sex."[62]

This measure was reported annually, hearings were held, and finally in 1882, select committees in both houses of the Congress were designated to consider woman suffrage. This effort was the major focus of Miss Anthony and the National Woman Suffrage Association when they convened each year in Washington for lobbying efforts. These attempts, despite setbacks, kept the national movement alive.

From 1870 to 1910 seventeen state referenda were held on woman suffrage, and only two were successful. These two approaches—national and state-by-state—proved to be prongs of a pincer movement which culminated in the 1920 victory. The gradual increase in the roster of states having woman suffrage enrolled more women who could vote for representatives in the Electoral College. This generated power and placed pressure on the major political parties, especially in presidential election years.

The election of 1876 marked the end of Reconstruction. The South had been readmitted with full representation in the Congress; the military occupation troops were withdrawn; the rights of blacks remained on paper with chattel slavery replaced by sharecropping and tenant farming; segregation and discrimination were practiced in employment, housing, public accommodation, and education; Liberal Republicans who had been in the forefront of the abolitionist movement turned their backs on blacks, some even becoming social Darwinist racists; Southern Democrats made common cause with Northern Republicans on matters of mutual concern in economic, financial, and industrial expansion. The hotly contested 1876 election between Samuel J. Tilden, the Democrat, and Rutherford B. Hayes, the Republican, ended up with Hayes the victor. No violence ensued because of back-stage efforts. The Gilded Age was in full swing, and woman suffrage remained in the political backwaters until more propitious reform impulses catapulted it to the forefront.

ORGANIZED LABOR
AND WOMAN'S RIGHTS—
THE POSITIVE PHASE

WOMAN'S RIGHTS AND LABOR—THEIR INTERRELATIONSHIP

In social composition, the woman's rights movement was essentially middle- and upper-class. As educated women, sensitive to the lack of fulfillment of women as persons in society, they were not content to remain at home and concern themselves only with domestic responsibilities of caring for the husband and children. Some were writers, lecturers, doctors, teachers— avidly interested in the world around them, particularly the conditions of women—social, economic, and political. They had demonstrated great organizing and occupational ability during the Civil War in the fields of med icine, nursing, war-related factory work, and education. Their sensitivity to their own rights as women was sharpened by discrimination visited against them in the very struggle to abolish chattel slavery of the blacks. Their attachment to abolitionism was an association with a belief in rights for all humanity, men and women. They were therefore concerned with exploitation wherever it arose, including the workplace, and such consequences as poverty, disease, prostitution, crime, and slums. They were aghast at the degree of child labor and were ardent advocates of expanded public education. To be sure, their focus was on securing the ballot for women as the talisman which would solve all the problems of society.

Working women, made up largely of two sectors who had to work— those who were young and single, and widows—exercised their right of association sporadically and formed unions. But these unions were mostly independent of the stronger male unions. The only significant exceptions were the Daughters of St. Crispin, who worked very closely with their male counterparts in the shoe industry, the Knights of St. Crispin (the women were restricted to working on the uppers, which required less skill and strength); the women cigar makers who came from Bohemia and were admitted to the Cigar Makers International Union only after their presence became a real threat to the men cigar workers; and the National Typographical Union of printers, which reluctantly admitted women into its ranks as typesetters because they often worked as strikebreakers, and provided for a while a separate division called the Women's Typographical Union.

Generally, the unions of women were shortlived because of a lack of resources for a permanent staff and the mobility of women in and out of work because of marriage and child rearing. Sectors of the woman's rights movement aided these women by focusing public attention on their conditions of work, occasionally organizing them into unions, and developing workingwomen's protective associations to act as employment exchanges and as agents securing wages improperly withheld from women workers.

Various labor reform organizations also took an interest in the welfare of woman workers. There the emphasis was on the political arena—securing legislative posts, enacting remedial legislation, focusing attention on working conditions by investigations and public hearings, and at various times fielding a political ticket independent of the major parties. Among the proposals in their platforms were the eight-hour day, equal pay for equal work, opening up all occupations to women, woman suffrage, producer cooperatives, and arbitration to forestall strikes. Women were in leadership posts and helped put out a variety of labor reform newspapers. While these reformers were allied to abolitionists and sympathetic to woman suffrage, independent labor reform politics came first.

Of the three woman's rights groups that could be differentiated, the National associated with Susan B. Anthony and Elizabeth Cady Stanton developed a most positive relationship with organized labor, although it was not sustained beyond 1869 with respect to the largest organization of unions, the National Labor Union. The American group, adhering to its exclusivist perspective of eschewing side issues, paid scant attention to organized labor, except to voice an occasional conservative hostility. In the group following Victoria Woodhull, aside from pro-labor rhetoric and ostensible labor reform aspirations, there was actually little if any effort on her part to organize women workers in unions. The unions that did exist shied away from Mrs. Woodhull and her political aspirations for the presidency under the banner of the Cosmo Political party.

The National Labor Union (N.L.U.), obviously working-class and predominantly male in composition, was a hybrid organization with affiliates of unions of skilled craftsmen seeking better wages and working conditions and a labor reform element initially looking to establish a national labor party for wide-ranging social reform. Through the period of 1866 to 1869 it was able to keep both elements together in a growing viable organization that claimed a membership of 600,000. The apogee of the N.L.U. was reached under the direction of a most remarkable labor leader, William H. Sylvis. His untimely death removed a person who was acutely conscious of the need to maintain unity. His successor, Richard Trevellick, stubbornly maintained his reform approach in the face of massive defection of union affiliates. It became increasingly a political captive, a prize for contention by agents of the major parties in its ranks, and gave up the ghost in 1872.

Even though the monumental documentary history of woman's rights written by Susan B. Anthony and her colleagues avoids mentioning the relationship between the National Woman Suffrage Association and the National Labor Union, and Eleanor Flexner in her comprehensive history of the Woman's Rights movement downgrades the importance of Miss Anthony and her followers being associated with the N.L.U., this aspect of woman's history is quite significant.[1] The insights this important close tie provides reflect on the possibilities and pitfalls in the necessary coalition building to realize a basic common goal in social reform.

DIFFERING PERCEPTIONS

While the term *working women* relates to those who actually work for wages, *working-class women* is a much more embracing concept. Included are women whose husbands, brothers, sisters, sons, and daughters may be working, but these women remain at home doing the arduous unpaid labor of rearing children, shopping, cleaning, laundering, and cooking. They had achieved the first rung of upward mobility—having left the factory, office, and store. Their unmarried daughters looked forward to the time when they too could escape the drudgery of low-paid, unskilled, monotonous, and repetitive work through the route of marriage and family life. Their outlook was identified with the struggles of their male breadwinners. They thought that woman's place was in the home and viewed single women beyond the marriage age and widows with pity. For them the workplace was no setting for the liberation of women; it was a place of degradation and exploitation.

The binding of women to the home certainly strengthened the family unit, but it also caused them to become preoccupied with the home, husband, and children to the exclusion of other more worldly concerns. This was a factor in the difficulty of organizing women in unions.

With the advance of technology, those aspects of work that lost human skills became degraded in status and became "woman's work". Thus it was with spinning machines, sewing machines, and the perfecting of the type-writer and the telephone. This term "woman's work" has been uttered "with the slight inflection of contempt" and there has been "created a . . . division of labor with jobs that are unskilled, underpaid and lacking in social distinction."[2] Theresa Wolfson, a distinguished historian of woman workers, cites the cultural anthropologist W. I. Thomas from his *Race Psychology*:

"In general it may be said on the lowest levels of culture, man has made a tool of her [woman] and on the higher, an ornament."[3]

The trade unions have developed a body of thought and traditions centered on the role of men as earners and caretakers of the economic concerns of the family.

The trade union was the workingman's club and though organized primarily for economic purposes it became his refuge from the worries of home and the family. It brought him in the company of his friends and fellow workers. The trade union language, therefore is a man's jargon. The rituals of procedure are suited for men, and the meeting place in the past was synonymous with the neighborhood saloon— that institution which was for years the central meeting place for the workers' social and economic activities in every industrial country.[4]

The saloon keeper would have the tables in the back for playing cards and transacting union business—formal and informal, while benefiting from the patrons quenching their thirst on beer and whiskey. The association of woman's righters with temperance did not endear them to male workers on this count as well.

Fundamentally, men regarded women in the workplace with pity, contempt, and as dangers to their standards of work—hours and wages. The men regarded themselves as protectors of women and were influenced by the propaganda of some employers who derogated their own women employees as "bad" women. An eloquent woman worker responded, "We do not estimate our liberty by dollars and cents—consequently it was not the reduction of wages alone, which caused the excitement, but that haughty, overbearing disposition, that purse-proud insolence, which was becoming more apparent. We beseech them not to asperse our characters or stigmatize us as disorderly persons."[5]

Well before the Civil War, the position of skilled male workers toward women entering their trade was expressed in a manifesto issued by the printers' union. In essence the male worker identified women working in male-dominated trades as equivalent to immorality and vice; that the efforts of publishers to recruit women were designed to lower wage costs and curtail unionism; that entry of women would force housewives to leave the homes and find work with the combined income of husband and wife being about the same in purchasing power as the wages brought home by the husband alone in the past.[6]

THE WOMAN'S RIGHTS ORGANIZATIONS AND THE LABOR QUESTION

The Anthony-Stanton group, organized around *Revolution* and the National Woman Suffrage Association, was more open than the 'American' group toward considering labor-capital problems and the condition of the woman worker. The close collaboration with the National Labor Union (N.L.U.) and occasional rhetoric of identification with labor's cause masks the basic approach to woman workers as being purely a woman question and that as long as women do not have the elective franchise they would be exploited. Their focus on feminism caused them to advocate women's entry into the crafts and trades dominated by men, even if it meant for a woman to be a strikebreaker. This is borne out even in the heyday of closeness between National and the N.L.U.

Talking of strikes; we heard a "male" compositor say the other day that "it was mean for women to step in and take work at the old price, when men had struck for higher wages; besides it was degrading." "Mean", is it? Well we're agreed. . . . Just as often as possible we shall step into new places, and then—get us out if you can. If you won't let us enter in any other way, we must enter in this; and as to its being degrading, we beg leave to differ with you there. *Woman* is not degraded, but *man* is. Every time that a strike is made, and woman in consequence enters some new branch of business, she is elevated and man degraded.[7]

The Anthony-Stanton later effort at training and recruiting strikebreaker women in the printing trade caused the rupture between their group and the N.L.U. When this sector courted the N.L.U. after losing control of the American Equal Rights Association, the concept of women's entry into male-dominated occupational fields no matter what the consequence was muted. As a matter of fact an effort by the proprietors of *Flake's Bulletin* of Galveston, Texas, to have a woman compositor work at a rate of pay below that paid to men was rejected. The Woman's Typographical Union No. 1, led by Augusta Lewis who worked in *Revolution*'s printshop, went even further: "the female compositors of New York take this occasion to inform all proprietors making such offers that they cannot be induced, under any plea, to place themselves in antagonism to any organization under the jurisdiction of the National Typographical Union."[8]

Miss Anthony accepted this position out of expediency in contrast to Miss Lewis's more solid trade union orientation. An interesting observation of an analytical nature was made by an early historian of women in unions:

By some this incident [Miss Anthony's encouragement of woman strike replacements] has been interpreted to show a wide difference of outlook between those women who were chiefly intent on opening fresh occupational responsibilities for women, and those who, coming face to face with the general industrial difficulties of women already in the trades, recognized the urgent need of trade organization for women if the whole standard of the trades wherein they were already employed was not to be permanently lowered.[9]

She further wrote that Miss Anthony "had forgotten what was likely to be the outcome for the girls themselves of training, however good, obtained in such a fashion. She had also forgotten how essential it was that she should work in harmony with the men's organizations as long as they were willing to work with her."[10]

The attitude of male-dominated unions constituted a severe provocation.

The bitter and often true complaints made by workmen that women have stolen their trade, that have learnt it, well or ill, they are scabs all the time in their acceptance of lower wages and worse conditions... and that they often act as strike-breakers when difficulties arise, form a sad commentary upon the men's own shortsighted conduct. To women, driven by need to earn their living in unaccustomed ways, men have all too often opened no front gate through which they could make an honest daylight entrance into a trade.[11]

Workingman's Advocate, a labor newspaper published in Chicago by A. C. Cameron, was designated as the official organ of the National Labor Union. Cameron wrote a frank editorial on the conduct of male-dominated unions toward woman workers.

If there is one act more than another in the conduct of our trades unions to which exception can be taken it is the tardy justice which they have doled out to the weaker sex, in their efforts to sustain themselves by useful industry.... Disguise the fact as they may, *woman* is destined to occupy a higher position in the future than she has in the past.[12]

As a *leit-motif* in the Anthony-Stanton views toward labor, the ballot in the hands of women is constantly sounded. Here in this devastating account of child labor, the theme emerges as the key element in the solution of this grave problem:

How far the law is observed appears from the report recently made by the officer appointed to have charge of its enforcement. In Fall River he found one thousand children employed in factories, mostly of foreign parentage, in a generally low condition, ignorant in many cases of their own ages, earning very low wages, and deprived in great part or altogether of the school privileges which the law requires... the officer inquired of the agent of one of the principal factories, whether it was the custom to do anything for the physical, intellectual, or moral welfare of the work people. The answer would not have been out of place in the master of plantations, or the captain of the coolie ship: "We never do; as for myself, I regard my workpeople as I regard my machinery; so long as they do my work for what I choose to pay them, I keep them and get out of them all I can. What they do, or how they fare outside my walls, I do not know. They must look out for themselves, as I do for myself. When my machinery gets old and useless, I reject it and get new; and these people are part of my machinery." Another agent... replied "that he used his mill-hands as he used his horse; so long as it was in good condition and rendered good service, he treated him well; otherwise he got rid of him as soon as he could, and what became of him was no affair of his."... When women, mothers have the ballot, how soon will many such outrages and cruelties be suppressed![13]

"We will show the hundred thousand female teachers, and the millions of laboring women, that their complaints, petitions, strikes, and protective unions are of no avail until they hold the ballot in their own hands; for it is the first step toward social, religious, and political equality.[14]

In a review of a book, Mrs. Stanton claimed that women's wages would go up if new avenues of employment would open up for women, thus decreasing the number of women for particular jobs. She then raises the talisman: "Now if woman had the ballot she would hold office, . . . be anything, go everywhere; hence there would not be so many to teach school and sew, and they would command better wages in these employments. Again the ballot dignifies the laborer, exalts whatever he touches, and thus again increases the value of his work."[15]

In essence the group around *Revolution*, particularly in 1868, was very close to the labor movement. They regarded the National Labor Union with a claimed following of over 600,000 members as an attractive force with which they could forge an alliance. In this association Anthony and Stanton saw an opportunity to put some male political muscle behind woman's rights, especially suffrage. They were willing to envisage organization of women in unions, not fully realizing the frustrating difficulties in that course. They were also willing to bide their time on direct support for woman suffrage from the N.L.U., but in William Sylvis they saw a sympathetic partner who personally believed in woman suffrage. In this relationship both had approached the Democratic party's 1868 convention with remarkably similar proposed platform planks. Despite opposition within the N.L.U., Sylvis accorded them a warm welcome.

THE NATIONAL LABOR UNION

The National Labor Union held its first convention in Baltimore on August 20, 1866, with seventy-seven delegates from thirteen states. Only two national unions were represented, but as an indication of the liberal approach to delegate status, there were seven delegates from five eight-hour leagues. John Hinchcliffe, the chairperson, expressed his feeling that this convention would have a great influence "upon the preponderating class of the land, the workingmen and women of the country." He further stated that the delegates were "no factious opponents of any system of politics. They are neither Radicals or anti-Radicals, and they would never introduce politics into their labor movement."[16]

Of critical importance was the adoption of a resolution: "*Woman Workers—Resolved*, that we pledge our individual and undivided support to the sewing women and daughters of toil in this land, and would solicit their hearty cooperation, knowing, as we do, that no class of industry is so much in need of having their condition ameliorated as the factory operatives, sewing-women, etc. of this country."[17] While there were no woman delegates, the chief officers elected, A. C. Cameron, J.C.C. Whaley, and Alexander Troup, were very sympathetic to woman's rights. The N.L.U.'s successful audience with President Johnson could not but impress militant woman suffragists. Indeed a law was enacted establishing the eight-hour day in government shipyards and arsenals, and it was no accident that the sponsor was none other than Representative George W. Julian, one of the staunchest supporters of woman suffrage.[18]

In Chicago at the N.L.U.'s 1867 convention great strides were reported in delegate strength and representation. The address to the convention not only recorded its ecumenical hope that all labor regardless of race or religion would unite, but also had an extended section on female labor. The immediate consideration was the spreading action of employers hiring woman as strike replacements under the guise of philanthropy. "We claim that if they are capable to fill the positions now occupied by the stronger sex— and in many instances they are eminently qualified to do so—they are entitled to be treated as their equals and receive the same compensation for such services."[19]

Of significance were two provisions incorporated into the N.L.U. constitution, which made it possible for Susan B. Anthony and her colleagues to participate as delegates in 1868 and 1869. Article 2, Section 1, provided that the N.L.U. "shall be composed of such labor organizations as may now or hereafter exist, having for their object the amelioration of the condition of those who labor for a living." Article 2, Section 3, set forth that "Ex-representatives, upon presentation of a certificate of good standing in their organization, shall be entitled to a voice, without a vote, in the National Labor Congress."[20]

The High Point of N.L.U.
Association with Anthony-Stanton, 1868

William H. Sylvis, who was to become president of the N.L.U. at the convention in 1868, was the subject of a new feature in *Revolution*. An article, which took up four-fifths of a page in small type, referred to Sylvis as "a prominent leader in the Labor Reform Movement which already counts hundreds of local associations with a membership of more than half a million, and will ere long, shape the policy of the nation. Most of the members are legal voters though some are women soon we trust to be voters."[21]

At a special conference prior to the convention, a platform was drawn up based upon positions the 1867 convention had endorsed. On women, the resolution read: "Resolved, that the low wage, long hours, and damaging service, to which multitudes of working girls and women are doomed, destroy health, imperil virtue, and are a standing reproach to civilization; that we urge them to learn trades, engage in business, join our labor unions."[22]

The key actor in the drama representing the N.L.U. in its relation to the Anthony-Stanton woman's righters in 1868 was William H. Sylvis. A foundry worker, he became a leading figure in the Molders Union. In politics Sylvis started out as a Whig follower of Henry Clay. Later he became a Democrat and supporter of Stephen Douglas. When the clouds of war gathered in the 1860s, he organized a company of Union volunteers after the Confederates led an attack on Pennsylvania. Later in politics he avoided any entanglements with the major parties, stating that they were guilty of breaking every promise made to labor. "If we resort to political action at all, we must keep clear of all entangling alliances. With a distinct workingman's party in the field, there can be no distrust, no want of confidence."[23]

He regarded unions as "purely defensive in character" and felt "that no permanent reform can ever be established through the agency of trade unions . . . and there will be no end to it until the workingmen of the country wake up to the necessity of seeking through the ballot-box. All the evils under which we groan are legislative."[24] He was in favor of paper currency inflation and producer cooperatives.

Since many woman's righters were active abolitionists, Sylvis's views would be significant. He was opposed to the Freedmen's Bureau, calling it "a huge swindle upon the honest workingmen of the country," because he strongly believed that it was unfair to spend millions on feeding and clothing one class of workers while having a work-or-starve policy for white workers, particularly returning soldiers. He didn't seem to be aware of the fact that freed blacks were designated as vagrants and returned to former slave owners as sharecroppers or tenant farmers in a form of outright peonage.

Nevertheless, he looked toward getting blacks into trade unions, knowing that blacks were used as strike replacements. Shortly before he died while touring the South for the N.L.U., he wrote:

We conversed with a number of intelligent negroes who were . . . well-pleased with our views, and in a short time there will be a second Labor Union in this city, composed exclusively of colored men. If we can succeed in convincing these people that it is their interest to make common cause with us in these great national questions, we will have a power in this part of the country that will shake Wall Street out of its boots.[25]

Sylvis could not fathom the devotion the blacks felt toward the Republican party, the political force associated with the end of slavery. On the other hand, he knew of the close connection of the Republicans to the employers, the bankers, and the businessmen.

On woman suffrage, Sylvis shared the common "belle-ideal" of women having special emotional qualities that called for being in the home as an educated person.

If there are reasons why man should be educated, there are many more and stronger reasons why woman should receive the soundest and most practical mental and moral training. She was created to be the presiding deity of the home circle, the instructor of our children, to guide the tottering footsteps of tender infancy in the paths of rectitude and virtue, to smooth down the wrinkles of our perverse nature, to weep over our shortcomings, and to make us glad in the days of adversity to counsel, comfort, and console us in our declining years..[26]

He scorned the spasmodic efforts of "superficial theorists" who "display their oratorical powers and tickle the public ear, but no good has been gained. The efforts were ephemeral, the effect fleeting. It is but a mockery of woman's woe to draw a fanciful picture of her sufferings, and then leave her in her misery, without hope of amelioration."[27] He urged three courses to aid women. One was to boycott all those manufacturers who refused to pay women a living wage. The second was to have women join unions. The third was the forming of cooperatives, a course he favored most.

On woman suffrage, Sylvis evolved from a view of limited suffrage to full universal suffrage. The former position was expressed in an essay he wrote for the International Moulders Union Journal: "Shall women vote? We answer, *yes*. We are in favor of *limited* female suffrage. We think our wives, sisters, and daughters should have a vote on all questions involving a moral issue."[28] Later he expressed a broadened view:

Many assert, and I fully endorse it, that they would add dignity to the elective franchise, and give it a moral power that would elevate it above the bribery, corruption, dissipation, dishonesty that now cling to it like a festering sore.... Why should women not enjoy every social and political advantage enjoyed by men? The time, I hope is not far off when universal suffrage and universal liberty will be the rule all over the world.[29]

The congruence of views between Sylvis and the Anthony-Stanton group seemed to augur well. The N.L.U. was on an upswing while without the financial help of George Train, *Revolution* was financially quite burdened. The loss of control to Lucy Stone of the American Equal Rights Association tended to isolate Miss Anthony and her followers. The N.L.U. offered a well-organized body of reformers with which the National group of woman's righters could work harmoniously.

The Woman's Righters at the N.L.U. Convention

For some weeks prior to September 21, 1868, when the N.L.U. convention was scheduled to convene, *Revolution* repeated the official call to the convention and urged that "women will not fail in some proper way to be represented there."[30] While it was noted that the call was "addressed to working*men* only; ... the voice and action of some former meetings and the liberal tone of the newspapers devoted to the interests of the Union lead us confidently to believe that working *women* also will be admitted to the body if they make the proper application."[31]

Susan B. Anthony made every effort to get as many woman organizations as possible to send delegates. She seized upon the portion of the N.L.U. constitution that stated that all organizations which worked for the "amelioration of the condition of those who labor for a living" could be represented and hoped that *"The Working Woman's Protective Union, The Working Woman's Home, The Young Woman's Christian Home,* and every association to ameliorate the conditions of working women will appoint delegates at once."[32] The actual efforts began at a meeting of women in the town of Mt. Vernon, New York, who were interested in voting on school and town improvements. Mrs. Mary MacDonald moved that an organization be formed "to be called 'The Woman's Suffrage and Protective Labor Association of Mount Vernon'-Carried.... Mrs. MacDonald moved that the Association select a delegate to the Workingmen's convention."[33]

Two days later a meeting was held in the office of *Revolution* to form a workingwoman's association.

Miss Anthony stated the object of the meeting to be an organization of working-women into an association for the purpose of doing everything possible to elevate women, and raise the value of their labor.

The meeting was then organized by the election of Mrs. Anna Tobitt as President, Miss Augusta Lewis, Miss Susan Johns, and Miss Mary Peers as vice-presidents, Miss Elizabeth C. Browne as Secretary and Miss Julia Browne as Treasurer.... Miss Lewis works upon the newly invented typesetting machine. Miss Johns and Miss Peers are both able compositors and profitably employed. The Misses Browne are clerks in *The Revolution* office.

Mrs. Stanton thought it should be called the Working Woman's Suffrage Association.

Miss Augusta Lewis said that woman's wrongs should be redressed before her rights were proclaimed, and that the word "suffrage" would couple the association in the minds of many with short hair and bloomers and other vagaries. She thought that the workingwomen should be brought together for business purposes, after which they could be indoctrinated with suffrage or any other reform.

Mrs. MacDonald coincided with Miss Lewis.

Mrs. Stanton that redressing woman's wrongs before her rights were asserted was placing the cart before the horse....

Notwithstanding Mrs. Stanton's argument, it was decided that the word "suffrage" should not be inserted and the Working Women's Association was adopted as the title.

Miss Anthony said if those present did not feel that the ballot was the fulcrum by which they could gain their ends, she was sorry; but did not desire them to pass resolutions beyond what their present mental status sanctioned.[34]

This account reveals an important divergence in the approach to the problems of the working women. The suffrage leaders emphasized the ballot as the panacea; the working women were looking for something more immediate and practical in some form of unionism to gain some improvements in wages, hours, and working conditions.

A motion was made at the same meeting to send Miss Anthony as the delegate to the N.L.U. convention.

> Miss Lewis came squarely to the point and said: "What good will that do?"
> Miss Anthony replied that the object was to gain recognition for women as members of men's societies, and gain for them the same wages as men for the same work.[35]

The third woman delegate was elected from the Workingwomen's Home, a boardinghouse for working women located at 45 Elizabeth Street on New York's Lower East Side. Mary Kellogg Putnam, the daughter of the monetary reformer, was chosen.[36]

These three delegates were admitted to the congress on the first day. Mrs. Stanton attempted to become accredited as a delegate from the Woman's Suffrage Association. There was a heated debate with the majority of leading officers-to-be voting for and speaking in favor of her admittance.

Sylvis was enthusiastic on her behalf and called her "one of the boldest writers of the age and had done more to elevate her class and his class too. (Applause)."[37] This view was supported by most of the delegates. Bourke of the Painter's Union led the opposition. He claimed that Mrs. Stanton's admission was an endorsement of woman suffrage and would bring the N.L.U. into politics. He also feared that woman suffrage would upset the harmony of the home.

> Now as for woman's suffrage, I might be in favor of it to a certain extent; but I tell you a woman is a very strange kind of being. If a man is a Democrat it is likely his wife would be a Republican, or, if a Republican, most likely his wife would be a Democrat—such is the nature of woman; and I think you would have a healthy old time in the family.[38]

The decisively favorable vote to admit Mrs. Stanton was followed by a bit of jocularity by a delegate asking that he be admitted representing the Grant and Colfax Club of the Seventeenth Ward. Behind these attempts at humor lay the stereotype of women as being irrationally contradictory and the fear of political action. The opposition to Mrs. Stanton as a delegate did not give up and threatened to withdraw from the convention. A. C. Cameron of the *Workingman's Advocate* then introduced a resolution stating that by seating Mrs. Stanton the N.L.U. "does not regard itself as endorsing her peculiar ideas, or committing itself to position on female suffrage, but simply as a representative from an organization having for its object the 'amelioration of the condition of those who labor for a living.' "[39]

"Worthy of a Talleyrand," was Mrs. Stanton's comment after the resolution was unanimously carried.

Of the four delegates associated with the *Revolution* woman's rights wing, none was a working woman. They were described as being "drawn from the better situated classes."[40] But their entrance to the convention floor provided a field day for the male delegates and the press.

Half an hour before the commencement of the proceedings three delegates from the weaker half of creation entered the hall and took seats at a table in front of the platform.... Miss Anthony was dressed in a suit of black alpaca striped with green. Mrs. Putnam had on a suit of light second mourning and Mrs. MacDonald wore a dress of gray material striped with brown. Miss Anthony carried a morocco leather bag and a bundle of *Revolutions* which she distributed for cash or for compliments all around. A good many of the sterner sex paid their respects to the distinguished champion of woman suffrage. Miss Anthony was delightfully insinuating and made no mean impression on the bearded delegates.[41]

There were thirteen convention committees concerned with a variety of topics for the preparation of resolutions. Three of these, Female Labor, Platform, and Prison Labor, had women delegates as members.

William H. Sylvis was elected president unanimously. For the position of second vice president, the women began to show their colors. "Mrs. Mary Kellogg Putnam and Miss Susan B. Anthony canvassed and caucused energetically while the ballot was being taken in favor of their standard-bearer, Miss K. Mullaney, Troy Collar laundry manufacturer, and with good result, as she had an immense majority on the first ballot."[42] (Kate Mullaney was the leader of the woman laundry workers of Troy who had aided the bricklayers and molders unions in their strikes, and despite reciprocity from these unions when the laundry workers left their jobs in a prolonged dispute, lost the strike. In an effort to maintain her supporters, Kate Mullaney then organized a producers cooperative.)

After Miss Mullaney's election, it was discovered that the N.L.U. constitution barred the first and second vice presidents from coming from the same state. Accordingly, Sylvis appointed her as assistant national secretary.[43]

The record provides ample evidence of widespread participation in debate by Miss Anthony. The influence of women was also seen in the president's report, committee reports, and the adopted platform. Outgoing President Whaley had an entire section of his remarks devoted to female labor. He asserted that it was to the self-interest of labor to protect itself against the depressing effects caused by the introduction of female labor into the trades at low wages. He advocated equal pay for equal work.[44]

The Committee on Female Labor in which Miss Anthony participated brought forth five resolutions. The first urged women to overcome their disabilities: to form unions, learn trades, engage in business, and "secure the ballot".[45] This resolution, although supported by the three men who were also on the committee, sparked extensive debate on the matter of woman suffrage, and it was voted to strike out the disputatious phrase. Other sections urged equality of pay for women and pledged support of the unions in the N.L.U. for the organization of women into unions, the application of the eight-hour day to women workers, and equality of treatment of women workers in federal employment.[46]

The Committee on Labor Organs adopted the following resolution, which met with convention approval: "*Resolved*, That we recognize in the *Revolution*, . . . an able and well conducted advocate of our principles, and call upon men and women of all occupations to render it a full and impartial support."[47]

Delegate Keating, out of reasons of chivalry, proposed that the women delegates be exempt from financial assessments. "Mrs. MacDonald appealed to the gentleman to withdraw his motion, as she would not consent to remain on the floor of the Congress except on the same money basis as the male members." The motion was withdrawn.[48]

In his final speech to the convention, President Sylvis stated that he hoped the delegates would go home determined to work hard to build up the National Labor Union.

I say this to both males and females, for we have now a recognized officer from the female side of the house—an assistant secretary—one of the smartest and most energetic woman there is in America, and from the great work which she has already done, I think it not unlikely that we may have delegations representing 600,000 working women. That you see has been promised to balance the 600,000 men—so I think those on our side of the house had better go to work and get 600,000 more, so that we will still be that number ahead of them.[49]

With this convention, the N.L.U. extended real recognition and cooperation to women and their particular representatives led by Miss Anthony. By admitting them as delegates with a status equal to that of men, by placing them on committees, permitting them to participate in debate, appointing a woman to high office, and adopting a program which, except for woman suffrage, echoed the position of *Revolution* the N.L.U. provided real evidence of affinity to the woman's righters centered around Miss Anthony and Mrs. Stanton.

The woman delegates on their part, by taking defeat on woman suffrage with good grace and by participating enthusiastically in the affairs of the convention which did not concern women directly exhibited a feeling that this labor reform movement was important and a vital vehicle of cooperation.

The impression that the N.L.U. convention made on Mrs. Stanton and the others of *Revolution* was powerful.

The great event of the last week has been the National Labor Congress.... There were about one hundred delegates representing the different Trades Unions in the country—all were of more than average ability, and the leaders equal to any men of the age.... We publish in our Financial column, their platform, which, in our opinion, is far superior to that of either Chicago or Tammany.

The admission of four women as delegates marks a new era in Workingmen's Conventions. And the appointment of Mrs. Catherine Melaney, President of the Collar Laundry Union of Troy, composed of five hundred women, as Assistant Secretary, whose duty it will be to organize labor unions all over the country, shows the recognition of woman to be the future policy of the National Labor Congress.... The producers—the workingmen, the women, the negroes—are destined to form a triple power that shall speedily wrest the sceptre of government from the non-producers—the land monopolists, the bondholders, the politicians....

One thing was clearly understood in the convention—that the workingmen would no longer be led by the nose by politicians, as they proposed to have a people's party in '72 ... so long as neither party proposes Universal Suffrage or a Sound Monetary System, it makes no different to the masses which succeeds; or, whether they are made slaves by brute force or cunning legislation.[50]

In the course of the convention, Miss Anthony extended an invitation to the delegates to attend meetings of the Workingwomen's Associations, which were held in the evening after the convention sessions were over. The invitation was met with applause and the record indicates that William H. Sylvis, Lewis A. Hine, Alexander Troup, and William Jessup did attend.[51]

REVOLUTION AND THE ORGANIZATION OF WOMEN WORKERS

At the time of the N.L.U. convention notices began to appear in *Revolution* calling meetings of women workers to organize into unions. "The Workingwomen's Association No. 1, invite the women compositors of this city and Brooklyn to attend their next meeting to be held at the offices of *The Revolution*, ... to form a Woman's typographical union. Officers and members of the men's unions promise to render every possible aid in securing to themselves equal pay for equal work."[52] What appear to be verbatim extracts of this meeting are quite revealing of the attitudes of woman workers toward male-dominated unions.

Mr. Alexander Troup, a delegate to the National Labor Congress from Typographical Union No. 6, denied that the association of which he was a member was in hostility to the female compositors. If the female compositors will work together with the members of the Union, they will get an equal remuneration for their labor.

Miss Peers: Will the Union allow ladies to join their ranks as members?

Mr. Troup: I never knew of any woman applying for admission. I can speak for
    Mr. McKechnie, the present foreman of the *World*, and President of the National

Typographical Union as being in favor of women working at case with equal rights and privileges as the men. But he is not in favor, nor am I, of women coming in to undermine the prices paid to men.

Miss Anthony: How much is the initiation in this union of yours?

Mr. Troup: One Dollar.

Miss Anthony: Oh, that is not much; I guess our girls can stand that. (Laughter)

Miss Peers to Mr. Troup: Will you take my initiation fee now, if you please?

Mr. Troup: Yes of course I shall; and will propose you as a member.

Miss Gussie Lewis: ...I have heard that there is a decided prejudice in the Union against women setting type among men.

Mr. Troup: ...I believe that the *World* could not have got its paper but for the assistance of the women compositors when the men struck for wages."[53]

This event was a momentous one, for here the women around *Revolution* organized something that went beyond a broad woman's organization dedicated to reforms for women with particular emphasis on the ballot. A specific woman's trade union was organized. It was a step that spelled out unity with the organized labor movement. The fear and suspicion of women toward male unions was very evident. The women were daring the men to exclude them. A romantic note may be added. Augusta (Gussie) Lewis, who became the leader of the Woman's Typographical Union, married Alexander Troup.

Within the ranks of the Workingwoman's Association, there were quite a number of articulate workingwomen who were not at all favorable to woman's suffrage. So eager were Miss Anthony and Mrs. Stanton to work with them and assist in organizing that the suffrage leaders were content to hope that the antisuffrage attitude would be overcome with time.

Perhaps the most clear-cut example of this current was the following statement of the compositor, Emily Peers:

In this city, where not only the poor of our land, but the ignorant, the degraded of all nationalities are herded together, forced by the instinct of self-preservation to the sharpest of competition one with another, it is especially necessary that efforts, organized and persistent, should be put forth by every well-wisher of humanity to better their condition.

And upon the very threshold of this movement, looking to the improvement, social, moral, and physical of woman, having only her welfare in mind, it becomes us to carefully, dispassionately consider what are her needs....Inequality between the sexes, as well as in the sex itself, we know has always existed....You, Mrs. Chairman, may have one opinion and I may have another. You may believe with good motherly Mrs. Stanton here, that the ballot is the great panacea for the correction of all evils, and I may hold an entirely different opinion; but waiving what is problematical, there is a broad common ground upon which we can stand, agreeing fully and entirely. We can reach out, one to another—the highest to the lowest—the hand of fellowship....

I confess...that I have but little faith in the ballot as a remedy for what we complain of...however we altered or amended the law, custom, more tyrannical than law would remain, and once possessed of the ballot, a moral force—woman's truer weapon, would, I fear be lost....All working women, be their trade or employment what it may, are welcome to our organization....That of compensation or cooperation should claim consideration....

I want to see labor dignified; I want to see my sex elevated; I want to see all of my inequality removed, and in the growing intelligence of the age, in the moral forces of the public mind, I build my faith that all will be accomplished.[54]

Two points represented common agreement—trade union organization and producer cooperatives. Miss Anthony proposed that *Revolution* be made up by a cooperative female printing office.[55] Lewis Hine of Ohio and William Sylvis came to the meeting to discuss the feasibility of organizing a cooperative printing office. Hine was the most erudite leading figure of the N.L.U. in the field of economics. Sylvis was not only the president of the N.L.U., but he had had some experience in setting up producer cooperatives.

Mr. Hine: ...The great mistake with capitalists is that they think they have a right to own labor. They have not. Labor should own itself. Teach economists, public men, and scholars to have a higher opinion of the dignity of labor.

Mr. Wm. H. Sylvis of Phila.: I am an iron-moulder and I am perfectly willing that ladies should come into our business....We have now come to the time when we can take hold of cooperation, and we shall yet utterly abolish the accursed system of wages for labor. I am in favor of universal liberty and universal suffrage, regardless of sex and color. They go hand in hand with universal labor and co-operation. I am not in favor of women working at all. I believe that every man should be able to derive profit from his toil to enable him to support his wife, daughter, or mother. I do not believe that woman was intended to live by the sweat of her brow.[56]

The presence of these two N.L.U. leaders at this woman's meeting is further evidence of the mutual attraction these two groups had toward each other. Hine emphasized the barrier of fashion in the way of women accumulating sufficient funds to establish a cooperative on a sound basis. While Sylvis would welcome women into any trade out of their economic necessity, he could not see the justice of women working outside the home. Their working was part of the inherent evil of the wage system.

The Woman's Typographical Union was soon formed. Robert Clark, the corresponding secretary of Typographical Union Local 6, addressed the meeting:

I will state here that it is necessary for the new Woman's Typographical Union to have on their roll eleven names of compositors in good standing before applying for a charter from the National Union, under whose jurisdiction the new association will come. When admitted, we will sustain and stand by them in every sense, providing that they establish a scale of prices and stick by them. We have no desire to work against the women or exclude them.[57]

Miss Anthony then made an ardent plea urging the women to work hard to make the union a success.

Girls, you must take this matter to heart seriously now, for you have established a union, and for the first time in woman's history in the United States you are placed, and by your own efforts, on a level with men, as far as possible, to obtain wages for your labor. I need not say that you have taken a great, a momentous step forward in the path to success. Keep at it now girls, and you will achieve full and plenteous success. (Applause) Mr. Clark, what are the obligations enforced on a member of the printers' union?[58]

In reply, Mr. Clark read the pledge of the Typographical Union to stand by each other until death did them part. The cooperative print shop was also formed.[59]

Not long after the Woman's Typographical Union was formed, a publisher of *Flake's Bulletin* of Galveston, Texas, wrote to Miss Anthony asking that female compositors be sent there to work below union wages. This was summarily refused.

Resolved, That the offer . . . is rejected, and that the female compositors of New York take this occasion to inform all proprietors making such offers that they cannot be induced, under any plea, to place themselves in antagonism to any organization under the jurisdiction of the National Typographical Union; the price in the above city being in advance of the offer made, it is wished to be understood that the object of this union is to raise wages instead of lowering them.

A. Lewis, Pres. Woman's T.U. #1"[60]

At the Workingwoman's Home on Elizabeth Street, Miss Anthony, with the help of N.L.U. leaders, helped organize another local of the Workingwoman's Association. The home itself was set up by philanthropists, and the upkeep was self-sustaining. It accommodated 225 women between the ages of fourteen and sixty-five. The charge for sleeping accommodations and washing was $1.25 a week. There was also a restaurant plan for $3 to $5 a week. The building itself was an old but spacious tenement. Cultural equipment included a piano, melodeon organ, and library. Lights were out after 10:30 P.M.[61]

At a meeting held at the home, Miss Anthony kept up her campaign for woman suffrage by stating that men were successful in strikes because they had the ballot. Women needed the franchise to undergird their demands for equal wages for equal work and decent conditions of work. At another such meeting, the assembled women were asked to recite some of the working conditions in their places of employment.

Revolution printed a tabulation of the women workers' testimony. Twenty-one occupations were represented with from ten to fourteen hours a day. The daily earnings varied from 66¢ to $1.20. Weekly wages ranged from $5 to $14.[62]

Anecdotal statements supplemented the tabulation. A typical example follows:

A girl looking very ill, weak in voice—I am a carpet sewer. I work for one of the largest carpet houses in the Bowery. The Brussels carpets are very stiff sometimes, and I blister my hands very badly (showing her blistered fingers). I worked nearly three days, and sewed fifty yards of carpet, and when I asked him to pay me for sewing the borders, which is additional work, he laughed and said it was "chucked in". (Sensation and cries of what's his name?)[63]

Mr. Hine of the N.L.U., sensing the cumulative effect of these descriptions, urged them to form unions as a matter of life or death.

The importance of laboring unions must be plain to you all. It is the only means of lifting you from this misery. Get together and form associations and establish scales of prices.... I don't see how it is possible for any girl after obtaining her majority to live ten years at this kind of work exhibited here tonight. You are here for a year or so and then you are gone forever. (Sensation)[64]

This meeting thoroughly frightened the backers of the Workingwomen's Home, and its further use was denied to Workingwoman's Association No. 2. They continued to meet in the offices of *Revolution*, and Miss Anthony urged that the garment workers organize a union.

She would advise them ... for the sewers, the embroiderers, and every other class represented to organize themselves and raise their prices higher, and go out and get other women to come into the society. It was impossible as the women stand single-handed and alone to compete with their employers ... as they all wish to get their work done at the lowest price. As they are they can only have starvation prices. They *must* combine. If the women of the city who work at different trades were to form an association, that association would at once inaugurate a scale of prices and then be able to say to the employers: "If you do not pay us that price we will not work for you."[65]

A committee was formed to help organize a woman's garment workers union. In addition to Miss Anthony, prominent woman suffrage leaders such as Sarah F. Norton and Dr. Clemence Lozier assisted. Within ten days a Sewing Machine Operator's Union was organized. They met in a hall on East Broadway with several dozen working women and some men in attendance. Officers were elected and a promise made for machines to set up a cooperative shop.[66]

Susan B. Anthony was indefatigable in her efforts and realized the staggering size of the task in organizing women into unions. She approached several prominent women active in Sorosis, the woman's social and cultural organization founded by Mrs. J. C. Croly, a popular woman writer known as Jenny June. Mrs. Croly was appalled at this attempt and wrote to a newspaper,

> The only foundation in fact consists in the expression of a wish, uttered in private conversation by Miss Anthony with a member of Sorosis....
> They cannot form a society for social purposes...without being hectored or scolded. Men meet in clubs and societies without being expected to directly aid in advancing the millennium; why not women?[67]

FROM UNIONIZATION TO AN UPLIFT SOCIETY

Toward the end of the year the efforts to organize women into unions slackened. The continued isolation of the group around *Revolution* and its severe financial difficulties drained its hopes and energies. The task of getting women into associations and unions proved to be a monumental task. The Workingwomen's Associations merged and composed a declaration of principles. The emphasis was now away from organizing and toward publicizing conditions and presenting educational lectures of a broad general nature.

> *The Dignity of Labor*—We have no sympathy with the ideas so prevalent with regard to the degrading tendency of labor. Honored be the individual who refuses to eat the bread of dependence....
> *Excellence of Performance*—... Without thoroughness and perfect mastery of our vocation we shall not only fail of doing justice to our employers, but shall be unable to take the positions and secure the salaries which real skill and excellence are sure to command.
> *Social Interchange*—Owing to the exhausting toil of workingwomen, their want of leisure and their countless hindrances, they have but little opportunity for social life, and that fine interchange of sentiment and cordiality which elevates the character and without which the soul pines in solitude and a feeling of friendlessness chills the heart.... Therefore we deem it advisable to meet once a month.[68]

The declaration averred that while all women's problems couldn't be solved all at once, organization could generate sufficient strength to better their conditions. "Therefore we urge...that at our monthly meetings we not only strike hands in friendship, but solicit from competent persons, hints, maxims, addresses, heroic songs, whatever will awaken our thoughts, and give us wisdom for future action and attainment."[69]

Provisions were made for the organization of a "Sickness and Misfortune Fund" and a lecture by Anna Dickinson to benefit the organization, the topic being "Temperance and Fashion." Actual workingwomen played little or no role. The leadership was firmly in the hands of suffrage leaders.

Committees were formed to find out the facts about women in various crafts and trades. Victims of grave social abuse, such as Hester Vaughn, accused of the murder of her illegitimate child, were to be championed.[70]

The association began to take on the character of an "uplift" society with a labor orientation. Emphasis was placed on craftsmanship and development of skills to break into industry. There was no longer any mention of the need for workingwomen to organize into trade unions. Women who were eager to alleviate the condition of the wage-earning women were quite dismayed at this turn away from unionism and the constant harping on woman suffrage as the key solution. Aurora H.C. Phelps articulated this view when she wrote:

The poor working-women do not, most of them, want the ballot; I do not; I believe the result of putting the ballot in the hands of woman at the present time would be disastrous in the extreme to herself and to the community. . . . to those who advocate female suffrage, or who desire the ballot, I say we want bread and clothes and *homes* first, and after we caught as good pay for our work as the men do for theirs . . . it will be time enough for you to talk to us about wanting the ballot. Almost all women feel by instinct, that their need is not of the ballot, but of homes.[71]

At a poorly attended meeting of the Workingwomen's Association, led by Miss Anthony and Mrs. Stanton, a Mr. Marvin lectured on marriage. He stated, "no one is fit for marriage who is not lovable. If I were a woman, I would rather be the mistress of the man I loved than the wife of the man I did not love. Not until man recognizes in woman a companion and equal will marriage succeed."[72]

Miss Anthony tried to fathom the reason for lack of attendance and blamed fatigue and inability to pay carfare. Mrs. Kirk took issue with this argument and urged that the association do something practical and discuss the work and wages of workingwomen. Referring to the topic of the lecture, she thought, "we had better leave marriage alone for the present." The facts are that when the association did attempt to organize women in unions and discussed those matters, women came in the hundreds despite the same fatigue and carfare. Mrs. Kirk claimed to have received many letters complaining that the working woman's association was really a suffrage association, and

though she was committed to the cause of suffrage, yet in that association it was her candid opinion the question had no place. (Applause). There was a cause deeper than suffrage and that was suffering. (Loud Applause). What did women who were starving care about the ballot? They always cried out for bread first. . . . She came there for the purpose mainly of taking a vote upon the question of keeping closely to the matter of woman's work and wages, and if the association was indisposed to take that course and let everything under the sun discussed, she would cut adrift and form an organization on her own hook. (Loud Applause).[73]

The question of support of the Troy woman collar workers came up at the Workingwoman's Association meeting in July. Miss Gussie Lewis, of the woman printers, Alexander Troup of Typographical Union No. 6, and Miss Kate Mullaney, the leader of the strikers, came and appealed for aid. The strikers had been out for five weeks, and only two of their number had gone back to work. Mr. Troup said, "They needed aid ... and now was the time for this association to show whether they were really working-women or not. They could now do something practical."[74]

Miss Mullaney said she thought that the association was composed of workingwomen, "but as she looked around the room they were not the workingwomen she had been accustomed to see. She had to work all day in the shop, and this she did not think judging from their appearance, that they did."[75]

A collection was taken up, which netted the sum of $35 for the strikers, not a substantial effort at labor solidarity. Mrs. Elinor Kirk continued her criticism of the Workingwoman's Association in a widely circulated magazine.

In reviewing the prominent reforms, the first which stares us in the face is that of Woman Suffrage—a grand and glorious cause, and one which could have been established years ago.... Had the twenty years which have been spent on discussion, in attempts to convert the wealthy and the aristocratic to the cause of the ballot, been passed in endeavors to raise the condition of working women, for every ten who now look upon suffrage as an inalienable and God-given right would have been found one thousand ready and willing....

The Workingwomen's Association of this city, started under the most favorable auspices, numbering shortly after its inauguration at least one hundred bona fide working women, has now on account of the plank of suffrage in its platform, dwindled down to less than ten; if indeed it be not altogether abandoned ... they reasoned and argued, presented the question in its broadest and not infrequently most impractical light—discoursed on the marriage question, the sin of infanticide, and the benefits to be derived from an extended socialism until the workingwomen, disgusted with their outspoken sisters seeing no chance of benefit to themselves, blushingly withdrew....

If in that association, labor and the interests of labor alone had been discussed— and suffrage and every other "ism" tabooed—it would today have been a stronger power in the cause of equal rights than any engine it now commands, not even excepting *The Revolution*.[76]

It must be remembered that this Workingwomen's Association from its inception was identified with Miss Anthony, Mrs. Stanton, *Revolution*, and therefore the National Woman Suffrage Association. Its change in character to a "do good" organization from one dedicated to the organization of women into unions reflects an alteration in the outlook of that wing of the woman's righters. Beset with financial difficulties centered on putting out

Revolution, increasingly frustrated because association with labor in organizing women proved to be so arduous, tired of keeping the issue of woman suffrage in the background so that the mass of workingmen and women would not be alienated, and being cast in the role of the less respectable group dedicated to women—all this caused the Anthony-Stanton group to embark on a course that could only cause a fundamental schism with organized labor and its national expression, the National Labor Union.

13

THE LABOR–WOMAN'S RIGHTS
COALITION BREAKS APART

THE LABOR MOVEMENT CONTINUES TO GROW

The period of fairly full employment that began in the latter part of 1868 continued through the next few years until rudely interrupted by the panic of 1873. It reflected an economy of postwar growth and expansion marked by speculation, westward migration, and a consistently high demand for labor. The cost of living tended to rise, and this engendered a drive on the part of organized labor to catch up with this trend. Trade unions grew both in membership and expanse. The demand for the eight-hour day became widespread and was a key element in the increase in the number of strikes. This activity was not labor reform but pure and simple trade unionism geared to better wages, hours, and working conditions.

Preparing for the 1869 convention to be held in Philadelphia, William H. Sylvis and his colleague Richard Trevellick toured the South and enlisted wide support, including unions of blacks. The N.L.U. under Sylvis "entered upon the most fruitful year of its existence. Sylvis now introduced systematic and persistent efforts in the management of the affairs of the National Labor Union."[1] He entered into a widespread correspondence, issued scores of circulars, and established a lobby in Washington. Sylvis composed a presidential address for the convention in which he detailed the growing respect of public opinion for the N.L.U.

Up to this time our fight was an uphill business. Our enemies denounced us as demagogues and disturbers of the peace—revolutionists endeavoring to stir up strife and contention, and array one class against another.... But when Congressmen and Senators of high standing and ability took up our platform and made speeches in its defence, the attention of the whole country was aroused and the "hush policy" could no longer answer.[2]

The convention, which was to see the fruits of his efforts, met without his presence. He died on July 27, 1869.

Sylvis's place was taken by Richard F. Trevellick. A worker at various trades, he had traveled widely at home and abroad. He was a great orator and an indefatigable organizer. He did not have Sylvis's knack of keeping diverse elements together and of staying close to the masses of workers. Trevellick, convinced of the soundness of his views, was persistent and doggedly determined to further them in spite of increased defections.

On two counts, Trevellick could rely upon the support of the woman suffrage movement. He was a strong advocate of temperance reform and a vigorous opponent of slavery.

He was a strong proponent of woman suffrage and claimed that woman, as an American citizen, was entitled to all human rights including the vote "for the assessor of her taxes and the judge who probated her estate or who might possibly try her son for alleged crime. . . . He claimed that a woman's property should not be taxed without representation."[3]

President William Jessup of the New York State Workingmen's Assembly at its convention in early 1869 referred to the organization of several "female labor unions" and claimed that there was a "disposition on the part of workingwomen generally to organize in most branches of trade in which they find employment. . . . This movement . . . should be seconded by all workingmen, and every aid and encouragement extended to them to persevere in the movement.[4] Later that year at the national convention of the printers union, the Women's Typographical Union No. 1 was granted a charter and its delegates, Misses Lewis and Howary, granted seats.

The year 1869 saw a host of job actions by unions, bordering on a general strike. Printers, tailors, bakers, sailors, blacksmiths, and building trades workers walked off their jobs. Strangely enough, *Revolution* was silent on this wave of labor discontent.

The employer printers met in conference and passed a resolution denouncing the printers' strike, which was organized "regardless of right and courtesy." They refused to meet with any union committee of the printers.

Despite the fact that Miss Anthony had been instrumental in organizing women into the printers union, she wrote a letter to the employing printers during the strike and even addressed their meeting. "Gentlemen: The Working Women's Association appeals to you to contribute liberally . . . to establish a training school for girls in the art of typesetting. . . . Give us the means, and we will soon give you competent woman compositors."[5]

When the men in the printers union heard about this, they were outraged. Susan B. Anthony attempted to mollify the opposition to her move by addressing a letter to J. Vincent, the secretary of the National Labor Union.

Sir: You fail to see my motive in appealing to the employers for aid to establish "a training school for girls." It was to open the way for . . . the hundreds of girls to "fit them to earn equal wages with men everywhere", and not to undermine Typographical Union No. 6. I did not mean to give the impression that, "Women, already good compositors, should work less per thousand ems than men." and I rejoice most heartily that Typographical Union No. 6 stands so nobly by the Women's Typographical Union No. 1, and demands admission for women to all the offices under its control; and I rejoice also that Woman's Union No. 1 stands so nobly and generously by Union No. 6 in refusing to accept most advantageous offers to defeat its demands. . . .

Every woman should scorn to allow herself to be made mere tool of, to undermine just prices of men workers; and to avoid this, "union" is necessary. Hence I say, girls, stand by each other, and by the men who stand by you.[6]

This exchange suggests that Miss Anthony projected a trace of irony implying that the male unions did not in fact open up the shops to women. Her rationale in seeking to open a school for women strikebreakers hardly squared with her avowed support of unions. This was but a prelude to the storm that descended upon her.

THE 1869 N.L.U. CONVENTION—THE ARENA OF THE CONTENTIOUS SPLIT

The overwhelming bulk of the convocation's time in Philadelphia was concerned with the seating of Miss Anthony as delegate. She put in an appearance toward the end of a eulogy to Sylvis and made a motion that it be made part of the record of proceedings. She was challenged by delegate Walsh of Typographical Union No. 6 of New York City on the grounds that her credentials had not been passed upon.

When her credentials were reported to the congress, Walsh said:

I am directed by Typographical Union No. 6 comprising 2,000 members to protest in their names the admission of Miss Susan B. Anthony. We claim she is not a friend of labor. I understand that the lady is here to represent a Workingwomen's Association of New York, composed of male and female agitators in a movement for female suffrage. . . . In the first place, the lady is the proprietor of a paper published in New York, called the *Revolution*, and while the columns of that paper proclaim the principle of equal wages for men and women, its forms are gotten out by as notorious "rats" as we have in our trade, and who are opposed to our organization at every point. The ladies working upon that paper do not receive the same wages men receive, and this, too notwithstanding the officers of our Union under the direction of that body called upon the proprietor of that paper and requested her to observe the same scale of prices which was observed in a union office. In the second place, during the struggle with their employers in which the Typographical Union No. 6 was engaged last spring—a struggle which cost us $24,000—a meeting of our employers was held at Astor House and the lady . . . waited on those employers and solicited aid to furnish a room wherein females could learn to set type, thereby enabling our employers to defeat our just demands by throwing upon the market unskilled labor....

We therefore protest against the admission of the lady, and trust that every man here who knows what strikes are and who is a member of a trades union will stand by us on this question.... We represent a large membership, pay a large tax, struggle hard for our principles, and I trust that no one who is not a genuine friend of labor will be admitted here.[7]

A motion was nevertheless made to admit Miss Anthony as delegate. It was tabled. She then advanced to the stage of the hall to offer her explanation.

Miss Anthony: With regard to the printing office in which my paper, the *Revolution*, is printed, before I knew anything of typesetters union or workingmen's associations my paper was in the hands of a printer, Mr. Johnston, in the city of New York.

A voice: A "rat".

Miss Anthony: I don't know whether he was a rat or not a rat. I never heard of such a thing; but I have this to say, that the girls in that office are paid forty cents per thousand ems, while in the *Independent* office, and in all other offices in the city, the pay is from thirty to thirty-five or thirty-seven cents. In that office they are paid more than in any other printer's office, as I understand the facts from the President of the woman typesetters union of New York. It is not my office any more than the Cooperative union office is mine; but if it is a rat office No. 6 must remember that the President of the first women's Typographical Union of New York No. 1 has, up to this time, been one of the head workers in that office receiving forty cents per thousand ems for her work and I have never heard the slightest objection from No. 6 or from any other source, to woman typesetters who were in full membership in typesetters' union working in that office.

Mr. Walsh of New York: Will the lady permit me to ask a question? Why was the President of the Woman's Typographical Union No. 1, a union which we support, turned out of the *Revolution* office a week ago?"

Miss Anthony: I did not know she was.

Mr. Walsh: I know she was for being a union woman.

Miss Anthony: Oh, no.

Mr. Walsh: Well, she tells that.

Miss Anthony: Well, I cannot help it if she was. I am not responsible for anything in that office, except I pay a job man for putting out my paper. My printer never told me that he had discharged the woman. Then again in regard to the employing printers. Last spring some one came into my office and said: "Miss Anthony, now is your time. You have been talking to your workingwomen's association about establishing a training school for learning girls to set type. Now is your time, while these employing printers are in distress to make them fork over some cash to establish a school. Well, of course, I am not in the Workingwomen's Association especially to advance men's wages; I am there specially to help women out of the kitchen and sewing-room, so I put my bonnet on in a twinkling and went over to Astor House. Those gentlemen with a broad grin on their faces, looked and sneered as I walked in the room, but I told them why I came there....I appealed to their self-interest to establish a school for the education of girls in typesetting. They appointed a committee to take the matter into consideration,...and I said to girls who applied to me by fifties, go in and learn your trade. I knew full well that when Union No. 6 came in line with the employers, or the employers with them, the girls would be turned adrift; but I said to myself, they will have acquired a little education, a little help, and I will have helped them this much. The result was that some forty or fifty young girls served with Gray and Green and others, during a few months while the strike was in progress. Last year when your noble President was here, women were for the first time admitted into your association and admitted without one objection.... I warn you of the disastrous effect of the vote which refuses me admittance to a seat in the convention.

A Voice: The workingwomen of New York will be satisfied with that vote.

Mr. James F. Hager of Trenton, N.J. remarked that the lady had talked very pathetically, but she failed to enunciate very clearly why a lady was discharged from an office over which the lady present had control.

Miss Anthony replied that she knew nothing of the matter, and had no control over it.[8]

On the second day of the convention a motion was made to the effect that the refusal to seat Miss Anthony on the previous day "was not on personal grounds but that the organization she represented was not a bona fide labor organization." This was seconded by Mr. Walsh of the Typographical Union No. 6.[9]

Mr. Puett of Indiana defended Miss Anthony, stating that she had a right to be seated under the N.L.U.'s constitution, and this purely local matter had no place in the deliberations of a national body.

Mr. Walsh in replying claimed that Miss Anthony was not a true workingwoman.

If Miss Anthony were a working woman I would willingly take her by the hand and welcome her. We have here one such woman from the Knights of St. Crispin (Miss Wallbridge of Mass.) and such as her I welcome. The lady (Miss Anthony) goes for taking women away from the kitchen and the work tub. Who in heavens name are going to be there if these are not? I believe in a man doing the work and taking a wife and supporting her and their children. (Applause) I am for that, and not for women going to set type or any other trade. But this is not merely a typesetters' affair....Fearing that there might be misunderstanding in the matter, I wrote to Miss Augusta Lewis and received an answer from her an hour ago.[10]

In summary, Miss Anthony was denied a seat at the convention based on the arguments that the Workingwomen's Association No. 1, which she sought to represent, was not a working-class organization in membership or program. To support this charge, it was asserted that she approached employer printers during a strike and asked their aid in setting up a school to train woman type-setters. The second charge was that the paper she published, *Revolution*, was printed by a nonunion printer and that the president of the Women's Typographical Union No. 1, Miss Augusta Lewis, was discharged.

Miss Anthony admitted the first charge to be substantially true. She stated that her purpose was not to advance men's wages but to open up occupational opportunities for women. She looked then upon the strike as a male device and did not at all blink at the fact that forty or fifty young women acted as strike replacements during that labor dispute. As for the second charge, Miss Anthony claimed that the *Revolution* office paid the union scale of prices and that if Miss Lewis was discharged, it was without her knowledge. She also stated that she had nothing to do with employment conditions in the printing plant.

Mr. Walsh then read Miss Lewis's letter to the convention, describing the character of the Workingwomen's Association, the organization Miss Anthony claimed to represent.

The Working-women's Association was organized immediately before the last session of the Labor Congress. I was first vice-president. Mrs. Stanton was to have it a Working-women's Suffrage Association. It was left to a vote and defeated.

The society at one time comprised over one hundred working-women; but as there was nothing practical done to ameliorate their condition, they gradually withdrew. I do not know who introduced the "Literary" in the society; but the debates and introduction of "suffrage" was introduced. . . . After the adoption of the Constitution and by-laws several members of the Sorosis joined and were on the committee to nominate officers which they did ignoring working-women. . . .

Although the Society comprises many wealthy ladies, they raised $30 for the laundresses of Troy. As a society, either the want of knowledge or the want of sense, renders them as a Working-women's Association, very inefficient. I wish I could assist you in your protest more than I have, and that it is not too late for the purpose.[11]

The debate raged on with Trevellick prominent in Miss Anthony's defense. He claimed that it was a local matter and that she was at least entitled to the floor as a delegate from last year: "last night this body committed an outrage against humanity when they refused that lady a voice in her own behalf. (Loud Cheers)"[12]

Miss Anthony again rose to her defense and challenged the Typographical Union.

As for the collision complained of between the men type-setters and women, the collision between men and women must come some time if the latter are ever to be given the privilege of entering the trade at all. When the type-setters struck for higher rates she urged women to take their places who had no fathers, brothers, or husbands to support themselves, girls who were on the streets looking in vain for work or washing at 25 or 30 cents a day, and who had consequently nothing before them but starvation and prostitution....I would like to ask the Typographical Union how many girls they have taken and educated thoroughly in the art of printing?[13]

As for the falling off of workingwomen membership in the Working-women's Association, Miss Anthony stated that it was because working-women expected no discussion of principles but immediate pecuniary aid.[14]

A motion was then made to have the matter of seating Miss Anthony decided by a roll-call vote. A. C. Cameron, who had authored the resolution finally seating Mrs. Stanton at the 1868 N.L.U. convention, was anxious to avoid a clear-cut decision. He conferred with Miss Anthony and got her to agree to voluntarily withdraw her credentials so as not to bring "disgrace" on the convention. She was to retain her seat as an ex-delegate without voting privileges.[15]

Susan B. Anthony was also vigorously championed by S. P. Cummings of the Knights of St. Crispin, Miss Wallbridge of the Daughters of St. Crispin, and Elisha M. Davis, the labor reformer. Mr. Davis based his argument on that part of the N.L.U.'s constitution calling for the admittance of any organization dedicated to the "amelioration" of the condition of the working people. The vote to seat Miss Anthony was close—fifty-five for and fifty-two against.[16]

At this point a resolution passed by Typographical Union No. 6 on August 16 was read to the N.L.U. convention. This resolution served to cast doubt on the integrity of Miss Anthony.

Whereas, the President of this Union and Mr. Alex. Troup waited upon Miss Anthony in New York, in April last and requested her to pay the scale of prices of Typographical Union No. 6 which she has agreed to do, but has not done;

Whereas, the statements made by her in the Labor Congress, at Philadelphia, that the *Independent* and other offices in New York City are not paying as high prices as the *Revolution* is false, as there are female compositors who are receiving 10 percent higher prices than are paid in the *Revolution*, and

Whereas, the statement made by her in the said Labor Union that she did not know that the President of the Women's Typographical Union No. 1 was discharged from her office is false, the latter lady having a long interview with her on the matter, therefore, be it

Resolved, that we consider it an insult to our entire organization to admit her as a delegate to the National Labor Congress.

In behalf of two thousand printers
Wm. Stirk
Pres. N.Y. Typographical Union No. 6[17]

The dispute spilled over to the third day when Walsh of the printers read a telegram to the effect that if Miss Anthony were to be seated as a voting delegate, he was to withdraw in the name of the printers union.

William Jessup, head of the central labor body of New York City, stated

that he had voted...in accordance with instructions from his constituents...the Workingmen's Union of New York, representing 5,000 members...The working-women's associations in New York City—the Women Capmakers Association and the Laundry Association—had no confidence in this association which Miss Anthony claimed to represent as a labor organization in the Congress last year; but since then other and similar organizations in New York City had lost all confidence in the concern.[18]

In her final plea, Miss Anthony returned to her talisman, the ballot.

There is an antagonism between men and women workers, and there must continue to be until men and women occupy an equal platform, civilly and politically. (Hisses and Applause). I am not in a passion, gentlemen. I am here for women as I have been everywhere for women for the last twenty years, whether on the floor of a teachers' convention, a woman's rights convention, or a labor organization. You have admitted these black men to your councils, but would you have admitted them...at any time prior to the issuance of that proclamation that enfranchised them? They hold in their hands that magic piece of paper, the ballot....Did I represent a class that held the ballot, my right never would have been questioned here.[19]

The final vote on seating her as a *voting* delegate was twenty-eight for and sixty-three against. She then remained with voice but no vote as an ex-delegate from last year.[20]

A newspaper correspondent described the convention from the woman "angle" by characterizing the six or more women participants:

One of these was the notorious Dr. Mary Walker, who appeared in full bloomer costume; another was Miss Wallbridge, of Stonehampton, Mass., delegate from a women's shoe-sewers' union there. The others were Philadelphia ladies, who came out of curiosity to hear the expected discussion on the question of...Miss Anthony....Miss Anthony formed (in a strictly metaphorical sense) the great bone of contention in the Congress..., and was well gnawed and mumbled by some 200 masculine mastiffs, including several coal-black ones. She took it serenely as she always does. Miss Wallbridge by the way, was admitted as a member of the Congress without any difficulty.[21]

As a coda to the dispute a discussion took place on the importation of coolie labor. A delegate stated that he "was opposed to bringing coolies here for the same reason that he was opposed to giving Miss Anthony a seat in the Congress. They would be employed by the employers when men were in strikes, just as Miss Anthony would furnish female labor to the employers under the same circumstances."[22]

THE AFTERMATH OF THE NATIONAL LABOR UNION CONVENTION

Mrs. Stanton took up the cudgels in defense of her colleague:

Their petty treatment of the proprietor of *The Revolution* was unworthy of common sense thinking men. She went simply as a delegate from a labor organization, not as a member bound by its rules.... Susan B. Anthony represents working women whether they know it or not.... Her action in all this matter does not show that she regards men less, but women more. To the petty charges made against Miss Anthony's honesty and rectitude, which should have promptly been ruled out of such a body her public life of twenty years is the best reply.[23]

Elizabeth Cady Stanton ended her editorial with one of the most significant and revealing passages:

Miss Anthony, hanging by the eyelids four days in a Working Man's Convention, has given the press a grand opportunity to manifest the manly elements of justice and chivalry.... The result has proved what *The Revolution* has said again and again, that the worst enemies of Woman's Suffrage will ever be the laboring classes of men. Their late action towards Miss Anthony is but the expression of the hostility they feel to the ideas she represents.[24]

Miss Anthony seized the occasion to hold a public meeting at which she would give a report of her ouster.

As to the charges which were made by Typographical Union No. 6, no one believes them, and I don't think they are worth answering. I admit that this Working Woman's Association is not a *trade* organization, and while I join heart and hand with the working people in their trade unions, and in everything else by which they can protect themselves against the oppression of the capitalists and employers, I say that this association is more upon the platform of philosophizing on the general questions of labor, and to discuss what can be done to ameliorate the condition of the working people generally.[25]

There was an exchange of views reported at the end of the meeting which indicated that even within the ranks of the Workingwoman's Association there were elements which thought that she deserved to be ousted.

Mrs. Norton: I have understood that Miss Anthony was rejected by the Congress, on the ground that this was not a labor association.... It was not from any personal feeling against Miss Anthony or the Suffrage question. Well I think the Labor Congress was right. This association is useless and a sham, and has never done anything for working women.

Miss Anthony: ... I believed it was a good plan to call women together to discuss their interests. And if the suffrage was sometimes mixed up with the discussions, it was to show how women's interests could best be secured. It was to show how the suffrage was the key which would unlock every door to them.[26]

With some misgivings a motion was adopted to draft a series of resolutions condemning the action of the N.L.U. Elinor Kirk replied to Miss Anthony's comments:

had I been there, I should have been prepared to say that S.B.A. has publicly deplored the same management which I make mention of in the magazine alluded to—that both she and Mr. Pillsbury, at a recent meeting of the Association, expressed the belief that the discussion of Suffrage, Marriage, Socialism and the like are damaging to the best interest of the Association.[27]

The press that reacted to Miss Anthony's ouster was divided. *The New York Star*, organ of Tammany Hall and widely read by the workers in the trades, was very abusive toward Miss Anthony.[28] The *New York World*, which provided the widest coverage to the convention, was quite sympathetic. The *World* called the delegates who voted to deny her a seat "ungallant men."[29]

Utica Herald sarcastically urged Miss Anthony to give up trying to become a man and to rejoin the female sex.

Who does not feel sympathy for Susan Anthony? She has striven long and earnestly to become a man. She has met with some rebuffs but has never succumbed. ...

At length Susan's case came up for consideration, and the congress committed the crowning act of rashness and without a thought of the consequences, made an everlasting enemy of Susan Anthony by ruling her out of the convention as a delegate ... denied the solace of being counted one-two-hundreth part of a man by a labor convention! ... This is not the first time that "man's inhumanity to woman" has made Miss Anthony mourn, and as it is not her first rebuff, we counsel her to seek admission again to the ranks of her sex, and cease to cast reproach upon it by struggling to be a man.[30]

The ties between the woman suffrage movement as represented by the Anthony-Stanton forces and the National Labor Union had been broken. Fundamentally, the trade union movement's purpose was to counter the untrammeled power of the employer with the combined strength of workers to negotiate collectively and to use their power to withhold services in a strike.

For Miss Anthony and her cohorts this concept was not on their basic agenda. If a movement or personality could be used to further woman suffrage, then the leadership of the National Woman Suffrage Association wouldn't hesitate to coalesce. In the context of the N.W.S.A. becoming more isolated, being regarded as less respectable, and having the onerous obligation of financing *Revolution*, the association with the National Labor Union was attractive. For a short time, Miss Anthony, despite the rejection of working-class women in the Workingwoman's Association of woman suffrage, helped organize women into unions, but this task was costly in both time and money.

There was a basic class difference in outlook. Miss Anthony, Mrs. Stanton, and their close colleagues were middle-class reformers who regarded men as an enemy of woman's rights and therefore did not hesitate to engage in strikebreaking against a male-dominated union to get women into skilled trades. To be sure, the labor reform element in the N.L.U. resisted Miss Anthony's ouster, since they felt that reforming society had to go beyond pure trade unionism.

The other major wing of the woman suffrage movement, the American Woman Suffrage Association led by Lucy Stone, kept its distance from organized labor because a coalition with that social force would necessitate endorsement of side issues that were not directly concerned with securing woman suffrage. Mary A. Livermore wrote about Miss Anthony's ouster as a voting delegate:

The head and front of Miss Anthony's offending seemed to be, that her paper is printed in what is called a "rat office", that is where printers work for less than the specified rates of the Typographical Union. Miss Anthony has no control over the office and is not responsible for its management. So after a great deal of violent wrangling... Miss Anthony was compelled to budge. Why? The honest truth is because *she was guilty of being a woman!*
... The 200,000 workingmen of the country, represented at Philadelphia have insulted the working women of the country in their treatment of Miss Anthony.[31]

While the A.W.S.A. asserted that it would not be lured away from the single issue of woman suffrage, the following excerpts of a *Woman's Journal* editorial philosophizing on labor will suffice to establish the middle- and upper-class antipathy to labor on the part of the Lucy Stone sector.

The combined effect of an easy money market and a high tariff has been to stimulate manufacturers. Thence has resulted an increased demand for skilled labor. Laborers have combined to take advantage of this increased demand and have forced employers to pay exorbitant wages....
On the one hand, the capitalist is threatened with ruin by the exactions of organized bodies of workingmen, who seek to advance the natural rate of wages to an artificial standard by concert of action, by intimidation of underbidders, and by compulsion of capitalists.[32]

In another issue a description of a labor situation in 1633 was reprinted from the *Nation*. In part it read:

The workingman must be protected against himself. He was growing poor by being overpaid. Because his wages were too high, he worked only two-thirds of his time, and for the rest of the week he was spending money instead of earning.... The General Court interposed for his relief and for the good of the State, by *lowering* his wages and compelling him to work six days in the week.[33]

The fundamental right of labor to organize was conceived to be a violation of the free market. Indeed, the newspaper prefaced this 1633 reprint with a challenge to organized labor: "What would the Crispins and Trades Unions think of such measures as are here described?"

Lydia Maria Child, a veteran of the woman's rights movement set forth the basic antiunion position.

I honor labor; I believe in labor.... But I am opposed to the "eight hour law."... I dislike all monopolies; and a monopoly of labor seems to me as wrong in spirit and principle.... For men to combine together to fix by a forcing process the price of the article in which they deal is monopoly, and nothing else....

The attempts to prevent men who want to work from working in any part of the world where labor is needed seems to me contemptible in spirit and shallow in policy.[34]

Victoria Woodhull, whose agenda included the support of the woman's rights movement and organized labor in her campaign for the presidency on her Cosmo Political party ticket, was incensed that the N.L.U. had decided in 1872 to ignore her blandishments and embark on a course of supporting a major party ticket.

Woodhull, whose movement was affiliated with the International Workingman's Association, led by Marx and Engels, until expelled for ideas on free love, expressed her views quite clearly after her grandiose plans fell flat.

We live under a despotism of political parties. If this set of persons... were to succeed, the despotism would only be shifted from that of the Republican party to that of the Trades Unionists. There is no more despotic body of people in the known world than these same Trades Unions. Skilled labor is their cry, and it would be still more unendurable than is that of capital now.[35]

Theodore Tilton, who had been so close to the woman's rights movement and led a campaign to unify its two wings, spoke out against militant trade unionism.

We do not pretend to have fathomed the depths of the yet unsounded question of Labor and Capital. On the one hand, we believe in the right of workmen to combine for higher wages, provided their strike is peaceable, and does not interfere with the liberty and choice of any fellow workman who refuses to engage in it. But a "union" by which a majority of workmen in any given trade or place, compels all others— at peril of life and limb—to join in its revolution, and to do its bidding as to whether he shall work or not, or for what pay—such a union is a disgrace to whomsoever is engaged in it, and deserves to have the riot act read against it, and its participants dispersed at the point of a bayonet.[36]

Tilton, the partisan of the Paris Commune and self-proclaimed communist, came out against the chief aim of the organized labor movement—the eight-hour day.

The strike has practically ended. Most of the workmen have accepted work upon such terms as they could make. The total effect of the demonstration has been exceedingly damaging.... Eight hours may be quite as long as anybody wants to work, but in our present industrial condition, it is impossible to universalize the eight hour rule, and there is neither reason nor justice in reducing manual labor to eight hours, while mental labor is obliged to give twelve or fifteen.... We learn that as a rule the families of eight hour workmen have fewer clothes and comforts and less money than those who work ten.[37]

Tilton was apparently unaware that the labor movement's goal of an eight-hour day was predicated on no reduction of wages.

Thus it may be established that all sectors of the woman's rights movement were in essence middle and upper class in social composition and unable to identify basically and persistently with organized labor. Laboring men and their families embraced the concept that woman's place was in the home. If women had to work, it was to be hoped that it was a temporary condition that single women and widows could overcome by marriage.

The labor newspaper, the *Workingman's Advocate*, ably edited for many years by A. C. Cameron, a friend of woman's rights, established a new feature column in 1870 devoted to the interests of workingwomen. Mrs. Goodrich Willard, the editor of this column, in the very first issue reiterated the position that woman's place was in the home, that women in industry should be organized in unions, and that women should use their intellectual faculties, which were deemed equal to those of men, as instruments in their proper roles of moral mentors and guides of the family. It was aimed at workingmen, working wives and daughters, and housewives.[38] She wrote, "The family is the basis of the State, but man as its business head represents only its business and pecuniary interests. As the moral head of the family, woman must have a voice and hand in the government, as the moral representative of the family and society."[39]

Mrs. Willard saw the community of interest between both men and women workers and the suffragists. She considered it to be part of a universal struggle for equality. She thus reflected a stand that transcended the narrower concerns of the woman's righters and the pure and simple trade unionists.

The inequality of the compensation of men and women for equal work . . . is one of the great evils of our system. . . . The low wages and salaries of women in the trades and professions in competition with men, as in school teaching, and the no wages of slave labor she performs for the family in the house has a constant tendency to degrade all labor, and to depress the wages of men. . . .

In denying to women the rights of labor and the means to protect their rights, the laboring man loses in numbers half the advocates and half the strength of the cause. . . .

The anti-slavery movement was a labor movement and so is the Woman's movement. The right of suffrage is only an incidental right. It is only a means to an end, and that end is the protection of the rights of labor and the property that comes from it. The laboring man must make common cause with woman in her struggles for the rights of labor, if he expects to obtain justice for himself. He must know that justice is not a one-sided principle. It knows no sex.[40]

This broad approach encompassed the concept of the work of the housewife being a form of unpaid slave labor.

THE END OF THE WOMAN'S TYPOGRAPHICAL UNION

Under the leadership of Miss Augusta Lewis, Woman's Typographical Union No. 1 attempted to function and broaden its membership. Even when her employment was terminated in the Johnston shop which printed *Revolution*, she continued to approach proprietors of newspapers who were advocates of woman's rights. She wrote:

Hoping to stimulate the women into action by opening an office where none but union girls would be employed and the full price would be paid, I wrote to Mrs. Livermore of the Woman's Advocate, asking the owners of that paper to adopt such a course. Her answer was courteous, but unsatisfactory, and I regret to say no practical assistance can be obtained from that "women's rights" organ for the working women.

Hoping the advocates of "women's rights" would place us on a "financial equality" with men, I waited on Theodore Tilton of the Golden Age. He promised to pay the same wages to women as men. On further inquiry, I learn men in his office are working under price. As he has promised to do "whatever is right", I hope we can persuade him to see "right" in the same light as we do. I also waited on the proprietors of the Revolution, who have solemnly promised when their present contract expires, to have the Revolution a union office, paying the full scale alike to men and women.[41]

As a woman who had made common cause with the union printers at the 1869 N.L.U. convention which ousted Miss Anthony as a voting delegate, and as one who was fired from her job as typesetter for union agitation

in the printshop that put out *Revolution*, one would expect more than lip
service in support of her efforts to get women into union printshops, which
had signed up with Typographical Union No. 6. She wrote sorrowfully:

we have never obtained a situation that we could not have obtained had we never
heard of a union. We refuse to take the men's situations when they are on strike,
and when there is no strike if we ask for work in union offices we are told by union
foremen "that there are no conveniences for us." We are ostracized in many offices
because we are members of the union: and although the principle is right, disad-
vantages are so many that we cannot much longer hold together.[42]

The result was that the women's local was absorbed into the men's local,
and no separation on the basis of sex existed in the printing field. It seemed
that the union brothers on the shop level were not very cordial to union
sisters attempting to break into the trade.

During Miss Lewis's heartbreaking nine-year attempt to keep the Woman's Typographical Union alive she was elected corresponding secretary of
the National Typographical Union, the first such national full-time post held
by a woman. Her reports were exemplary, and she was informed about the
activities of the union, salary scales, union negotiations, and other matters
throughout the country.

THE DECLINE OF THE NATIONAL LABOR UNION

In 1870, the year after Miss Anthony's exit from the National Labor
Union, the labor organization held its own. There were four women delegates and three black representatives. This convention decided to hold two
conventions annually—one to be the regular union delegated body, the other
to consider political action.

The trade unions became disenchanted with the N.L.U. As one perceptive
analyst wrote: "The 'National Labor Union', a loose sort of federative
association, grew out of the trades union, but has nearly lost its direct
relations therewith, being now in the main representative of a number of
political clubs and leagues...which are the chief representatives of the
political labor movement in America."[43]

In 1870 there was, according to another observer of the N.L.U., "a strange
mixture of mechanics, workingmen, ministers, lawyers, editors, lobbyists,
and others of no political occupation, some intent upon organizing a political
labor party, others using their efforts to defeat that measure and benefit
existing parties."[44] A report to the National Typographical Union in 1871
was in the same vein:

we attended said Labor Congress from the opening to the close of the session, and
failed to discover anything in the proceedings, with the exception of the report of

the committee on obnoxious laws, that would entitle the congress to representation from a purely trade organization. The congress was made up of delegates, with few exceptions, who openly avowed the object to be the formation of a political party. Played-out politicians, lobbyists, woman suffragans, preachers without flocks, representatives of associations in which politics are made a qualification for membership, declaimers on the outrages perpetrated on poor Lo, formed the major part of the congress. The session was one of continuous confusion, in which personalities abounded, and charges and counter-charges were made of attempts to run it in the interest of both old political parties. The only thing accomplished was the formation of the Labor Reform party, and the adoption of a platform announcing its principles.[45]

As the presidential year 1872 neared, plans were laid for the political convocation of the N.L.U. in 1871. The leadership was not discouraged by the defections of unions. Their hope was for the Labor Reform party's showing at the polls. Victoria Woodhull relied on the N.L.U.'s endorsement of her candidacy. Trevellick, the N.L.U. president, was eager to support her and by letter invited her to be a delegate at the Columbus, Ohio, political convention. In this letter, Trevellick wrote under a dateline of February 2, 1871:

Personally and otherwise, I would like Mrs. Woodhull to be a delegate.... First: She is a remarkable woman and understands matters of State and the politics of our country as few do.

Second: Because I am convinced that women should not be debarred the right to vote.

Third: Because the National Labor Party, if successful, must be established upon the principle of equal and exact justice to all....

The female suffrage question may be laughed at, belittled, aye, even lowered in the estimation of men by its advocates, but for all that, it is second to none of all which are before the people today.[46]

The N.L.U. became weaker and weaker, and the *Workingman's Advocate* made a public appeal for funds to enable the organization to pay President Trevellick's salary. At its convention in St. Louis in August 1871 there were only twenty-two delegates, among whom was one woman. Not a single national trade union was represented.

While the N.L.U. was diddling around in presidential politics centering on its February 1872 political convention in Columbus, Ohio, all around it the unions swirled in successive strike waves with shorter hours and higher wages as chief goals. In the spring of 1872 over 100,000 building craft workers were on strike in New York. Fearful employers responded by using a blacklist against union workers and locking out strikers until they would come back to work on the employers' terms.

The political convention met and called itself the National Labor Reform party with ninety-three delegates from seventeen states. Each state delegation could vote its strength equal to that in the electoral college. Very few delegates were connected with organized labor. A resolution calling for "equal rights and suffrage for all" was tabled. A newspaper reported, "New and small parties are generally incisive and aggressive in their platform declarations, but this labor party is as vague, and inoffensive, and ambiguous in its resolutions as if it were a party which had been long in power, which had nothing to fear but positive principles."[47]

The candidates nominated were Supreme Court Justice David Davis for president and Governor Joel Parker of New Jersey for vice president. One pamphlet was issued on behalf of the National Labor Reform party calling it:

A rallying ground for the people to fight Monopolies and every species of Thieving, Corruption, and Rascality.
A Party for the People, and not the People for a Party
Honesty, Economy, Anti-Monopoly, Equality and Prosperity the Watchwords.
A new Era in American Politics, a new Leaf turned over.[48]

The Liberal Republicans and the Democrats united behind the candidacy of Horace Greeley, whereupon the candidates of the National Labor Reform party withdrew. Confusion reigned with small groups moving in all directions. One sect led by A. C. Cameron and the N.L.U. Executive Board met in August in Columbus, Ohio, and decided to dissolve on the grounds that it was too late to mount a campaign. Thus the National Labor Union, which had attracted 600,000 members and the Anthony-Stanton forces, lost its trade union adherents and became a political prize balloon that collapsed in the welter of vying interests in the 1872 election campaign. It will be recalled that Mrs. Woodhull became embittered because her political efforts came to naught; the N.W.S.A. and the A.W.S.A. both supported Grant and Wilson, the standard bearers of the Republican party, which promised to give serious attention to the needs of women.

Historically the N.L.U. had pressed for equal pay for equal work, organization of women into unions, admission of women into the trades, and improvement of conditions of work for women. Women came as delegates from reform organizations as well as unions. Despite its demise, the National Labor Union's achievements were carried forward in subsequent national labor organizations. The concerns of women, as they increasingly entered the labor force, particularly during the two World Wars, were consistently on the agenda of the labor movement. The government, both state and federal, became intervenors in matters affecting the conditions of work for women.

The woman suffrage movement of the early twentieth century found ready allies in the trade union women in the final struggle for the Nineteenth Amendment. Women in organized labor developed organizational expression in the Women's Trade Union League and in the present-day Coalition of Labor Union Women.

Some basic conclusions which may be drawn from the N.L.U.–woman's rights movement experience are that coalitions needed for fundamental social reform must respect the critically important values and aspirations of the coalition members; emphasis on woman's rights need not take the form of feminist exclusivism; and unnecessary divisive issues are to be avoided if they conflict with the attainment of the broadest possible consensus in the pursuit of the goal.

14

THE WOMAN'S RIGHTS PRESS

Until 1868 the woman's rights movement had no sustained press of its own. It relied as a rule on the daily general newspapers, particularly *The Tribune*, edited by Horace Greeley; the periodicals of the abolitionist movement, such as the *Anti-Slavery Standard*; the weekly of the liberal Protestant establishment, *The Independent*; and occasional articles in labor newspapers such as the *Workingman's Advocate* and *Fincher's Trade Review*. Periodicals devoted to women's interests, such as *Godey's Lady Book*, avoided woman's rights and were concerned with the role played by middle-class women as homemakers and child rearers dedicated to making life pleasant for the husband, the earner; the topics covered were sewing, embroidery, furniture, cooking, health, child care, and fashion.

In 1867, it will be recalled, Kansas was the scene of an intense political battle involving as distinct issues to be decided by separate referenda, black and woman suffrage. Susan B. Anthony entered this electoral contest after Lucy Stone and Henry Blackwell had returned despondent. There was no support forthcoming from the abolitionist-Republican press back East, particularly *The Independent* and *The Tribune*. Whatever funds were available for the woman suffrage campaign were exhausted.

The Kansas State Republican Committee came out against woman suffrage and in a fit of desperate frustration, Lucy Stone departed from her equal-rights-for-all-without-any-priority principle to opposition to giving blacks voting rights ahead of women.[1]

Led by a dissident Republican, Sam N. Wood, who had broken from the anti–woman suffrage position of the Kansas Republican leadership, Susan B. Anthony and Elizabeth Cady Stanton embarked on a new course. They invited a Democrat, George Francis Train, to join the campaign in Kansas for woman suffrage. Both Miss Anthony and Mrs. Stanton had demonstrated their independence of the Republican party by supporting a proposed change offered by a Democrat, Senator Cowan, to eliminate the word "male" from the proposed Fourteenth Amendment. Furthermore they were cognizant of Lucy Stone's opposition to granting suffrage to blacks ahead of women.

THE BIRTH OF *REVOLUTION*

During the Kansas campaign in a speech at Junction City, Train hurled a thunderbolt from the platform that took Miss Anthony and Mrs. Stanton by complete surprise. He said:

When Miss Anthony gets back to New York she is going to start a woman suffrage paper. Its name is to be The Revolution; its motto "Men, their rights and nothing more; women their rights, and nothing less". This paper is to be a weekly, price $2 a year; its editors, Elizabeth Cady Stanton, and Parker Pillsbury; its proprietor, Susan B. Anthony."[2]

This was quite in keeping with Train's flamboyant style. Now, after paying the cost of the lecture tour—a sum of $2,500—he determined, without consultation, the name of a new woman suffrage newspaper, its ownership and editors, and announced that he would finance the venture into militant journalism to the tune of $100,000. He even advanced Miss Anthony $3,000 with another $7,000 coming from David Melliss, the financial editor of *The New York World*. The only stipulation given by Train was that one-third of the space was to be provided for the exposition of his views. Although opposed from the beginning by all the daily press, criticized violently by the Radical Republican abolitionists, the more forthright advocates of woman's rights were going to get a voice to express their views to the public.

With a dateline of January 8, 1868, the first issue of *Revolution* appeared in an edition of 10,000 copies. In an editorial it announced its purposes:

SALUTATORY

A newspaper is the promise of new thoughts; of something better or different, at least from what has gone before.

With the highest idea of the dignity and power of the press, this journal is to represent no party, sect, or organization, but individual opinion; ... The enfranchisement of woman is one of the leading ideas that calls this journal into existence.... "The Revolution" is a fitting name that will advocate so radical a reform as this involves in our political, religious and social world.... [3]

This modest statement wasn't representative of the broader nature of the newspaper. The back section was devoted to the writings of Train and

Melliss, but on the front page there appeared the statement of principles that was carried for many issues over the names of Anthony, Stanton, and Pillsbury.

The Organ of the National Party of New America

Principle, not policy—individual rights and responsibilities.

The Revolution will advocate:

1. *In Politics*—Educated suffrage, irrespective of Sex or Color; Equal pay to Women for Equal Work; Eight Hours Labor; Abolition of Standing Armies and Party Despotisms; Down with Politicians—Up with the People!

2. *In Religion*—Deeper Thought; Broader Idea; Science not Superstition; Personal Purity; Love to Man as well as God.

3. *In Social Life*—Morality and Reform; Practical Education not Theoretical; Facts not Fiction; Virtue not Vice; Cold Water not Alcoholic drinks or medicines; It will indulge in no Gross Personalities and insert no Quack or Immoral advertisements.

4. *The Revolution proposes a new Commercial and Financial Policy*—America no longer led by Europe. Gold like our Cotton and Corn for sale. Greenbacks for money. An American system of finance. America products and labor free. Foreign manufactures prohibited. Open doors to artisans and immigrants. Atlantic and Pacific Oceans for American Steamships and Shipping, or American goods in American bottoms. New York, the Financial Centre of the World. Wall Street emancipated from the Bank of England, or American Cash for American Bills. The Credit Foncier and Credit Mobilier System, or Capital mobilized to Resuscitate the South and our Mining Interests, and to people the country from Ocean to Ocean, from Omaha to San Francisco. More organized labor, more Cotton, more Gold and Silver bullion to sell foreigners at the highest prices. Ten millions of Naturalized citizens. *Demand A Penny Ocean Postage*, to strengthen the Brotherhood of Labor; and if Congress vote one hundred and twenty-five millions for a Standing Army and Freedman's Bureau, cannot they spare one million to Educate Europe and to keep bright the chain of acquaintance and friendship between those millions and their fatherland?

> Elizabeth Cady Stanton,
> Parker Pillsbury, Eds.
> Susan B. Anthony,
> Proprietor and Manager[4]

There is no doubt that much of this mélange emanated from the fertile brain of Train. He, a world traveler, who had made a fortune in shipping, railroading, and on the stock exchange, impressed the woman's righters with the justice of his ideas. Train was cast in a favorable light as the "angel" of the organ of opinion they had so ardently longed for. Nevertheless, these ideas were, in part, well taken and trumpeted often in the pages of *Revo-*

lution and at various times at conventions and meetings in which the editors and proprietor participated.

The statement also served to antagonize the traditional Republican-abolitionist sector of the woman's rights movement. "Educated Suffrage" was a phrase considered by these groups as code words meaning the exclusion of blacks from voting by advanced literacy tests. "Abolition of Standing Armies and Party Despotisms" clearly meant to this same group the ending of the military occupation of the South—effectively causing the loss of every gain made by the ex-slaves and the restoration of the Southern Democrats to a position of challenge to the power of the dominant Republicans. Advocacy of "Capital mobilized to Resuscitate the South and our Mining Interests, and to people the country from Ocean to Ocean, from Omaha to San Francisco" was an appeal to the ex-Whigs of the Confederacy by supporting internal improvements through government land subsidies to railroads and federal aid for turnpikes, levees, and harbor dredging. Support of greenbackism earned them the enmity of the conservative financial circles, while support of the eight-hour day gave them the plaudits of organized trade unions.

Other aspects of the statement become clearer when it is understood that Train was an ardent supporter of Irish independence from Great Britain through the Fein. He was the champion of the Irish-Americans who wished to communicate with their relatives and have all restrictions lifted against immigrants, particularly the Irish, coming to the United States.

The close identity of the supporters of woman's rights with temperance reform made it desirable for the plank against alcoholism to appear in the programmatic statement. Train himself was a teetotaller and a leader of the Father Matthew Society of Irish-Catholics dedicated to anti-alcoholism education among the Irish.

REVOLUTION AND THE GENERAL PRESS

The newspapers were quick to respond to the appearance of the new journalistic upstart. *Revolution* printed these editorial comments verbatim. As a sign of the tone of the opposition, some representative citations follow:

The Ladies Militant—It is out at last. If the women as a body have not succeeded in getting up a revolution, Susan B. Anthony, as their representative, has. Her Revolution...is said to be charged to the muzzle with literary nitroglycerine. If Mrs. Stanton would attend a little to her domestic duties and a little less to those of the great public, perhaps she would exalt her sex quite as much as she does by Quixotically fighting windmills in their gratuitous behalf....As for the spinsters, we have always said that every woman has a natural and inalienable right to a good husband and a pretty baby. When by proper agitation she has secured this right, she best honors herself and her sex by leaving public affairs behind her.[5]

The Revolution, advocating "love to man as well as God", is edited by Miss Parker Pillsbury and two gay young fellows named Mrs. Elizabeth Cady Stanton and Miss Susan B. Anthony. It advocates "Equal pay to women for equal work". Why does it not go for exact justice to all, irrespective of sex or color, and also demand "Equal pay to men, for equal work for women"? This, we take it, would save a good many dollars to a good many good fellows. As society is now organized, we men have to do all the work and the women get all the money. In the dictionary of Fifth Avenue the word husband is thus defined: Husband—a useful domestic drudge; a machine that makes dollars.[6]

As to woman's suffrage, we would mildly suggest to the editors that their labors are thrown away in writing for men. What they need to do is to convert women to their way of thinking; for from the days of Eve to the present time women have generally had no difficulty in making men do everything they wanted them to. That women do not vote in this State, side by side with men, is owing, not to the opinion of men against it, but to those of women themselves.[7]

The traditional tailors of Tooley Street, three in number, met and resolved themselves into "We the people of England". Susan B. Anthony, as proprietor and manager, and Elizabeth Cady Stanton and Mrs. Parker Pillsbury, have issued a new paper called *The Revolution*, which is announced as the organ of the "National Party", whatever that party is, "of New America" wherever that may be. The first number is a sharp and spicy sheet with a considerable show of Stanton, plenty of Pillsbury paragraphs, and an almost inexhaustible volcano of Train.[8]

In addition to the tone of ridicule and vulgar reference to Parker Pillsbury, the comments of the press reflected the customary attitudes toward women. At the same time women really controlled everything through domination of their husbands, and were better off taking care of homes and babies because suffrage and participating in world affairs were the exclusive province of men.

THE LABOR PRESS LOOK AT *REVOLUTION*

The was a direct contrast in attitude between the trade union organs, which were generally positive, and the sarcastic hostility of the general newspapers.

The Revolution. We welcome with much pleasure the appearance of the first number of this new journal of reform. . . . Its articles are able, radical, timely and interesting, striking telling blows upon old error and wrong, mainly in unison with our own humble sheet. Its appearance is an encouraging sign of the times.[9]

"We have no doubt it will prove an able ally of the labor reform movement."[10]

To these statements *Revolution* commented, "Yes, labor and the ballot go hand in hand. As soon as workingmen come to understand how the degradation and disfranchisement of women cheapens all labor she touches, they will demand the ballot for her, for their own protection."[11]

"The Revolution"—"...We place it with pleasure to our list of exchange; and take occasion to say to our readers of both sexes, that *The Revolution* should be read by every lover of reform. Revolution is the watchword and nothing short of a *mighty* revolution will redeem the downtrodden and oppressed from the galling yoke placed upon them by petty tyrants and political snobs.[12]

The editors of *Revolution* responded, "We would call the attention of workingmen to the fact that cheap labor of a woman cheapens their labor also. Capitalists are asking women and children today to prevent a strike among men. Give women the ballot, you dignify and exalt her, make her labor valuable and increase the price of the laborer."[13]

The Revolution—In conning the columns of *The Revolution*, we find but a little to condemn and much to admire. In "Woman's Suffrage" we cannot see...how either of our present political parties can consistently oppose the movement in its favor.
We do not commit ourselves to the support of the principle of suffrage without regard to race, color, or sex; neither do we oppose it.[14]

At the New York convention of the National Labor Union in 1868, a resolution was adopted urging the *Workingman's Advocate* of Chicago and the *Arbeiter Union* of New York as national labor organs, and recognizing the *Revolution* as "an able and well-conducted advocate of our principles; and entitled to full and impartial support."[15]

Thus the reception given *Revolution* by the labor press and by the N.L.U. was cordial. In the comments of Anthony, Stanton, and Pillsbury may be found repeated the tremendous power they ascribe to the possession of the ballot by woman. It is described as the means by which she will get equality of pay. And since equal pay will prevent the use of women as sources of cheap labor, it is to the self-interest of organized male labor in trade unions to support woman suffrage.

REVOLUTION AND THE ABOLITIONISTS

The attitude of the abolitionist wing of the woman's rights movement may be summed up in a letter written to Miss Anthony by William Lloyd Garrison:

In all friendliness, and with the highest regard to the women's rights movement, I cannot refrain from expressing my regret and astonishment that you and Mrs. Stanton should have such leave of good sense, departed so far from true self-respect,

as to be travelling companions and associate lecturers with that crack-brained har-
lequin and semi-lunatic, George Francis Train!...The colored people and their
advocates have not a more abusive assailant than this same Train; especially when
he has an Irish audience before him, to whom he delights to ring the changes upon
the "nigger", "nigger", "nigger" *ad nauseam*....

It seems you are looking to the Democratic party, and not to the Republican, to
give success politically to your movement....The Democratic party is the "anti-
nigger" party, and composed of all that is vile and brutal in the land, with very
little that is decent or commendable. Everything that has been done, politically for
the cause of impartial freedom has been done by the Republican party.[16]

Mrs. Stanton's reply was couched in calmer language.

If Mr. Garrison may judge parties by their action on slavery alone, is it not fair to
judge them by their action on woman alone?

...Though we travelled with him [Train] through nine states we never heard him
in public or in private ignore the black man's rights. On the contrary, he always
demanded educated suffrage, without respect to sex or color.[17]

Train continued as an issue in the woman's rights movement for the entire
year of 1868 and well into 1869 despite the fact that after the first few
issues of *Revolution* appeared, he had practically no influence on that paper
except for letters he wrote from a British prison. One of the most frequently
hurled epithets at Train was "Copperhead," which was used to describe
people, particularly Democrats, of doubtful loyalty who wanted to reestab-
lish the South to the same position it had before the war without any
intervening Reconstruction military occupation.

Train lost no time in using the columns of *Revolution* to reply. "Copperhead. I deny the right of leagues and clubs to coin words giving their
own definitions. My meaning is Union, Constitution, Law, independent
thought."[18]

George Train, as an ardent partisan of Fein, the militant Irish independence movement, was the idol of the Irish immigrants in America. He even
participated in the ill-fated movement to seize Canada from the British. As
soon as *Revolution* was established, he embarked for Great Britain and
Ireland, his pockets stuffed with the first issue of the paper. Knowing his
reputation, the authorities arrested him upon arrival and put him in prison.
The possession of the woman's rights paper entitled *Revolution* was enough
to damn him in the eyes of the authorities as a dangerous revolutionary.

Elizabeth Cady Stanton quickly reacted to the incarceration of her Kansas
ally.

The position of England towards the Irish is precisely what that of America has
been towards the African; and it is as great an outrage for England to arrest American
Fenians today, as it would have been for us to have arrested English abolitionists
thirty years ago....

Verily it is time for all true men to rebuke tyranny wherever they find it, remembering that "*Our country is the world and all mankind our countrymen.*"[19]

TRAIN WITHDRAWS

Train, himself, felt the abuse directed against Miss Anthony and Mrs. Stanton, because of his association with them. In a letter from his British prison he asked that he be allowed to withdraw from the paper.

I knew the load I had to carry in the woman question, but you did know the load you had to carry in Train.... I saw the theoretical breeching had broken in Kansas, and with voice, with pen, with time, and, what none of your old friends did, with purse, I threw myself into battle....

... You no longer need my services. The Revolution is a power. Would it not be more so without Train? Had you not better omit my name in 1869?... I cannot better show my unselfishness than by asking you to forget my honest exertions for equal rights and equal pay for women, and to shut me out of the Revolution in the future, in order to bring in again the Apostates.[20]

REVOLUTION CHANGES CHARACTER

George Francis Train continued his association with the paper even though he had written that perhaps he was handicapping its success. Upon his return from abroad, he insisted that he no longer be a contributor. "Out of my Bastille cell I asked you to omit my name from THE REVOLUTION ... On my return I found the antagonism on the increase. You remember L.S. [Lucy Stone] turned her back when you wished to introduce her. W.L.G. [Garrison] exhausted the vocabulary in slandering me. H.G. [Greeley] did the same. And all your friends said, '*Do drop that man, Train*'."[21]

No sooner had Train left, when the paper changed its legend under the masthead. It now read:

THE REVOLUTION
Devoted to the discussion of
SUFFRAGE
The only means by which
EQUAL RIGHTS
can be secured to
WOMAN
in the *State*, the *Church*, the *home* and the *world of work*.
AN AMERICAN MONETARY SYSTEM
Greenbacks for money, as well as for Bondholders and Capitalists, as
  for working classes[22]

With the loss of Train and his financial backing, *Revolution*, from 1869 on, faced a persistent crisis. The split in the ranks of woman's righters found the group around Lucy Stone, not only forming a rival organization, the American Woman Suffrage Association, but also publishing a competing newspaper, *The Woman's Journal*. The abolitionist–Radical Republicans were alienated from the Anthony-Stanton group because of its opposition to the Fourteenth Amendment and its having consorted with an antiblack Democrat, George Francis Train. Whatever funds could be raised for a woman's rights organ were more easily directed toward the more "respectable" A.W.S.A. which was also more readily attuned to the major national political focus of battling Andrew Johnson in favor of a Radical Republican Reconstruction in the South.

A letter from Miss Anthony in a new periodical, a rival to the more conservative newly managed *Revolution*, provides an insight into the difficulties faced by Miss Anthony and her methods in attempting to overcome them.

My financial recklessness has been much talked of. . . . .Always when there was *need of greater outlay*, I never thought of *curtailing the amount of work* to lessen the amount of cash needed, but always doubled, quadrupled, if need be efforts to raise the needed sum. . . . None but the good Father *can* ever begin to know the terrible struggle of that twenty-nine months; . . . I am not complaining, for mine is but the fate of almost every originator, pioneer who has ever opened up the way. I have the joy of knowing that I have showed the thing possible—to publish a live out-and-out woman's paper.[23]

The effort by Miss Anthony to run a training school for women printers to act as strike replacements in 1869, served to alienate yet another ally—organized labor in the N.L.U. *Revolution*, possibly to save money, was printed by an antilabor, nonunion firm, and the leading union women typographers putting out *Revolution* were fired.

On May 22, 1870, *Revolution* passed out of the control of Miss Anthony and her colleagues and sold for $1 to Mrs. Laura Curtis Bullard, who assumed the $10,000 debt. The motto of *Revolution* in its third version canceled the original: "The True Republic—Men, their rights and nothing more; women their rights and nothing less." It was succeeded by: "What God hath joined together, let no man put asunder." It was transformed into a literary and society journal, established in elegant headquarters in Brooklyn, and inaugurated with a fashionable reception. Mrs. Bullard conducted *Revolution*'s affairs for eighteen months, when she tired of it, or her father tired of advancing money.[24]

When Mrs. Bullard ended her relationship with *Revolution*, its one-time arch-rival, Lucy Stone's *Woman's Journal* editorialized with fulsome praise.

We regret Mrs. Bullard's withdrawal from the *Revolution*, which was only kept in existence for a long time through her munificence...we rejoice that it has fallen into good hands who will keep its flag flying—not "a rag of offense" flaunting license and demoralization but summoning all to work with clean hands and true purpose for woman's elevation. The *Revolution* has our best wishes. We hope it will flourish.[25]

The full circle had been orbited by that once disturbing journal, *Revolution*. It lost Train, the founding angel, Fenian Irish partisan, opponent of military reconstruction and blanket voting rights to illiterate blacks while women of education were disenfranchised; then Anthony, Stanton, and Pillsbury who did not hesitate to consider side issues, sought allies among the ranks of organized labor and Victoria Woodhull; then it became more and more respectable until it expired altogether at a point where its policy was indistinguishable from that of *Woman's Journal*, the organ of the A.W.S.A. As a matter of fact, Lucy Stone and her Bostonian associates were sorry to see it go and this confirmed the programmatic proximity of *Revolution* and the perspective of the A.W.S.A.

WOMAN'S JOURNAL

The existence of *Revolution* under the Anthony-Stanton control was long a painful thorn in the side of Lucy Stone, Henry Blackwell, and their abolitionist-Republican supporters. They finally launched their own weekly periodical, *Woman's Journal*, with the first issue appearing on January 8, 1870.

Below *Woman's Journal* was inscribed "A Weekly Newspaper...devoted to the interests of woman, to her education, industrial, legal, and political Equality and especially to her right of suffrage."[26]

The very first issue described the structure of the organization it represented and set forth its views.

A political organization, to be national in fact as well as in name, must not only be specific in its object and logical in its methods, but also widely representative in its character. We must not only confine ourselves to woman suffrage as the end and aim of our efforts, but we must recognize the equal personal rights and responsibilities of every friend of the cause. No one, in any part of the country, should have just occasion to say that he or she has been deprived of a voice in the selection of officers or in the declaration of principles.... It is sufficient to say that however identical in principle, negro suffrage and woman suffrage may be, the questions have never to any considerable extent been identified in the public mind, and must therefore be urged separately upon their respective merits.

Moreover, its very name of "Equal Rights" gave a breadth to the discursions of the old society quite incompatible with political efficiency. Even the term "woman's rights" covers too wide a field....

A mass-meeting held annually in the city of New York elected an executive committee, of which a majority were always residents of the city and its vicinity. Everybody who attended its meetings voted, whether friend or foe....

The Cleveland movement is an attempt to organize upon a better basis. It seeks to limit the range of discussion to woman suffrage....

The provisions of its constitution are so broad that it can never be controlled by any individual, clique, newspaper, or locality—so impartial it can never be perverted to advocate or assail side-issues.[27]

It should be noted that powerful figures in the abolitionist movement leadership, such as Garrison and Higginson, were on the editorial board. The separation of black male suffrage from woman suffrage made it possible for *Woman's Journal* to support the Fourteenth and Fifteenth amendments, despite the inclusion of "male" in the amendments' text. The rationale that this was the "negroes' hour" was based on the twofold consideration of keeping control of the Congress in the hands of the Radical Republicans and preventing a return to antebellum conditions for the Southern blacks.

The words "side issues," as matters to be avoided, referred to the host of social questions the Anthony-Stanton group raised. In a decided slap at the administrative control by Susan B. Anthony and Elizabeth Cady Stanton over the day-to-day affairs of the Equal Rights Association, *Woman's Journal* and the A.W.S.A. made certain that its direction would be more representative and broadly based.

With the full backing of the liberal Protestant, abolitionist, Radical Republican establishment, *Woman's Journal* was not lacking in funds. It had incorporated *Woman's Advocate* of Ohio and increased its circulation by as much as a thousand a month.

As the Cleveland convention of the A.W.S.A. neared, the *Woman's Journal* shrilly expressed its anxiety over the growing strength of the unification movement led by Theodore Tilton. In an effort to blunt the thrust of the effort to merge the two wings of the woman suffrage movement, the views of Mrs. Stanton were subjected to an attack which bordered on the demogogic. *Woman's Journal* commented on a speech by Elizabeth Cady Stanton in which she had stated that a marriage that holds either party against his or her will was pronounced an outrage.

We are still reluctant to believe that Mrs. Stanton has been correctly reported by the papers. Herself a matronly wife of the one husband of her youth, to whom she has been wedded for thirty years or more, the accomplished mother of a family of seven children ... we cannot believe she is lending her masterly intellect to the propagation of such mischievous doctrines....

Legitimately carried out, these theories abrogate marriage, and we have then the hideous thing known as "free love". Be not deceived—free love means free lust.[28]

Sarah F. Norton, who had been associated with *Revolution* in its earlier militant phase, attacked *Woman's Journal* on its position with respect to the marriage question. To her it was bondage, and the measure of any woman's rights movement was its attitude toward marriage. She wrote:

The *Woman's Journal* has been almost blatant in denying that the Marriage and Suffrage questions have any bearing upon each other: and yet how eagerly it seizes every item of domestic discord and makes the most of it, as an additional reason why women should be enfranchised.

. . . But how is legislation to remedy the wrong growing out of a certain condition, if the condition itself is not to be interfered with? . . . Thus, if marriage remains the same, and husbands still hold the power which it confers to command their wives, of what use will suffrage be to women if husbands see fit to assert that power? . . .

The Revolution discussed marriage and its kindred evils fearlessly for a time.

Soon, however, it began to grow conservative, and continued growing in that direction until it became sort of mongrel. Thence it became an orthodox truckler of the weakest type, and then at last, it blazoned forth with this ridiculous motto: "Whom God hath joined together, let no man put asunder!"[29]

Woman's Journal continued as the house organ of the American Woman Suffrage Association, and when the split with the National Woman Suffrage Association was finally overcome in 1890, it became the official voice of the merged National American Woman Suffrage Association. It survived the effort engineered by Theodore Tilton for an earlier merger. It overcame the association with "free loveism" as a result of the notoriety given by Victoria Woodhull to the Tilton-Beecher scandal. It avoided association with Mrs. Stanton's exposé of antiwoman attitudes in established religion and remained the more staid and prudent voice for woman suffrage.

WOODHULL AND CLAFLIN'S WEEKLY

A new woman's newspaper appeared on the scene edited by two sisters, Victoria Woodhull and Tennie C. Claflin. They had set up a stockbroker's office in New York's financial district with the rumored aid of Commodore Cornelius Vanderbilt and launched their weekly journal called *Woodhull and Claflin's Weekly*. It had a special section called "The Sixteenth Amendment" devoted to a discussion of woman's rights. Items appeared on French gossip, literature, drama, and baseball. Its prospectus stated:

This journal will be primarily devoted to the vital interests of the people, and will treat of all matters freely and without reservation. It will support Victoria C. Woodhull for President, with its whole strength; otherwise it will be untrammeled by party or personal considerations, free from all affiliation with political and social creeds, and will advocate suffrage without distinction of sex! The harmonious co-operation of labor and capital; liberal national education; the widest action of the citizen compatible with the dignity of the state. . . .

Woodhull and Claflin's Weekly affirms that the Democratic party has long been only a shade of a name—that the Republican party is effete, and only coheres by reason of place and power.[30]

Among the chief contributors was Stephen Pearl Andrews, a philosophical anarchist. He often wrote articles illustrating his version of the Bible and the universal language he invented called Alwato. The principles he espoused were as follows and printed in most issues of the weekly: "1. United States of the World—Pantarchy. 2. Universal Religion—New Catholic Church—devotion to truth. 3. Universal home—Palaces for people—Reconciliation of Capital and Labor. 4. Universology—universal laws. 5. Universal language. 6. Universal Canon of Art. 7. Unism, duism, trinism.* 8. Universal Reconciliation of all differences."

One of the first individuals singled out for praise by Mrs. Woodhull was Elizabeth Cady Stanton.

In the Woman's Rights movement, pure and simple, of 1870, however, there is probably no one who ranks with Elizabeth Cady Stanton....

What good will woman's suffrage do for the women? is the frequent inquiry of men. Not the least in life perhaps.... Utility, however is not the main issue in the adjustment of rights. It is for you to give me my own; for me to do as I will with my own.[31]

Woodhull and Claflin's Weekly remained an object of curiosity to the established leaders of the woman's rights movement. Occasionally, one of them would send in a letter or an article. At the end of 1870 an event took place that established a positive relationship between Victoria Woodhull and the woman's rights leaders, especially those around Mrs. Stanton, Miss Anthony, and Mrs. Hooker. This was a memorial written by Mrs. Woodhull to the Congress on woman suffrage. She appeared, a woman, for the first time in American history to testify before the Joint Judiciary Committee.

Thereafter both Susan B. Anthony and Elizabeth Cady Stanton wrote regularly for *Woodhull and Claflin's Weekly*. The growing conservatism of *Revolution* under Mrs. Bullard's editorship also contributed to the turn toward Woodhull.

Bravo! My Dear Woodhull: Everybody chimes in with the new conclusion that we are free here already. But how absolutely dead, dead are The Woman's Journal and The Revolution. One would think them in the midnight of a "Rip Van Winkle" sleep. It is beyond my comprehension how anybody can be so dull, so behind the times....

I have never in the whole twenty years' good fight felt so full of life and hope.... I am sure you and I and all the women who shall wish to vote for somebody, if for Geo. F. Train or Victoria Woodhull....

---

* A form of dialectics—thesis, antithesis, and synthesis.

Go ahead! bright, glorious, young and strong spirit and believe in the best love and hope and faith of

S.B. Anthony[32]

Victoria Woodhull
Dear Madame:—The majority report presented by Mr. Bingham against your memorial to Congress is really one of the feeblest public documents I ever perused....
When the women in Boston sold out to the Republican party and declared themselves Republicans in the Massachusetts State Convention, I blushed for my sex....
In view of these monstrous wrongs of our sex,—patience and calmness and a willingness to wait—in those of us that can speak and write are not virtues but crimes.

ECS[33]

The impress of the Woodhull memorial was so great that even *Woman's Journal* endorsed the arguments and printed verbatim the supporting speech and the minority report of the committee signed by Loughridge and Butler.[34]

Mrs. Woodhull had her own agenda. She was going to ride this wave of popularity among woman's righters to capture control of the newly reconstituted National Woman Suffrage Association. The presidential election year was 1872, and the Woodhull forces were gearing up for the May Anniversary convention of the N.W.S.A.

In 1871 Victoria Woodhull solidified her support within National by addressing that May Anniversary meeting, openly proclaiming the complete program of the new party that she would form, the "Cosmo Political party" with herself as candidate for the presidency of the United States.

Radical as the speech must have sounded then, the reforms proposed were not only relatively mild but anticipated many things in effect or seriously discussed in the contemporary world—proportional representation, the United Nations and the World Court, and the abolition of capital punishment.[35]

As far as the National Labor Union was concerned, there was only one segment of the woman's rights movement in 1871 toward which it exhibited any positive relationship at all—the group around *Woodhull and Claflin's Weekly*. Mrs. Woodhull reciprocated with the hope that the N.L.U. would endorse her candidacy in 1872. The president of the N.L.U., Richard Trevellick, addressed a letter to Victoria and her sister Tennie: "I am thankful indeed that our country's metropolis has one paper that dares speak the truth, and that paper is the *Woodhull and Claflin's Weekly*."[36]

Even in 1871, the identification of Woodhull with the Anthony-Stanton group was widely accepted. The newspaper most widely read by the working people of New York City commented on the May Anniversary of the N.W.S.A.: "The anniversary of the 'Woodhull' branch of the Woman's Suffrage Convention was the more spicy.... We are sorry... that Mrs.

Woodhull-Blood or Blood-Woodhull (her relations toward her two husbands, past and present seem somewhat mixed) . . . in her speech which was a gradual crescendo of *wants* and *wills*, reached a climax astounding and admonitory."[37]

The American group and its liberal Protestant supporters joined in incessant attacks on Mrs. Woodhull. Henry Bowen, publisher of *The Independent*, a publication closely associated with Henry Ward Beecher, together with Henry Blackwell led the assault centering on her alleged advocacy of free love and her life-style of living in one household with her current husband, Colonel Blood, and her former husband, Dr. Woodhull. Isabella Beecher Hooker and Mrs. Stanton took up the cudgels for Mrs. Woodhull. She was virtually the only issue of the 1871 May anniversaries of both the N.W.S.A. and the A.W.S.A.

As May 1872 rolled around, Susan B. Anthony became increasingly apprehensive of the designs of Mrs. Woodhull on the N.W.S.A. Miss Anthony wanted the organization to preserve its character as a militant advocate of woman suffrage about to approach both major political parties to include woman suffrage in their platforms. She wrote a letter to Mrs. Stanton and Mrs. Hooker articulating her fears to little avail. The call of the N.W.S.A. convention referred to a political convention to consider nomination of candidates for president and vice president of the United States.

Worried by this state of affairs, Miss Anthony cut short her lecture tour and came to the New York City convention at Steinway Hall. She proclaimed, "I say to the Internationalists today and to all who recognize the question of rights at this convention, that the basis of woman suffrage and the recognition of the question of the rights of woman is the chief cornerstone."[38]

The platform adopted reflected the views of *Woodhull and Claflin's Weekly*, an out-and-out reform document ranging over many questions. Mrs. Woodhull then moved that a session be held the next day to consider the nomination of candidates for the presidency and vice presidency. Miss Anthony declared the motion out of order, and the convention ended in confusion. This drama was the end of the positive relationship between the National Woman Suffrage Association and Mrs. Woodhull.

Goaded to fury by the attacks on her as a free love advocate, Victoria Woodhull blurted out the entire story of the Henry Ward Beecher–Elizabeth Tilton amatory escapade. That issue of *Woodhull and Claflin's Weekly* was sold at a tremendous premium and she was clapped into jail.

The woman's rights press represented a broad spectrum: at one extreme *Woodhull and Claflin's Weekly* representing a thoroughgoing radical approach toward restructuring society and fearlessly embracing the concept that relationships between men and women were bound only by love and not by marriage vows. It also vigorously supported woman suffrage. *Revolution* focused on woman suffrage as the key toward redressing all of the wrongs directed against women and thus liberating all of society. It discussed a wide range of questions and did not hesitate to enter coalitions with reform groups including labor unions to further the cause of woman enfranchisement. *Woman's Journal* prudently avoided antagonizing men as a class, supported the Radical Republican–abolitionist alliance in favor of the Fourteenth and Fifteenth amendments, even though these measures barred women from voting, and was thoroughly conventional in support of the institution of the family and the marriage process. Still amidst the welter of deep differences among woman's righters, the fact remains that women were capable of putting out their own periodicals to advance their views.

Women shoebinders of Lynn, Massachusetts parading in a turnout (strike) during a raging snowstorm, March 1860. The banner read "American Ladies Will Not Be Slaves." Courtesy of Crown Publishers, Inc.

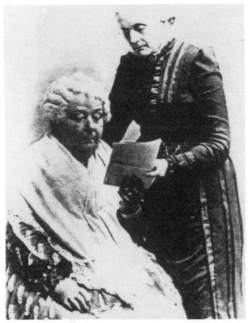

Lucy Stone. Courtesy of the Schlesinger Library, Radcliffe College.

Elizabeth Cady Stanton (seated) and Susan B. Anthony. Courtesy of the Library of Congress.

Frances E.W. Harper

Lucretia Mott. Courtesy of the Schlesinger Library, Radcliffe College.

William H. Sylvis, President of National
Labor Union in 1868 who worked
closely with Susan B. Anthony in organizing women. Courtesy of the AFL-CIO.

Augusta Lewis Troup, Linotype operator for *Revolution*. Head of Woman's
Typographical Union, No. 1. Courtesy
of the Library of Congress.

Women casting their ballots for the first time in Wyoming, September 6, 1870

Victoria Woodhull testifying before a Joint Committee on the Judiciary of the Congress in January 1871. This was the first time a woman had testified before a congressional body. Courtesy of the New York Public Library.

An engraving describing conditions in a sweatshop in 1888. Courtesy of the United States Department of Labor.

Fellow Workers!

Join in rendering a last sad tribute of sympathy and affection for the victims of the Triangle Fire. THE FUNERAL PROCESSION will take place Wednesday, April 5th, at 1 P. M. Watch the newspapers for the line of march.

צו דער לויה שוועסטער און ברידער!

די לויה פון די היילינע קרבנות פון דעם טרייענגעל פייער וועם זיין מיטוואָך, דעם 5טען אפריל, 1 אודר נאכמיטטאָג.

קינדער און אייך מער ניט פערבלייבען אין דער שטוב! שליסם זיך אן אין די רייהען פון די טרארירענדע! דריקם אוים אייער סימפאסיע און מיטנעפיל בעזוירערן אייך דעם נדרויקט בקרלוסם וואם די ארבייסערוועלט האָם געהאָם געפייענעם די קנע – סים זימעתרען הערצער שלינן סיר גיהרען אונזערע פעהייקטע שפערערם צו וייער לעצטער רוה.

זאלסם די ציפוניען הוץ זיילכע סיר זועלן לוזנן וויסען זואס איהר קענם זיך בענעמעני סען.

צו דער לויה פון די היילינע קרבנות,

קומם שוועסטער און ברידער!

Operai Italiani!

Unitevi compatti a rendere l'ultimo tributo d'affetto alle vittime dell'imane sciagura della Triangle Waist Co. IL CORTEO FUNEBRE avra luogo mercoledi, 5 Aprile, alle ore 1 P. M. Traverete nei giornali l'ordine della marcia.

A call to attend the funeral of the victims of the Triangle Waist Company fire of 1911 where 146 workers, mostly women, died. Courtesy of Crown Publishers, Inc.

PART THREE

EPILOGUE

The woman's rights movement in the Reconstruction Era following the Civil War is our major focus. This period is of critical importance toward gaining some basic insights and understanding of this continuing reform urge for equality between men and women. One of the most astute scholars of this field wrote: "In general, the monographs on the suffrage aspects of the woman's movement are good, but there is a particular need for more intensive investigation of feminism during the years between the Civil War and the turn of the century."[1]

Women "had succeeded in focusing attention on their grievances only at a time of generalized reform. The feminist movement began when abolitionism provided female activists with an opportunity to organize and exposed them directly to the physical and psychological reality of discrimination based on sex."[2]

The alternation between stagnation and dynamism in the historic drive for women's rights is related to the presence and absence of a pervasive reform impulse emerging from a national crisis. The Civil War and Reconstruction made up the social milieu for the earlier phase of the drive toward ending discrimination based on sex.

The organization for woman suffrage, the concrete goal of the movement until the passage of the Nineteenth Amendment, became weak and ineffective in great measure because the societal context of reform had been transmuted into the urge of industrial and financial expansion. This enervation persisted until the Progressive Movement of the early 1900s and World War I provided a new setting for woman's rights to assert itself as a key social question.

Features of the woman's rights movement from the Reconstruction Era were the building blocks of a connecting historic bridge to later developments. Here we found expressed variegated views on burning issues, but despite diversity, there were attempts at coalition. Thus, trade unions, abolitionists, and other social reformers cooperated with woman's rights forces. There were rifts as well. Here, too, was the expression of gender hostility, with men cast in the roles of conscious oppressors of women. Divergent outlooks arising out of social class perspectives—upper, middle, and working class—found reflection in differing goals and values. The woman's rights movement created national permanent organizations operating on a year-'round basis requiring staff and funds. Woman's rights periodicals were established, further testifying to this movement's ability to articulate its needs to the reading public.

In the sphere of political action there were activities directed toward legislation including constitutional amendments. Campaigns entailed flyers, demonstrations, state and national legislative lobbying, lecture tours, referenda drives, and direct action in defiance of law and convention in women running for office and seeking to vote. Questions arose around the alternative of a purist devotion narrowly limited to woman suffrage as against a broader conception involving other issues related to the condition of woman. There were some who viewed enfranchisement as a magical talisman capable of solving all society's problems. Differences also emerged on strategy between those who favored getting woman suffrage on a state-by-state basis as opposed to those who favored concentrating on Congress and the president. Elements of the movement wanted to work with the established major political parties; others urged a new independent political direction. There were the advocates of confrontationist and militant tactics as against the prudent gradualists.

These questions of strategy and tactics recur in the woman's rights movement in the period culminating in the achievement of votes for women as well as in the contemporary scene.

From the Suffrage Victory
to the Future of
Woman's Rights

OUT OF DOLDRUMS TO RENEWED DYNAMISM

In the late nineteenth century period of conservative self-interest, known as the Gilded Age, there was little societal anguish to generate a surge for reform. The efforts to achieve woman suffrage were well-nigh fruitless in concrete results, but the attempts developed a rhythm of activity that served to keep the organizations alive. From the comparative test of national versus state-by-state approaches, the movement assumed a country-wide character.

Woman's rights leaders in the early struggles of the twentieth century gave this assessment of these efforts:

> To get the word "male" in effect out of the Constitution cost the women of the country fifty-two years of pauseless campaign.... During that time they were forced to conduct fifty-six campaigns of referenda to male voters; 47 campaigns to get State Constitutional conventions to write woman suffrage into state constitutions; 277 campaigns to get state party conventions to include woman suffrage planks; 30 campaigns to get presidential party conventions to adopt woman suffrage planks in party platforms, and 19 campaigns with 19 successive Congresses.[1]

By 1890 the competing efforts of the National Woman Suffrage Association and the American Woman Suffrage Association in the face of glacial progress no longer made sense to the aging and tiring leadership. A merger agreement came about combining the old organizational designations into the National American Woman Suffrage Association (NAWSA). Susan B. Anthony remained the dynamic head of the movement, but against her will, the secondary leadership decided to forego the annual lobbying convocation in Washington, D.C. As the most respected woman's rights historian commented:

Events confirmed Miss Anthony's worst forebodings. Although formal hearings were held in the years when the suffrage association convened away from Washington, neither House gave the bill a favorable committee report after 1893. To all intents and purposes, the federal woman suffrage amendment vanished as a political issue until 1913.[2]

The old leadership began to leave the scene. Lucy Stone died in 1893; Elizabeth Cady Stanton in 1902. Miss Anthony remained active until her death in 1906. While Anna Howard Shaw remained heir-apparent, it was Carrie Chapman Catt who emerged as the field-general with organizational sagacity to develop the appropriate strategy and tactics to carry the campaign to victory. Her steady pragmatism was complemented by the militancy of Alice Paul.

The NAWSA combined efforts to secure woman suffrage in the states with annual attempts to secure an amendment. Mrs. Catt firmly insisted that every state organization be fully staffed with professional functionaries and activist volunteers. It was the liquor lobby on both the state and federal levels which lobbied against woman suffrage, fearing that giving the women the vote would inaugurate prohibition. The long-standing historic relationship between temperance reform and woman's righters gave credence to the fears of the liquor interests. Indeed as sentiment for prohibition rose, the fortunes of woman suffrage rose as well.

More and more states with women voting were racked up in the electoral college column. By 1918 there were twenty such states. The next year there were six more. A formidable weapon of reprisal against those politicians who resisted woman suffrage was forged by these state efforts.

Alice Paul formed her own group in rivalry to Mrs. Catt and the NAWSA, the Woman's party. Her efforts were directed against the party in power, the Democratic party, led by Woodrow Wilson, president of the United States from 1912 to 1920. Her militancy included parades, picket lines, jailings, hunger strikes causing prison officials to resort to force feeding— all emulating the activities of the Pankhursts in England. Her campaigns kept the issues alive and stirred up sympathy against brutal police action as well as physical and verbal abuse from male vulgarians.

Carrie Chapman Catt was more adroit in her leadership of the NAWSA. She adopted the tactic of rewarding your friends and punishing your enemies, regardless of party affiliation. Originally a pacifist, she abandoned her antiwar convictions and, unlike Rebecca Rankin, the congresswoman who voted against the U.S. entry into World War I, Miss Catt threw herself into the war effort in securing woman workers for defense industries, job replacements in areas where men had left for the armed forces, campaigning for war bonds, aiding in medical care, and fashioning supplies for soldiers and sailors. These patriotic activities were consciously and openly coupled to her insistent demand for woman suffrage.

Ms. Catt used this growing public support and political clout represented by woman suffrage states to court Woodrow Wilson. He agreed to address the national convention of the NAWSA in Atlantic City in 1916.

Unlike the Civil War period when the woman's righters submerged their struggle for the franchise, the NAWSA supported the effort involved in the war but kept up a drumfire of publicity for suffrage. In the public mind the American people appreciated the patriotism of the American women and felt that simple gratitude dictated granting them the right to vote. Victory with the final ratification of the Nineteenth Amendment came about because of a combination of circumstances. The Progressive Movement reached national prominence in the competition between Wilson and Theodore Roosevelt in 1912. Wilson came out in support of woman suffrage as a "war measure." The liquor lobby went down to defeat with the passage of the Eighteenth Amendment establishing prohibition in 1919.

WORKINGWOMEN AND TRADE UNIONS—A CONTINUING RELATIONSHIP

The year following the demise of the National Labor Union in 1872 ushered in a severe economic depression that lasted until 1877. Union membership, which grew in times of prosperity, plummeted. Of the work force 20% were totally unemployed. Wages approached the starvation level with the jobless acting as a labor reserve ready to take any job. In the winter of 1873 it was reported that 900 people died of starvation and mothers abandoned 3,000 infants.[3] Defiant demonstrations took place in New York, Omaha, and Chicago.

In January 1874 a rally took place in Tompkins Square Park on the east side of Manhattan to protest the terrible conditions. Just before the time of the demonstration the authorities withdrew the permit without informing the demonstrators. The police charged the crowd ordering them to disperse. Men, women, and children were literally mowed down in a most brutal fashion.

The anthracite coal pits of Pennsylvania became a scene of violence and secrecy where miners, calling themselves Molly Maguires, resisted the mine owners. In 1877 a nationwide wave of strikes, involving 100,000 workers, hit the railroads. Twenty men, women, and children lost their lives in battle against public authorities and company police. As a symbol of the times, young Eugene Victor Debs, the outstanding railroad union leader and later socialist, twice, in 1878 and 1880, invited Susan B. Anthony to address a discussion club in his native city of Terre Haute, Indiana. In these dramatic labor struggles women played a prominent part in support of their brothers and husbands seeking decent wages and good working conditions.

A new national trade union organization, the Knights of Labor, led by Terence Powderly, emerged after some years of existence as a secret society. Its doors were open to all—black, white, men, women, skilled, and unskilled. About 50,000 women joined its ranks from the fields of work usually associated with women workers. Most unusual was the fact that there were women assemblies of houseworkers, some of them black women from the South. The Knights did not hesitate to seek remedial legislation ending child labor and sweatshops, limiting hours and night work for women, workmen's compensation for job-related injuries, health and safety laws, and arbitration as a substitute for strikes. The Knights of Labor became associated in the public mind with the hysteria following the riot in Haymarket Square in Chicago near the McCormick Harvesting Works in 1886. Despite the decline of the Knights and its replacement by the American Federation of Labor, the role played by women in its ranks was significant. Sizable numbers were delegates and officers, and housewives were welcomed into its ranks.

THE WOMEN'S TRADE UNION LEAGUE

In comparison to the women millworkers who came in the 1850s from Ireland and other poverty-stricken areas, the women unionist leaders were educated and quite articulate. Leonora Barry played a notable role in the Knights of Labor as full-time functionary. She was followed by bindery worker, Mary E. Kenney, in the American Federation of Labor, appointed by Samuel Gompers as a national organizer. Ms. Kenney helped found the Women's Trade Union League (WTUL) in 1903.

The WTUL combined upper- and middle-class philanthropic women and trade union woman members to help organize, support strikes, provide strike relief, publicize poor working conditions, establish health clinics, and seek protective legislation for women and children. They fought for equal pay and opportunity for women, including securing leadership posts. One restriction based upon getting support from the American Federation of Labor (AF of L), was that the strike support the WTUL sought to extend had to be for unions affiliated with the AF of L. Often to preserve unity within the ranks of the WTUL, the unionists had to defer to the prominent wealthy women who were in the leadership.

Significantly, not until 1921 was the president of the WTUL a trade unionist. For the most part the WTUL and its prominent union leaders were solidly behind woman suffrage. While the leadership of the WTUL believed in the greater degree of freedom for women in society, the predominantly male membership and leadership of the AF of L, while supporting organization of women workers and equal pay for equal work, still held that marriage and raising a family was the ideal goal of women.

Rose Schneiderman and Pauline Newman, garment workers; Maud Anderson, shoeworker; Maud Swartz, typographer; Elizabeth Christman and Agnes Nestor, gloveworkers; and Leonora O'Reilly, shirtworker were the outstanding trade unionists in the WTUL. They made common cause with such women as Jane Addams and Lillian Wald of the settlement house movement and Maude Nathan and Florence Kelley of the National Consumers League. Thus the WTUL was at the center of the Progressive movement.

The strike of shirt-waist workers in 1909–1910 brought the WTUL into national prominence. The popularity of the shirt-waist through Gibson Girl illustrations caused a burgeoning of production in garment shops. After 30,000 women walked off their jobs, monumental logistical problems developed: members had to be enrolled into the union at the rate of a thousand a day; for those who suffered severe privation as a result of a loss of income rent, food, clothing, and other forms of strike relief had to be provided; picket lines around each garment shop had to be staffed; arrested unionists needed representation in court and money for bail. The fledgling union, with the aid of the WTUL, came through with flying colors helping to establish the International Ladies Garment Workers Union as a permanent national labor organization with a predominance of woman workers in its ranks. This was to be followed by solid trade unions in men's garments, millinery, textiles, and shoes—all with heavy female composition in the work force.

THE TRIANGLE FIRE

In 1911 a monumental tragedy placed conditions of labor squarely in the middle of the Progressive Movement. In the Triangle Shirt Waist Company fire 146 workers, mostly women, died from burns, smoke inhalation, drowning, and being smashed to death from jumping from the upper stories. Windows were nailed shut; doors opened in and were locked; the fire escapes were inadequate and flimsy; fire ladders could not reach the affected landings. Just as Upton Sinclair's *The Jungle* raised indignation about the conditions where food was prepared, the Triangle Fire created waves of sympathy and determination to improve the conditions of health and safety in the workplace.

The entrance of the radical, syndicalist, industrial unionist Industrial Workers of the World (IWW) complicated matters for the WTUL. Strikes led by the IWW in Lawrence, Massachusetts, and Paterson, New Jersey, were not sanctioned by the AF of L. Sectors of the WTUL leadership defied this ban and caused attenuation of support by the AF of L and wealthy women supporters. These militant strikes brought forth activist women who were able to dramatize these struggles by enlisting writers and artists in staging pageants, and securing protection of children of strikers by care with families in other cities.

AFTER WOMAN SUFFRAGE

The women were now enfranchised and had the political tool—the ballot. This was described as the talisman, the panacea, and the supreme weapon in securing equality for women, morality in politics, and much more—the solution to all of society's grave problems. This much can be gleaned from the protagonists of woman suffrage in the writings and speeches of Lucy Stone, Elizabeth Cady Stanton, and Susan B. Anthony. With the ratification of the Nineteenth Amendment a note of caution was sounded by Carrie Chapman Catt. In 1920 she stated that suffrage was only a means of entry and that relentless activism would be required to go through the door to the citadels of political power "You will have a long hard fight before you get behind that door, for there is the engine that moves the wheels of your party machinery.... If you really want women's votes to count, make your way there."[4]

Most of the economic gains of women entering industry during World War I evaporated with the return of the servicemen. The brief recession of 1921 gave way to a sustained period of prosperity, which lasted until the crash of 1929, which ushered in the Great Depression. The old "belle-ideal" of women having the goal of marriage, motherhood, and housewifery continued to hold in the minds and hearts of most women and men. Economically, the male could still be the sole breadwinner to sustain the family.

The 1920s was a period of turning away from the idealism of the Progressive Movement and becoming isolationist in foreign affairs. The vitiation of Wilson's Fourteen Points and the refusal of the Congress to join the League of Nations were but two manifestations of this nationalist trend. Europe settled back into the imperial design of the Versailles Treaty. Social upheavals in Europe, particularly the Bolshevik Revolution, engendered fierce antiforeignism, antiunionism, and antiradicalism here in the United States. Attorney General Mitchell Palmer organized raids on organization headquarters of the IWW and the Socialist and Communist parties. Severe restrictions were enacted in immigration legislation virtually closing the doors of the United States to the peoples of southern and eastern Europe. Foreigners were considered to be the bearers of subversive doctrines, crime, and disease. Employers inaugurated the "American Plan" to destroy union gains made during World War I.

The bonds of the war effort broke in an *individual* manner for young women in the public eye. They defied convention and inaugurated the "Flapper" era with bobbed hair, short skirts, lipstick, smoking, jazz, and suggestive dancing. Women entered colleges and universities, but they did not symbolize the serious scholar and the professional. Rather, they appeared in the public mind as the racoon-coated coed, nipping illicit liquor from hip-flasks carried by their beaus in the football stadiums and the rumble seats of roadsters.

The business office became the growing center of woman employment—typewriting, stenography, filing, and reception—for graduates of business schools. It was the place to meet men, not an avenue to positions of business authority. The professional businesswoman was characterized as a misfit who hid her sexuality behind the facade of a business suit.

Yet among groups of upper- and middle- class women who were college graduates, a vulgarization of Freudian psychoanalysis took hold in the form of resisting the repression of the basic natural urges of the id by the conventions of society, the superego. Women became more free to examine their roles in life.

The voting patterns of women since they had achieved woman suffrage proved to indicate no discernible difference from those of men. The Woman Suffrage Amendment did, however, help to enact statutes in a number of states affecting women by dealing with property, citizenship, child custody, jury duty, inheritance, and other basic rights. Alice Paul of the Woman's party in 1923 sensed the incompleteness of suffrage in achieving full equality for women and proposed an Equal Rights Amendment to alter the basic law of the land, the Constitution, for a frontal assault on sexist discrimination against women in all manifestations—social, economic, and political. The National American Woman Suffrage Association transformed itself into the League of Women Voters—an informational and lobbying group designed to educate women and the public generally on political issues.

THE GREAT DEPRESSION

Massive unemployment, the closing of banks, and numerous bankruptcies smashed the somnolence of the American people. This social cataclysm of breadlines, soup kitchens, shanty towns dubbed Hoovervilles, evictions from homes, and unemployed pathetically selling apples opened up a new era of social reform. Families were shaken to their very foundations.

Society was becoming polarized with extremism of the left and right securing more and more support from a desperate population. Franklin D. Roosevelt, a patrician pragmatist, was elected largely as an alternative to colorless Hoover so identified with the depression. Roosevelt's rhetoric of hope and a New Deal catapulted him to power. The host of legislative acts and federal governmental agencies set in motion a return of courage.

Roosevelt wanted to "prime the pump" of the faltering economy by restoring purchasing power through government employment projects touching every sector of the population—youth in work camps in reforestation and soil preservation, men in the skilled construction trades building public housing, schools, post offices and other public buildings, roads, and parks; price support for farm crops to help family farmers; codes of fair industrial practice to curb cutthroat competition; minimum wages, maximum hours, and collective bargaining rights to help unions elevate the depressed standard of living; and for the elderly the hope of social security. In this context the basic reforms also raised the hopes of women. Frances Perkins, the first woman cabinet member as secretary of labor, and Mrs. Eleanor Roosevelt, the social activist wife of the president, were but two notable role models among a host of women in government social agencies giving birth to rising expectations for women.

The war clouds of 1939 in Europe had unleashed the firestorm of World War II. By becoming the supplier of ammunition, food, ships, military equipment, the United States government became the effective agent of full employment. When the U.S. became an active combatant, women joined men in the armed forces and took up all the usual male occupations in defense and nondefense industries. This was but the second phase of a social upheaval and reform impulse that gave the woman's rights movement another grand opportunity.

THE CIVIL RIGHTS REVOLUTION

A. Philip Randolph, the black trade union leader, confronted President Roosevelt with a real dilemma in the midst of the war effort. Randolph insisted on equality in the workplaces of all companies having defense contracts. He threatened to organize a "March on Washington" in a grand demonstration against racial discrimination. All efforts to dissuade Randolph failed, and the promulgation of a Fair Employment Practices Executive Order established the public policy of ending racial discrimination in the places where presumably the war effort was directed against the dictatorial and racist policies of Hitler, Mussolini, and Hirohito.

For more than a decade after the end of the war against Fascism and Nazism the returning servicemen came back to a society still wracked with racism and sexism. Blacks were segregated in schools and places of public accommodations—washrooms, buses, trains, restaurants, and hotels—or simply barred. Jobs women held during the war went to the ex-servicemen; blacks in defense jobs were also bumped into low-skill and low-pay positions or thrown out of work. The time seemed ripe for massive nonviolent actions to correct these conditions. The U.S. Supreme Court decision in *Brown* v. *Board of Education*, which overturned the separate but equal doctrine of *Plessy* v. *Ferguson*, was met by persistent forms of arrogant and brutal defiance by local and state government authorities and violence-prone vigilantes. A roster of martyrs—blacks and whites, Jews and Gentiles, women and men—developed out of these struggles.

President John F. Kennedy's pronouncements for freedom were taken seriously, and in August 1963 A. Philip Randolph organized a march on

Washington that brought hundreds of thousands of blacks and whites together in the nation's capital. The galaxy of speakers, which included Martin Luther King, Jr., proclaimed the need for jobs and freedom to permeate all of society, not only in governmental civilian agencies, not only in the armed forces, not only in industries holding government contracts, but in all areas of human interaction—political, economic, and social.

PHILOSOPHIC DEBATES

The new opportunity for woman's rights was then another nationwide reform impulse born out of the succession of cataclysmic events—the Great Depression, the New Deal, World War II, and the Civil Rights Revolution. It was a thematic repetition of the Civil War and Reconstruction, which gave birth to the organized movement for woman's rights and the combination of the Progressive Movement and World War I which enacted the woman suffrage Nineteenth Amendment.

Against the newest backdrop of reform, philosophic debates continued among intellectuals on the societal role of women. In one sense it was a repetition of the old controversy of nature versus nurture. Mary Wollstonecraft first asserted that woman's social inferiority was an outgrowth of the difference in training and education between males and females. Sigmund Freud and his disciples placed their focus on the hereditarily determined libidinous urge being tempered by the mores of society. However, his theory that women had a "castration complex" because they did not possess penises was deemed to be the anatomical and physiological constitutional basis for woman's natural passivity and emotionalism as opposed to the male personality of autonomy, activism, and completeness. This selective reading of Freud had enough justification to cause feminists to rise up against psychoanalysis as a rationale for woman's continuing inferior role in society. Indeed this view was articulated by psychoanalyst Marynia Farnham and eminent sociologist Ferdinand Lundberg in their book, *Modern Woman: The Lost Sex*, which urged that women return to the natural feminine functions, especially motherhood, as against feminism and its ideal of equality of opportunity with men. For them a woman who became an active intellectual in a professional calling was to exhibit unnatural masculinization.

Schools of psychoanalysis associated with Karen Horney and the Center for Modern Psychoanalytic Studies took an opposite view, holding that what was considered masculine and feminine in society was in essence a product of historic patriarchal culture and could be altered by environmental historic experience or psychoanalysis.[5]

Feminists also took issue with the woman anthropologist Margaret Mead, who emphasized that nature defined societal roles—breast-feeding and other manifestations of child rearing—and for women to defy these was to invite chaos and confusion.

It remained for Betty Friedan to provide the intellectual underpinning for the modern feminist movement on behalf of the middle- and upper-class educated women who were relegated to the life of the wife in suburbia. This work, *The Feminine Mystique*, published in 1963, sounded the tocsin for these women to fulfill their humanity by liberating themselves from the narrow femininity of caring for the children, the husband, and the home. She described the potential that could be realized through further education and careers in the professions. The unhappiness and anxiety that plagued these middle- and upper-class women were engendered and perpetuated by the mass media and their emphasis on a new form of conspicuous consumption of goods and services attached to the homemaking model for women.[6]

Her book did not address the problems of married workingwomen who had to do double duty of laboring in the world of work and come home to another world of shopping, cooking, housekeeping, and child care. Nor did she realistically depict the world of work as it is for most men and women—the tyranny of drudgery of a nine-to-five day in the office, shop, or factory. She tended to concentrate on the goal of becoming a creative person in the arts and professions, neglecting to point out how limited this objective is in terms of attainment in present-day society.

Since the ideological leadership of the woman's rights movement did come from the middle and upper classes, Friedan's book served the same function as Mary Wollstonecraft's *Vindication of the Rights of Woman* in raising the consciousness and making women aware of their lack of personal fulfillment. Through growing contact between women's groups in the technique of "networking" a new woman's rights leadership was born, but one that inadvertently established a dichotomy between being a housewife and a professional worker. This served to antagonize segments of woman housewives who saw nothing unfulfilling in seeking to maintain the home, rear the children, and improve the schools. They did not think it wrong to assure safety and health standards for their neighborhoods; establish sound consumer standards for food, clothing, appliances, and home construction; to engage in community electoral and legislative pressure activities. However, Friedan did underscore the need for adequate child-care facilities of professional quality in the workplaces and parental leaves to equalize the task of child rearing between husband and wife. The organizational culmination was the creation in 1966 of the National Organization of Women (NOW).

THE EQUAL RIGHTS AMENDMENT

As an authority on the history of the Equal Rights Amendment (ERA) wrote: "The sixties had been a catalyst. The seventies was going to be a decade of enormous growth and change. For women it would swell and burst forth with a whole new universe of new ideas and actions. Many would come to see themselves differently and to believe they were entitled to much more than their mothers had ever dreamed of."[7]

The tragedy of President John F. Kennedy's assassination ushered in civil rights legislation, which affected women. In 1961 he had stated, "In every period of national emergency women had served with distinction in widely varied capacities but thereafter have been subject to treatment as a marginal group whose skills have been inadequately utilized."[8]

In 1964 Congress enacted the Civil Rights Act Title VII. Opportunist efforts by die-hard Southern segregationists to kill this legislation by tacking on "sex" to "race" and "color" failed. The Equal Employment Opportunity Commission was formed to enforce the law. Earlier in 1963, the Equal Pay Act amended the Fair Labor Standards Act by outlawing inequality in pay for equal work. (The concept of "equal work" required not identity of occupational tasks but substantial equality.) NOW was the watchdog to see that employers and unions did not discriminate in hiring, firing, training, promotion, and other job-related areas. Sexual harassment was considered to be an act of sexual discrimination. Improvements in the minimum wage also helped women, since they clustered heavily in low-pay occupations.

The Occupational Health and Safety Act (OSHA), adopted in 1970, required employers to provide workers with healthful and safe working conditions in accordance with standards, rules, and regulations. This was also of great benefit to women who work in such places as textile mills and chemical plants plagued by polluted air and toxic substances.

These measures were now on the books, but they could be gutted by lack of enforcement, outright repeal, and prolonged litigation. The new organization which was formed in the heat of the struggle, the National Organization of Women (NOW), was appealed to in 1967 to campaign for the Equal Rights Amendment to the Constitution to solidify the gains developed through legislation.

Opposition initially developed against ERA, not by conservative elements, but by progressive labor and liberal forces who had been deeply involved in the Progressive Movement to enact special protective legislation for women in working conditions and hours, statutes that were not applicable to men. Their fear was that these measures would be vitiated by ERA. This opposition was overcome by convincing the erstwhile opponents that equality would create desirable conditions for both men and women.

With the support of the AFL-CIO, women in its leadership formed a new organization to replace the Women's Trade Union League which had gone out of existence. This association was called Coalition of Labor Union Women (CLUW) and unlike the WTUL, only union members—men as well as women—could belong. In addition to backing ERA, CLUW supported affirmative action on the job, legislation, political action, and the organization of the unorganized. The current president, Joyce Miller, was the first woman elected vice president of the Amalgamated Clothing and Textile

Workers Union, and one of the two women to be on the AFL-CIO's Executive Council. CLUW understood that as an organization, it could not form union locals but it could assist existing unions in organizing campaigns. Recent concerns of professional women in publishing and on college and university nonteaching staffs found CLUW playing an important role in galvanizing this interest. But CLUW did not act parochially and concern itself only with struggles on behalf of women. It did not hesitate to join with the rest of the labor movement in organizing, strike support, and seeking to repeal the "right to work" laws which undermine union security in various states.

An estimate of CLUW by a woman historian states:

The working women of America are moving toward full participation for the first time. In the past, home responsibilities kept us from being active even when we had a union, and isolated us from one another. Our role at home released men for union activity. Now we seek a partnership role in the job, in the home, in unions, in politics.[9]

THE ERA CAMPAIGN—DEFEAT FROM THE JAWS OF VICTORY

"Equality of rights under the law shall not be denied or abridged by the United States or any State on account of sex." This is the simple text of the Equal Rights Amendment, an idea that lay dormant since 1923 but whose time had come. NOW took up the cudgels for this measure, and it won widespread support not only from liberals and labor, but also from the Republican and Democratic parties, the American Bar Association, the Girl Scouts, the Ladies Auxiliary of the Veterans of Foreign Wars, the National School Boards Association, the U.S. Conference of Mayors, the Association of Junior Leagues, the National Council of Church Women and such staid and even conservative individuals as Strom Thurmond, Richard Nixon, and George Wallace. The wives of presidents Ford, Johnson, and Carter gave approval.

By 1973, one year after approval by both houses of the Congress, thirty states had voted to ratify ERA. By 1977 the number of supportive states increased slowly to thirty-five. Thirty-eight were needed for ratification. In November of that year an International Woman's Year Conference was held in Houston, Texas, and there the opposition began to crystallize. There were 2,000 delegates and 12,000 observers from fifty-six states and territories. The task of the conference with a $5 million budget was to "identify barriers that prevent women from participating fully and equally in all aspects of national life" and to recommend ways to eliminate these barriers.[10]

There were three areas of controversy—the Equal Rights Amendment, legalization of abortion, and lesbian rights. Of the delegates, 30 percent labeled themselves "pro-family" and opposed all three issues, claiming that in combination they represented a monster that would destroy the home. On the other side there was equal solidification in support of these three issues, creating an almost indissoluble linkage.

The head of the opposition was Phyllis Schlafly, who astutely developed a strategy of mobilizing religious and ethnic elements of the working and lower middle classes in every legislative district, particularly in rural and semirural areas. There was greater emphasis in the South. The Catholic Church, Mormons, Orthodox Jews, and fundamentalist Protestants contributed recruits to the "pro-family" group.

A poll taken in the mid–1970s revealed that most women were uninformed about ERA. Claims were made by the opposition that women would be subject to the military draft and combat duty; that ERA would legalize homosexual marriages; and that it would do away with segregation between the sexes in public restrooms, college dormitories, and gymnasiums. Any measure that used the words "spouse" or "person" instead of "husband," "male," or "female" was targetted for defeat by the anti-ERA forces.

The convention was the scene of a pyrrhic victory for supporters of ERA, lesbian rights, and the freedom to choose abortion. Additional polls taken in 1978 showed clear majorities for ERA, but time was running out. An attempt by ERA supporters to secure a seven-year extension for ratification failed in the Congress. Only thirty-nine months were added with a deadline of June 30, 1982. States that did ratify had sizable sectors of the public demanding rescission of ratification. The opposition was growing stronger while support was weakening.

The anti-ERA forces were effective. "From the time of the Houston Conference, ERA became synonymous with gay rights in many people's minds."[11] It was a repetition of the earlier history of the woman's rights movement when "free love" became identified with both the Stanton-Anthony group and the Lucy Stone sector as a result of Victoria Woodhull's pronouncements and her exposé of Henry Ward Beecher.

The opposition to ERA emphasized its defense of tradition, the family, and the housewife. The economic climate had changed, and funds that would be mandated by ERA enforcement became scarce, causing some second thoughts in Congress. Ronald Reagan's slogan of "Getting the Government Off Our Backs" met with positive response not only with respect to funds, but also because of the fear that government agents would invade the privacy of the home and the workplace. ERA ratification lost in Illinois, Florida, North Carolina, and Virginia.

In the wake of the Iranian hostage crisis and the Soviet invasion of Afghanistan, President Carter promulgated nationwide registration. This served to dramatize the draft distortion in anti-ERA propaganda. The confrontationist tactics of NOW backfired. Statements such as those by Kate Millett that since males dominated society, the family is the locus of brainwashing women and children into servility, and therefore the family was to be abolished added fuel to the anti-ERA cause. Millett went further in identifying sexism and male chauvinism with racism and called for consciousness-raising groups to be formed as substitutes for the family. This was dubbed derisively as "women's lib."

Another ultra-militant feminist associated with NOW, T. Grace Atkinson, gained great prominence in the media when she broke from NOW, calling it too tame because it did not advocate the abolition of marriage, which she characterized as being a form of slavery. Marlene Dixon, another out-and-out feminist, went even further: "Women must learn the meaning of rage. The rhetoric of invective is an equally essential stage, for in discovering and venting their rage against the enemy—and the enemy in everyday life is men—women also experience the justice of their own violence.[12] While these positions were not the official stands of NOW, the identification in the public mind was there and helped prevent NOW from getting the broad national consensus of support for the enactment and final ratification of ERA.

In January 1983 the ERA was reintroduced in the House of Representatives and was six votes shy of the necessary two-thirds majority. Strategic differences broke out over whether or not to have the states pass state forms of the ERA. The movement for ERA effectively fell apart. In addition to this numerical index of failure, the hopes associated with a woman, Geraldine Ferraro, being the running mate of Walter Mondale in the contest for the presidency against Ronald Reagan and George Bush, were dashed when the Democratic ticket in 1984 failed to win more than Minnesota and the District of Columbia. The reform urge arising from the Civil Rights Revolution had been replaced by a conservative trend.

The woman's rights movement remained intact but weakened. NOW became the scene of internal bickering, and its damage caused the doyenne of the contemporary woman's rights movement, Betty Friedan, to articulate her concerns.

In an extensive article she called for a new round of consciousness-raising and networking. She was upset that young urban professional women seemed content, believing that the woman's rights struggle was over. The campaign against pornography as an assault on woman she considered to be unproductive, divisive, and extraneous. Friedan called for concentration on efforts to resist the Reagan government's attempts to cut legislative gains. Far from divorcing NOW from the abortion issue, she advocated strong counteractivity to the "right-to-life" forces, as the anti-abortionists called themselves, by promulgating the concept of "pro-choice."

Her program of revitalization embraced ten points.[13] 1. Consciousness-raising with respect to the untenable division of the home as the province of women and the world of work for men. Support for parental leave and professional child-care facilities. 2. Concentration on retaining legislative gains. Put ERA on the back-burner. 3. End the actions against pornography. 4. Confront the illusion of equality in divorce, when according to the Weitzman study, women have a 73 percent drop in standard of living while men gain 42 percent after a divorce.[14] 5. Return abortion to woman's own choice. 6. Affirm the difference between men and women and end the illusion of complete identity. Stress the restructuring of work and training to take into account childbirth. 7. Break the youth cult by championing the needs of elderly women for shared housing, social security, and adequate pensions to keep them independent and productive. 8. Bring men into alliance with women. End the concept that men are the enemies of women. 9. Mount political action campaigns on behalf of women involving both men and women. 10. Move beyond single-issue thinking. "I do not think women's rights are the most urgent business for American women," she wrote. She urged a multifaceted approach that would oppose fundamentalism in favor of liberalism, humanism, pluralism, environmentalism, civil liberties, and peace.

This remarkable litany of advice not only reveals the sad state of the woman's rights movement, but it also serves to raise some questions with respect to Betty Friedan's approach. One can understand that antimale attitudes and campaigns against pornography may be divisive and unproductive. It is difficult to fathom her view that woman's rights are no longer most urgent for American women. Is she on solid ground when she suggests ending campaigning for ERA? After all, even in periods of historic defeat, both Lucy Stone and Susan B. Anthony kept the woman suffrage amendment alive. It has been suggested that NOW's advocacy of abortion rights as its centerpiece of activity perpetuates division and makes it difficult if not impossible to achieve a broad consensus for those woman's rights affecting most women. Would abortion rights, however justifiable, be better handled by Planned Parenthood than NOW?

Such critical issues as equality of pay, comparable worth, child care, and promotional opportunities could prove to be more conducive in attracting more women and gain support among men. These questions are raised because when the next historic opportunity arises in a new reform movement, the woman's rights tendency must have a broader base and unified purpose.

WHERE ARE THE WOMEN TODAY?

According to the Consumer Research Center of the Conference Board, more than 51 million women are employed outside the home, up 26 percent in the past decade. In more than half of all married couples both spouses work.[15] The myth of women working for "pin money" has been shattered. A rising standard of living combined with inflation has been a powerful factor in propelling women into the labor force. Another has been the increase in divorces and separations, as well as the postponement or negation of the marriage option forcing women to support themselves and their families.

Women are still concentrated in low-pay, dead-end jobs. The median wage or salary income for women is $14,192 as of 1984, as compared to $22,410 for men. Women who are high school graduates earn less than men who have completed less than eight years of elementary school.

Women with children, including mothers of preschool children, have poured into the labor force. Of all mothers of children under eighteen, 61 percent are working and 52 percent of mothers of preschool children are also working. This underscores the need for child-care facilities.

Women continue to constitute large proportions in fields which are traditionally female—clerical and sales. Only 8 percent are in precision production, crafts, and repair services. Managers, administrators, and executives in retail and personal services account for 32 percent, while women constitute 70 percent of the work force in that area.[16] While incidents are publicized of women being employed as machinists, carpenters, bricklayers, plumbers, truck drivers, miners, and so on, the fact is that only 6.8 percent of apprentices entering the skilled trades were women.[17]

What emerges from these statistics are persistent pay discrepancies between men and women. These stem from outright discrimination; lower wages for occupations traditionally associated with women and compensated for on the outmoded concept that women, particularly married women, do not have to work; and the needs of childbirth, child rearing, and home care interrupting working. These breaks serving to reduce seniority, training and educational opportunities, as well as chances for promotion.

While women are entering nontraditional areas of blue-collar work and the professions, the trend is still quite low, with women objects of open and subtle sexual harassment while facing barriers that often are not job-related. As for the professions, such as law, medicine, and accounting, the obstacles to executive promotion are quite evident with women who are able to reach high administrative positions facing men below them who are reluctant to have women above them in line authority; being required to outproduce men conspicuously; and facing problems of coming home to the old domestic household chores, while their husbands sit back and relax.[18] In teaching, one of the original fields for women, the hierarchal system of power is one where males predominate as principals and superintendents; where women are relegated mostly to the elementary grades where the compensation and entry requirements are lower than the secondary schools. In higher education, again the needs of childbirth, child care, and homemaking create interruptions in seeking the doctorate degree, the key credential for professorships; in pursuing publication and research, the *de facto* considerations for the granting of tenure and promotion. The result has been a disproportionate number of women in the positions of lecturers and adjunct professors without job security, health and other fringe benefits, or adequate compensation.

The chief challenges in changing the work status of women in a decided and basic direction of equality include: employer and public supported child care of professional quality for children of working parents; expansion of preschool public education coupled with professional facilities for after-school child care; parental leave offering both father and mothers opportunities for home infant and child tending; increasing opportunities for women to gain entry into skilled trades and nontraditional jobs; expansion of the number of women executives in corporations and government; job availability and training opportunities, particularly for economically disadvantaged and middle age minority women enabling them to get out of menial and dead-end jobs; monitoring the effect of technology on clerical jobs; and securing flexible work schedules.

WHAT OF THE FUTURE?

The woman's rights movement remains a continuum of struggle with a big unfinished agenda. The implications of this societal tremblor go far beyond the simplistic concept of men versus women. The cultural baggage of centuries of patriarchal institutional arrangements have to be put aside, but cultural inertia inhibits movement in every such direction. The social costs are enormous, but they will have to be met. The permanent entry of women in the work force, where their work is needed and they vitally require the necessary compensation, presents women as having the roles of coequal partners with men. This is the material economic basis for deep-seated societal change. It is the foundation for associative political and social consciousness on the part of society.

The increased role of men in the local and regional leadership and direction of NOW can enlarge the population of supporters of woman's rights. Reaching out to women and men in working- and middle-class ethnic and religious groups by addressing basic economic and material concerns can broaden the consensus of public support. As great as the gains have been in legislation, consciousness, and linguistics, the fundamental fact of woman's low status requires the woman's rights movement to develop the necessary strategy and tactics of a broadly based movement which avoids the narrower issues, no matter how appealing they may be to the vanguard of the woman's rights leadership. The key cadres of the movement must recognize the danger of a narcissistic attachment to the organization as an end in and of itself.

It is time to listen to supportive and constructive critics and avoid, in this time of slow movement, the polarization of this great driving force into contentious factions reading each other out of the struggle for woman's rights.[19] When the next swing of the societal pendulum veers toward reform, the campaign of women for complete equality with men must be the product of preparation to succeed. In that success, society will approach realizing the goal of a humanity where all women, men, and children can realize their fullest potential.

The woman's rights movement has a history. The study of the dynamics of this drive for equality between man and woman is an inherent part of the struggle itself. The paths of societal reform blazed by Susan B. Anthony, Elizabeth Cady Stanton, and Lucy Stone have developed into broad highways marked by the milestones of the transformation of ladies into women.

NOTES

CHAPTER 1

1. Harvey Wish, *Society and Thought in Early America* (New York: David McKay Company, 1950), p. 416.

2. Belle Squire, *The Woman Movement in America* (Chicago: A.C. McClurg, 1911), pp. 34–35.

3. Andrew A. Sinclair, *The Better Half: The Emancipation of the American Woman* (New York: Harper & Row, 1965), p. 22.

4. Sidney Ditzion, *Marriage, Morals and Sex in America* (New York: Bookman Associates, 1953), p. 16.

5. Ibid., pp. 14–15.

6. Ibid., pp. 35–48.

7. Ibid., pp. 23–24.

8. Philip Foner, *The Complete Writings of Thomas Paine*, 2 vols. (New York: Citadel Press, 1945), 2:1119.

9. Ibid., pp. 1115–1118.

10. Ibid., pp. 34–38.

11. Squire, *The Woman Movement*, p. 41.

12. Page Smith, *A New Age Now Begins: A People's History of the American Revolution*, 2 vols. (New York: McGraw-Hill, 1976), 2:1810.

13. Barbara Mayer Wertheimer, *We Were There: The Story of Working Women in America* (New York: Pantheon Books, 1977), pp. 42–43.

14. Susan B. Anthony, Elizabeth C. Stanton, and Matilda J. Gage, *History of Woman Suffrage*, 6 vols. (New York: Fowler and Wells, 1881–1922), 1:32.

15. Smith, *A New Age*, pp. 1808–1809.

16. Ibid., p. 1809.

17. Inez Hayes Irwin, *Angels and Amazons* (New York: Doubleday Doran, 1933), p. 82.

18. Anthony, Stanton, and Gage, *History of Woman Suffrage*, 1:55.

19. Ibid., p. 59.

20. Ibid., p. 58.

21. Wertheimer, *We Were There*, pp. 103–104.

22. Henry Steele Commager, *Documents of American History*, 4th ed. (New York: Appleton-Century-Crofts, 1948), p. 315.

23. Eleanor Flexner, *Century of Struggle: The Woman's Rights Movement in the United States* (Cambridge, Mass.: Belknap Press, 1959), p. 77.

24. Irwin, *Angels and Amazons*, p. 71.

CHAPTER 2

1. Barbara Mayer Wertheimer, *We Were There: The Story of Working Women in America* (New York: Pantheon Books, 1977), pp. 8–11.

2. Quoted in Andrew A. Sinclair, *The Better Half: The Emancipation of the American Woman* (New York: Harper & Row, 1965), p. 14.

3. Wertheimer, *We Were There*, pp. 74–76.

4. Philip Foner, *Women and the American Labor Movement* (New York: The Free Press, 1979), p. 52, citing *Workingman's Advocate*, April 12, 1834.

5. Ibid., p. 72, citing *Voice of Industry*, June 13, 1847.

6. Helen L. Sumner, *History of Women in Industry in the U.S.*, Vol. 9 of Report of the United States Labor Bureau (Washington, D.C.: U.S. Government Printing Office, 1910–1911), p. 11.

7. Ibid., p. 12.

8. Ibid., p. 14.

9. J.B. Andrews and W.D.P. Bliss, *History of Women in Trade Unions*, Vol. 10 of Report of the United States Labor Bureau (Washington, D.C.: U.S. Government Printing Office 1910–1911), pp. 11–13.

10. Ibid.

11. Ibid., p. 23.

12. Inez Hayes Irwin, *Angels and Amazons* (New York: Doubleday Doran, 1933), p. 68.

13. Ibid.

14. Ibid.

15. Andrews and Bliss, *Women in Unions*, p. 16.

16. Ibid., p. 104.

17. Ibid., p. 105.

18. Ibid., p. 106.

19. Don D. Lescohier, *The Knights of St. Crispin*, Economics and Political Science Series, 7, No. 1 (Madison: University of Wisconsin, 1910), p. 28.

20. Barbara J. Berg, *The Remembered Gate: Origins of American Feminism, The Woman and the City, 1800–1860* (New York: Oxford University Press, 1978), chapter 4.

21. Barbara Welter, "The Cult of True Womanhood: 1820–1860," *American Quarterly* 18, (Summer 1966): pp. 151–174.

22. Irwin, *Angels and Amazons*, p. 54.

23. Lloyd Morris, *Incredible New York, 1850–1950* (New York: Random House, 1951), p. 82.

24. Ibid., p. 44.

25. Wertheimer, *We Were There*, p. 102.

26. Morris, *New York*, p. 46.

27. Berg, *Remembered Gate*, p. 145.

28. Morris, *New York*, pp. 37–43.

29. Wertheimer, *We Were There*, pp. 132–144.

30. Eleanor Flexner, *Century of Struggle: The Woman's Movement in the United States* (Cambridge, Mass.: Belknap Press, 1959), p. 108.

PART TWO

1. William A. Dunning, *Reconstruction, Political and Economic* (New York: Harper and Brothers, 1907); and Claude G. Bowers, *The Tragic Era: The Revolution After Lincoln* (Cambridge, Mass.: Houghton Mifflin, 1929).

2. C. Vann Woodward, *Reunion and Reaction: The Compromise of 1877 and the End of Reconstruction* (New York: Doubleday, 1956); Kenneth M. Stampp, *The Era of Reconstruction, 1865–1877* (New York: Random House, 1965); John Hope Franklin, *Reconstruction: After the Civil War* (Chicago: University of Chicago Press, 1961).

CHAPTER 4

1. Henry Steele Commager, *Documents of American History*, 2 Vols. (New York: Appleton-Century-Crofts, 1948), 2:14.

2. Ida Husted Harper, *The Life and Work of Susan B. Anthony*, 3 vols. (Indianapolis: Bowen, Merrill, 1898–1908), 1:256.

3. Theodore Stanton and Harriet Stanton Blatch, *Elizabeth Cady Stanton, As Revealed in Her Letters, Diary, and Reminiscences*, 2 vols. (New York: Harper and Brothers, 1922). 2:108.

4. Harper, *Susan B. Anthony*, 1:250.

5. *New York World*, May 10, 1866.

6. Ibid., May 11, 1866.

7. Ibid.

8. National Woman's Rights Convention, May 1866, *Proceedings*, p.3.

9. Ibid.

10. Ibid., p. 62

11. Ibid., p. 63.

12. Ibid., p. 64.

13. Ibid.

14. Ibid.

15. Ibid., p. 65.

16. Ibid., p. 5.

17. Ibid., p. 10.

18. Carrie Chapman Catt and Nettie R. Shuler, *Woman Suffrage and Politics: The Inner Story of the Suffrage Movement* (New York: Charles Scribner and Sons, 1923), p. 39.

19. *Proceedings*, May 1866, pp. 24–26.

20. Ibid., p. 40.

21. Ibid., p. 43.
22. Ibid., p. 44.
23. Ibid., p. 46, 48.
24. Ibid., p. 6.
25. Ibid., p. 48.
26. Ibid., p. 48–49.

CHAPTER 5

1. *New York World*, May 11, 1866.
2. Ida Husted Harper, *The Life and Work of Susan B. Anthony*, 3 vols. (Indianapolis: Bowen, Merrill, 1898–1908), 2:264.
3. Woman's Rights Convention, 1866, *Proceedings*, p. 52.
4. Anna Davis Hallowell, *James and Lucretia Mott, Life and Letters* (Boston: Houghton Mifflin, 1896), p. 4l8.
5. Ibid., p. 4l9.
6. Woman's Rights Convention, *Proceedings*, pp. 52–53.
7. Ibid., p. 56.
8. Ibid., p. 57.
9. Susan B. Anthony, Elizabeth C. Stanton, and Matilda J. Gage, *History of Woman Suffrage*, 6 vols. (New York: Fowler and Wells, 1881–1922), 2:179.
10. *New York World*, October 11, 1866.
11. American Equal Rights Convention, *Proceedings of First Anniversary*, 1867, pp. 62–63.
12. Ibid., p. 4.
13. Ibid., p. 6.
14. Ibid., p. 9.
15. Ibid., p. 17.
16. Ibid., pp. 39–41.
17. Alice Stone Blackwell, *Lucy Stone* (Boston: Little, Brown and Company, 1930), p. 210.
18. American Equal Rights Association, *Proceedings*, p. 43.
19. Ibid., p. 49.
20. Ibid., p. 66.
21. Ibid., p. 52.
22. Ibid., p. 53.
23. Ibid.
24. Ibid.
25. Ibid.
26. Ibid.
27. Ibid., p. 54.
28. Ibid., p. 55.
29. Ibid., p. 58.
30. Ibid., p. 52.
31. Ibid.

CHAPTER 6

1. *New York World*, January 24, 1867.
2. Ibid.
3. Susan B. Anthony, Elizabeth C. Stanton, and Matilda J. Gage, *History of Woman Suffrage*, 6 vols. (New York: Fowler and Wells, 1881–1922), 2:287.
4. *New York Times*, June 29, 1867.
5. Carrie C. Catt and Nettie R. Shuler, *Woman Suffrage and Politics: The Inner Story of the Suffrage Movement* (New York: Charles Scribner and Sons, 1923), p. 56.
6. *New York World*, July 12, 1867.
7. Alice Stone Blackwell, *Lucy Stone* (Boston: Little, Brown and Company, 1930), p. 208.
8. Ida Husted Harper, *The Life and Work of Susan B. Anthony*, 3 vols. (Indianapolis: Bowen, Merrill, 1898–1908), 2:275.
9. Harper, *Anthony*, p. 275.
10. Ibid., p. 283.
11. *New York Times*, September 29, 1867.
12. Harper, *Anthony*, 2:287.
13. Blackwell, *Stone*, p. 209.
14. Anthony, Stanton, and Gage, *History*, 2:245.
15. Ibid., p. 247.
16. Ibid., p. 255.
17. Ibid., p. 265.
18. Ibid., p. 264.
19. Ibid., p. 267.
20. Ibid., p. 320.
21. George Francis Train, *The Great Epigram Campaign of Kansas: Championship of Woman* (Leavenworth, Kans.: Prescott and Hume, Daily Commercial Office, 1867), front cover.

CHAPTER 7

1. *Revolution*, May 14, 1868.
2. Ibid.
3. *New York Herald*, May 15, 1868.
4. Susan B. Anthony, Elizabeth C. Stanton, and Matilda J. Gage, *History of Woman Suffrage*, 6 vols. (New York: Fowler and Wells, 1881–1922), 2:310.
5. Ibid., p. 311
6. Ibid.
7. Ibid.
8. Ibid., p. 312.
9. *New York Herald*, May 15, 1868.
10. Ibid.
11. *New York World*, May 15, 1868.

12. Ida Husted Harper, *The Life and Work of Susan B. Anthony*, 3 vols. (Indianapolis: Bowen, Merrill, 1898–1908), 2:300.

13. Anthony, Stanton, and Gage, *History*, 2:309.

14. *Revolution*, July 2, 1868.

15. Ibid., July 9, 1868.

CHAPTER 8

1. Susan B. Anthony, Elizabeth C. Stanton, and Matilda J. Gage, *History of Woman Suffrage*, 6 vols. (New York: Fowler and Wells, 1881–1922), 2:345.

2. Ibid., p. 347.

3. Ibid., p. 349.

4. Ibid.

5. Ibid.

6. Ibid., pp. 350–351.

7. Ibid., p. 353.

8. Ibid., p. 358.

9. Ibid.

10. Ibid., p. 367.

11. Ibid., p. 357.

12. Ibid., p. 322.

13. Anthony, Stanton, and Gage, *History*, 2:391.

14. Ibid., pp. 383–384.

15. Anthony, Stanton, and Gage, *History*, 2:384-385.

16. *Revolution*, May 20, 1869.

17. Anthony, Stanton, and Gage, *History*, 2:389.

18. Ibid., p. 401.

19. *Revolution*, June 10, 1869.

20. Anthony, Stanton, and Gage, *History*, 2:403.

21. Ibid., p. 404.

22. *New York World*, August 27, 1869.

23. Ibid., June 2, 1869.

24. Ibid.

25. Anthony, Stanton, and Gage, *History*, 2:764.

26. *Revolution*, December 2, 1869.

27. *New York Times*, December 2, 1869.

CHAPTER 9

1. *Revolution*, December 16, 1869.

2. Susan B. Anthony, Elizabeth C. Stanton, and Matilda J. Gage, *History of Woman Suffrage*, 6 vols. (New York: Fowler and Wells, 1881–1922), 2:420.

3. *The Independent*, November 4, 1869.

4. *Revolution*, March 24, 1870.

5. Ibid., March 31, 1870.

6. *The Independent*, March 31, 1870.

7. Ibid.

8. Ibid.

9. *Woman's Journal*, April 9, 1870.

10. Ida Husted Harper, *The Life and Work of Susan B. Anthony*, 3 vols. (Indianapolis: Bowen, Merrill, 1898–1908), 2:347.

11. *Revolution*, April 14, 1870.

12. Ibid.

13. *Woman's Journal*, April 9, 1870.

14. *Revolution*, December 1, 1870.

15. Ibid.

16. Anthony, Stanton, and Gage, *History*, 2:428.

17. Ibid., p. 429.

18. Ibid., p. 435.

19. Ibid., p. 436.

20. Ibid., p. 437.

21. *New York Times*, October 22, 1870.

22. *New York Star*, October 21, 1870.

CHAPTER 10

1. *Woman's Journal*, January 8, 1870.

2. Ida Husted Harper, *The Life and Work of Susan B. Anthony*, 3 vols. (Indianapolis: Bowen, Merrill, 1898–1908), 2:353.

3. Ibid., p. 309.

4. *Revolution*, October 6, 1870.

5. Lloyd Morris, *Incredible New York: High Life and Low Life of the Last Hundred Years* (New York: Random House, 1951), p. 82.

6. Ibid.

7. Ibid.

8. *Woman's Journal*, October 22, 1870.

9. *Revolution*, October 27, 1870.

10. Emanie Sachs, *The Terrible Siren, Victoria Woodhull* (New York: Harper and Brothers, 1928).

11. Paxton Hibben, *Henry Ward Beecher* (New York: George H. Doran, 1927).

12. *Golden Age*, March 4, 1871.

13. Ibid., April 22, 1871.

14. Ibid.

15. Ibid., June 3, 1871.

16. *Woman's Journal*, citing *Golden Age*, August 19, 1871.

17. Ibid., August 19, 1871.

18. Ibid., September 2, 1871.

19. Ibid., March 4, 1871.

20. *Golden Age*, August 26, 1871.

21. Ibid., September 9, 1871.

22. Ibid., October 14, 1871.

23. Sidney Ditzion, *Marriage, Morals and Sex in America* (New York: Bookman Associates, 1953), p. 182.

24. *New York World*, November 21, 1871.

25. Ibid.

CHAPTER 11

1. Eugene A. Hecker, *A Short History of Women's Rights* (New York: G.P. Putnam and Sons, 1910), pp. 175–235.

2. Carrie C. Catt and Nettie R. Shuler, *Woman Suffrage and Politics: The Inner Story of the Suffrage Movement* (New York: Charles Scribner's Sons, 1923), p. 107.

3. Eleanor Flexner, *Century of Struggle: The Woman's Rights Movement in the United States* (Cambridge, Mass.: Belknap Press of Harvard University Press, 1959), p. 178.

4. Ida Husted Harper, *The Life and Work of Susan B. Anthony*, 3 vols. (Indianapolis: Bowen, Merrill, 1898–1908), 1:382.

5. *Woodhull and Claflin's Weekly*, February 25, 1871.

6. Ibid., March 4, 1871.

7. Ibid., March 11, 1871.

8. *Woman's Journal*, February 18, March 4, March 11, 1871.

9. *Woodhull and Claflin's Weekly*, December 16, 1871.

10. Susan B. Anthony, Elizabeth C. Stanton, and Matilda J. Gage, *History of Woman Suffrage*, 6 vols. (New York: Fowler and Wells, 1881–1922), 2:481.

11. Ibid., p. 495.

12. Ibid., p. 496.

13. Ibid., p. 497.

14. Flexner, *Century of Struggle*, pp. 164–168.

15. Harper, *Susan B. Anthony*, 1:305.

16. *Revolution*, June 4, 1868.

17. Harper, *Susan B. Anthony*, 2:304.

18. Anthony, Stanton, and Gage, *History*, 2:312.

19. *Revolution*, July 2, 1868.

20. Ibid.

21. Ibid.

22. Ibid., July 9, 1868.

23. *New York Herald*, July 7, 1868.

24. *New York Tribune*, July 7, 1868.

25. *The Evening Express*, July 6, 1868.

26. *New York Sun*, July 7, 1868.

27. *New York World*, July 7, 1868.

28. *New York Herald*, July 9, 1868.

29. *Revolution*, July 16, 1868.

30. National Labor Union, *Proceedings of Convention*, 1868, p.39.

31. *New York Herald*, September 28, 1868. The "wicked men of Water Street" was a tough, cut-throat waterfront gang used as "enforcers."

32. *Revolution*, August 22, 1868.

33. *New York World*, August 27, 1869.

34. *New York World*, May 13, 1871.

35. *New York Star*, May 13, 1871.

36. *New York World*, May 11, 1871.

37. Ibid.

38. *Golden Age*, September 9, 1871.

39. Harper, *Susan B. Anthony*, 2:416.
40. *Woman's Journal*, May 11, 1872.
41. *Golden Age*, May 11, 1872.
42. Ibid., June 8, 1872.
43. Katherine Devereaux Blake, *Champion of Woman* (New York: Fleming H. Revell Company, 1943), p. 93.
44. Emanie L. Sachs, *The Terrible Siren, Victoria Woodhull* (New York: Harper and Brothers, 1928), p. 156.
45. Harper, *Susan B. Anthony*, 2:413.
46. Anthony, Stanton, and Gage, *History*, 2:517.
47. Ibid.
48. *Golden Age*, April 27, 1872.
49. Ibid.
50. *New York World*, May 10, 1872.
51. Ibid.
52. *Woman's Journal*, May 18, 1872.
53. Ibid., June 15, 1872.
54. *Golden Age*, June 15, 1872.
55. *Woman's Journal*, June 22, 1872.
56. *New York World*, October 11, 1866.
57. Anthony, Stanton and Gage, *History*, 2:181.
58. *New York World*, November 7, 1866.
59. Ibid., May 11, 1872.
60. Ibid.
61. Ibid.
62. Flexner, *Century of Struggle*, p. 173.

CHAPTER 12

1. Eleanor Flexner, *Century of Struggle: The Woman's Rights Movement in the United States* (Cambridge, Mass.: Belknap Press of Harvard University Press, 1959), p. 352.
2. Theresa Wolfson, *The Woman Worker and the Trade Unions* (New York: International Publishers, 1927), p. 20.
3. Ibid., p. 21.
4. Ibid., pp. 55–56.
5. Ibid., p. 103 (citation without source).
6. George A. Stevens, *History of Typographical Union No.6* (Albany, N.Y.: J. B. Lyon and Company, 1913), p. 427.
7. *Revolution*, March 19, 1868.
8. *New York World*, October 20, 1868.
9. Alice Henry, *The Trade Union Woman* (New York: D. Appleton, 1915), p. 250.
10. Ibid., p. 252.
11. Ibid.
12. *Revolution*, April 21, 1868.
13. Ibid., April 9, 1868.
14. Ibid., January 8, 1868.

15. Ibid., February 19, 1868.
16. *New York World*, August 21, 1866.
17. John R. Commons, Ulrich B. Phillips, Eugene A. Gilmore, Helen L. Sumner, and John B. Andrews, *American Industrial Society*, 10 vols. (Cleveland: A. H. Clark, 1910–1911), 9:138.
18. *Congressional Globe*, Washington, D.C., 40 Congress, 1 session, 1867, 425.
19. Commons, *Documentary History*, 2:156.
20. Ibid., p. 174.
21. *Revolution*, July 2, 1868.
22. Ibid., July 9, 1868.
23. James Sylvis, *The Life, Speeches, Labors, and Essays of William H. Sylvis, Late President of the Iron Molders Union and Also of the National Labor Union* (Philadelphia: Claxton, Remsen, Heffelfinger, 1872), p. 72.
24. Ibid., p. 77.
25. Ibid., p. 337.
26. Ibid., p. 119–120.
27. Ibid., p. 220.
28. Ibid., p. 400.
29. Ibid., p. 222.
30. *Revolution*, August 20, 1868.
31. Ibid., September 3, 1868.
32. Ibid., September 17, 1868.
33. Ibid., September 24, 1868.
34. Ibid.
35. Ibid.
36. Ibid.
37. *New York World*, September 23, 1868.
38. Ibid.
39. *Proceedings*, N.L.U., 1868, pp. 19–20.
40. Commons, *Documentary History*, 2:127.
41. *New York Herald*, September 22, 1868.
42. *New York Herald*, September 25, 1868.
43. Ibid.
44. *Proceedings*, N.L.U., 1868, p. 7.
45. Ibid., pp. 24–25.
46. Ibid.
47. Ibid., p. 21.
48. Ibid., p. 51.
49. Ibid., p. 56.
50. *Revolution*, October 1, 1868.
51. *Proceedings*, N.L.U., 1868, p. 15.
52. *Revolution*, September 24, 1868.
53. Ibid., October 1, 1868.
54. Ibid.
55. Ibid.
56. Ibid.
57. Ibid., October 8, 1868.
58. Ibid.

59. Ibid.
60. Ibid., October 20, 1868.
61. *Revolution*, October 20, 1868.
62. Ibid., October 1, 1868.
63. Ibid.
64. Ibid.
65. *New York World*, October 7, 1868.
66. Ibid., October 16, 1868.
67. Ibid., October 19, 1868.
68. Ibid., November 11, 1868.
69. *New York World*, October 27, 1868.
70. Ibid., November 24, 1868.
71. Ibid., May 22, 1869.
72. Ibid., May 20, 1869.
73. Ibid., June 18, 1869.
74. Ibid., July 2, 1869.
75. Ibid.
76. Elinor Kirk, "Woman and Labor," *Packard's Monthly* (September 1869): 260–261.

CHAPTER 13

1. John R. Commons, Ulrich B. Phillips, Eugene A. Gilmore, Helen L. Sumner, and John B. Andrews, *Documentary History of American Industrial Society*, 10 vols. (Cleveland: A. H. Clark, 1910–1911), 2:130.
2. *New York World*, August 17, 1869.
3. Obadiah Hicks, *Richard F. Trevellick* (Joliet, Ill.: J. E. Williams and Company, 1896), p. 56.
4. New York Workingmen's Assembly, *Proceedings of Fifth Annual Session* (Albany, N.Y., 1869), p. 7.
5. George A. Stevens, *History of Typographical Union No. 6* (Albany, N.Y.: J. B. Lyon and Company, 1913), p. 434.
6. *Revolution*, February 4, 1869.
7. *New York World*, August 17, 1869.
8. Ibid., August 18, 1869.
9. Ibid.
10. Ibid.
11. Ibid.
12. Ibid.
13. Ibid.
14. Ibid.
15. Ibid.
16. Ibid.
17. Ibid.
18. Ibid., August 19, 1869.
19. Ibid.
20. Ibid.
21. Ibid., August 18, 1869.

22. Ibid., August 21, 1869.
23. *Revolution*, August 26, 1869.
24. Ibid.
25. Ibid., September 9, 1869.
26. Ibid.
27. Ibid., September 16, 1869.
28. Ida Husted Harper, *The Life and Work of Susan B. Anthony*, 3 vols. (Indianapolis: Bowen, Merrill, 1898–1908), 2:367.
29. *Revolution*, August 26, 1869.
30. Harper, *Anthony*, 2:367.
31. *Revolution*, September 23, 1869.
32. *Woman's Journal*, July 16, 1870.
33. Ibid., December 7, 1872.
34. *Revolution*, November 3, 1870.
35. *Woodhull and Claflin's Weekly*, March 9, 1872.
36. *Golden Age*, April 5, 1873.
37. Ibid., July 6, 1872.
38. *Workingman's Advocate*, February 12, 1870.
39. Ibid., May 7, 1870.
40. Ibid., October 22, 1870.
41. George A. Tracy, *History of the Typographical Union* (Indianapolis: International Typographical Union, 1913), pp. 254–266.
42. Stevens, *History of Typographical Union No. 6*, p. 437.
43. Richard F. Hinton, "Organization of Labor: Its Aggressive Phase", *Atlantic Monthly* 27 (May 1871): p. 557.
44. Philip S. Foner, *History of the Labor Movement in the United States* (New York: International Publishers, 1947), p. 431.
45. Tracy, *History of the Typographical Union*, p. 256.
46. *Woodhull and Claflin's Weekly*, February 18, 1871.
47. *Cincinnati Daily Gazette*, February 24, 1872.
48. Ibid.

CHAPTER 14

1. Ida Husted Harper, *The Life and Work of Susan B. Anthony*, 3 vols. (Indianapolis: Bowen, Merrill, 1898–1908), 1:275.
2. Ibid., p. 290.
3. *Revolution*, January 8, 1868.
4. Ibid.
5. Ibid., January 22, 1868, citing *The New York Times*.
6. Ibid., citing *The New York Citizen*.
7. Ibid., citing *The New York Sun*.
8. Ibid., citing *The New York World*.
9. Ibid., February 5, 1868, citing *Boston Daily and Weekly Voice*.
10. Ibid., February 19, 1868, citing *The Workingman's Advocate*.
11. Ibid.
12. Ibid., April 16, 1868, citing *The Dayton Workingman's Appeal*.
13. Ibid.

14. Ibid., May 28, 1868, *Coach-Makers International Journal.*

15. John R. Commons, Ulrich B. Phillips, Eugene A. Gilmore, Helen L. Sumner, and John B. Andrews, *Documentary History of American Industrial Society*, 10 vols. (Cleveland: A. H. Clark, 1910–1911), 9:216.

16. *Revolution*, January 29, 1868.

17. Ibid.

18. Ibid., January 15, 1868.

19. Ibid., January 22, 1868.

20. Ibid., January 9, 1869.

21. Ibid., May 6, 1869.

22. Ibid., May 13, 1869.

23. *Woodhull and Claflin's Weekly*, July 23, 1870.

24. Harper, *Life of Susan Anthony*, 1:363.

25. *Woman's Journal*, October 21, 1871.

26. Ibid., January 8, 1870.

27. Ibid.

28. Ibid., November 5, 1870.

29. *Woodhull and Claflin's Weekly*, September 3, 1870.

30. Ibid., May 14, 1870.

31. Ibid.

32. Ibid., February 25, 1871.

33. Ibid., March 11, 1871.

34. *Woman's Journal*, February 18, March 4, 11, 1872.

35. *New York World*, May 13, 1871.

36. *Woodhull and Claflin's Weekly*, March 4, 1871.

37. *New York Star*, May 13, 1871.

38. *New York World*, May 10, 1872.

PART THREE

1. William H. Chafe, *The American Woman: Her Changing Social, Economic, and Political Roles, 1920–70* (New York: Oxford University Press, 1972), p.5.

2. Ibid., p.233.

CHAPTER 15

1. Eleanor Flexner, *Century of Struggle: The Woman's Rights Movement in the United States* (Cambridge, Mass.: Belknap Press of Harvard University Press, 1959), p.173, citing Carrie Chapman Catt and Nettie Rogers Shuler, *Woman Suffrage and Politics* (New York: Charles Scribner's Sons, 1923), p. 107.

2. Ibid., pp. 221–222.

3. Barbara Mayer Wertheimer, *We Were There: The Story of Working Women in America* (New York: Pantheon Books, 1977), p. 177.

4. Flexner, *Century of Struggle*, p. 372.

5. Mimi Grand-Jean Crowell, "Feminism and Modern Psychoanalysis: A Response to Feminist Critics of Psychoanalysis," *Modern Psychoanalysis*, 6, no. 2 (1981): pp. 221–235.

6. Betty Friedan, *The Feminine Mystique* (New York: W. W. Norton and Company, 1963).

7. Sharon Whitney, *The Equal Rights Amendment: The History and the Movement* (New York: Franklin Watts, 1984), p. 21.

8. Ibid., p. 19.

9. Wertheimer, *We Were There*, p. 376.

10. Whitney, *Equal Rights Amendment*, p. 29.

11. Ibid., p. 82.

12. Marlene Dixon, "Why Women's Liberation," *Ramparts*, 8 (December 1969), reprinted in Thomas R. Frazier, ed., *The Underside of America History, Volume 2: Since 1865* (New York: Harcourt Brace Jovanovich), p. 294.

13. Betty Friedan, "How to Get the Women's Movement Moving Again," *New York Times Magazine*, November 3, 1985.

14. Lenore J. Weitzman, *The Divorce Revolution: The Unexpected Social and Economic Consequences for Women and Children in America* (New York: The Free Press, 1986).

15. *New York Times*, October 3, 1985.

16. U.S. Department of Labor, Women's Bureau, *20 Facts on Women Workers*, 1984, and *Facts on U.S. Working Women*, Fact Sheet No. 85–7, July, 1985.

17. Ibid.

18. Helen Rogan, "Top Women Executives Find Path To Power Is Strewn With Hurdles," *Wall Street Journal*, October 25, 1984.

19. Sylvia Ann Hewlitt, *A Lesser Life: The Myth of Women's Liberation in America* (New York: William Morrow, 1986).

SELECTED BIBLIOGRAPHY

BOOKS, PAMPHLETS, AND REPORTS

Abbott, Edith. *Women in Industry*. New York: D. Appleton & Co., 1910.

American Equal Rights Association. *Proceedings of 1st Anniversary*. New York: R. J. Johnson, 1867.

Anthony, Susan B., Stanton, Elizabeth C., and Gage, Matilda J. *History of Woman Suffrage*, 6 vols. New York: Fowler and Wells, 1881 1922.

Banner, Lois. *Women in Modern America: A Brief History*. New York: Harcourt, Brace, Jovanovich, Inc., 1974.

Beard, Mary R. *A Short History of the American Labor Movement*. New York: Harcourt, Brace and Co., 1920.

Berg, Barbara J. *The Remembered Gate: Origins of American Feminism, The Woman and the City, 1800–1860*. New York: Oxford University Press, Inc., 1978.

Bimba, Anthony. *The History of the American Working Class*. New York: International Publishers, 1927.

Blackwell, Alice Stone. *Lucy Stone*. Boston: Little, Brown and Company, 1930.

Blake, Katherine Devereaux. *Champion of Woman*. New York: Fleming H. Revell Company, 1943.

Campbell, John T. *The Great Problem of the Age: An Address on Labor Reform, January 31, 1872*. Philadelphia: Labor Tribune, 1872.

Carlton, Frank T. *The History and Problems of Organized Labor*. Boston: D. C. Heath and Company, 1911.

Catt, Carrie C., and Shuler, Nettie R. *Woman Suffrage and Politics: The Inner Story of the Suffrage Movement*. New York: Charles Scribner and Sons, 1923.

Chafe, William H. *The American Woman: Her Changing Social, Economic and Political Roles, 1920–70*. New York: Oxford University Press, 1972.

Claflin, Tennie C. *Constitutional Equality: A Right of Woman*. New York: Woodhull and Claflin, 1871.

Commager, Henry S. *Documents of American History*. New York: Appleton, Century, Crofts, Inc., 1948.

Commons, John R., David J. Saposs, Helen L. Sumner, E. B. Mittelman, H. E. Hoagland, John B. Andrews, and Selig Perlman. *History of Labor in the United States*. 4 Vols. New York: The Macmillan Co., 1918-1935.

Commons, John R., Ulrich B. Phillips, Eugene A. Gilmore, Helen L. Sumner, and John B. Andrews. *Documentary History of American Industrial Society*. 10 vols. Cleveland: A. H. Clark, 1910–1911.

Demos, John. *A Little Commonwealth: Family Life in Plymouth Colony*. New York: Oxford University Press, Inc., 1970.

Ditzion, Sidney. *Marriage, Morals, and Sex in America*. New York: Bookman Associates, 1953.

Dubois, Ellen Carol. *Feminism and Suffrage: The Emergence of an Independent Women's Movement in America, 1848–1869*. Ithaca, N.Y.: Cornell University Press, 1978.

Faulkner, Harold U. *American Political and Social History*. New York: F. S. Crofts and Co., 1943.

Fine, Nathan, *Labor and Farmer Parties in the United States (1828–1928)*. New York: Rand School Press, 1929.

Flexner, Eleanor. *Century of Struggle: The Woman's Rights Movement in the United States*. Cambridge, Mass.: Belknap Press of Harvard University Press, 1959.

Foner, Philip S. *History of the Labor Movement in the United States*. New York: International Publishers, 1947.

Foner, Philip S. *Women and the American Labor Movement*. New York: The Free Press, 1979.

Franklin, John Hope. *Reconstruction: After the Civil War*. Chicago: University of Chicago Press, 1961.

Friedan, Betty. *The Feminine Mystique*. New York: W. W. Norton, 1963.

Grossman, Jonathan. *William Sylvis, Pioneer of American Labor*. New York: Columbia University Press, 1945.

Groves, Ernest R. *The American Woman: The Feminine Side of Masculine Civilization*. New York: Greenberg, 1937.

Hallowell, Anna Davis. *James and Lucretia Mott, Life and Letters*. New York: Houghton Mifflin and Co., 1896.

Harper, Ida Husted. *The Life and Work of Susan B. Anthony*. 3 vols. Indianapolis: Bowen, Merrill, 1898–1908.

Hecker, Eugene. *A Short History of Women's Rights*. New York: G. P. Putnam and Sons, 1910.

Henry, Alice. *The Trade Union Woman*. New York: D. Appleton, 1915.

Hewlitt, Sylvia Ann. *A Lesser Life, The Myth of Women's Liberation in America*. New York: William Morrow, 1986.

Hibben, Paxton. *Henry Ward Beecher*. New York: George Doran, 1923.

Hicks, Obadiah. *Richard F. Trevellick*. Joliet, Ill.: J. E. Williams and Company, 1896.

Irwin, Inez H. *Angels and Amazons: A Hundred Years of American Women*. New York: Doubleday, Doran and Co., 1933.

Kennedy, Susan Estabrook. *If All We Did Was to Weep at Home: A History of*

White Working Class Women in America. Bloomington: Indiana University Press, 1979.

Kessler-Harris, Alice. *Out to Work: A History of Wage-Earning Women in the U.S.* New York: Oxford University Press, 1982.

Lescohier, Don D. *The Knights of St. Crispin*. University of Wisconsin Economics and Political Science Series 7, No. 1. Madison: University of Wisconsin, 1910.

Lightner, Otto C. *The History of Business Depressions*. New York: Northeastern Press, 1922.

Livermore, Mary A. *The Story of My Life*. Hartford, Conn.: A. D. Worthington & Co., 1897.

McMahon, Theresa S. *Women and Economic Evolution: The Effects of Industrial Changes Upon the Status of Women*. Bulletin of the University of Wisconsin, No. 496, Economic and Political Science Series, VII, No.2, 1912.

National Labor Union. *Proceedings of the Session in Convention 2nd, 1868*. Philadelphia, 1868.

National Woman's Rights Convention. *Proceedings*. New York: 1866.

Nevins, Allan, ed. *The Diary of George Templeton Strong*. 4 vols. New York: The Macmillan Company, 1952.

Rayback, Joseph G. *A History of American Labor*. New York: The Macmillan Co., 1959, 1956.

Rosenberg, Rosalind. *Beyond Separate Spheres: Intellectual Roots of Modern Feminism*. New Haven, Conn.: Yale University Press, 1982.

Sachs, Emanie L. *The Terrible Siren, Victoria Woodhull*. New York: Harper and Brothers, 1928.

Schlesinger, Arthur Meier. *The Rise of the City, 1878–1898*, A History of American Life, Vol. 10. New York: The Macmillan Company, 1933.

Sinclair, Andrew A. *The Better Half: The Emancipation of the American Woman*. New York: Harper and Row, 1965.

Squire, Belle. *The Women Movement in America*. Chicago: A. C. McClurg, 1911.

Stammp, Kenneth M. *The Era of Reconstruction, 1865–1877*. New York: Random House, 1965.

Stanton, Theodore, and Blatch, Harriet Stanton. *Elizabeth Cady Stanton, As Revealed in Her Letters, Diary and Reminiscences*. 2 vols. New York: Harper and Brothers, 1922.

Stevens, George A. *History of Typographical Union No. 6*. Albany, N. Y.: J. B. Lyon and Co., 1913.

Sylvis, James. *The Life, Speeches, Labors, and Essays of William H. Sylvis, Late President of the Iron Molders and Also of the National Labor Union*. Philadelphia: Claxton, Remsen, Heffelfinger, 1872.

Todes, Charlotte. *William H. Sylvis and the National Labor Union*. New York: International Publishers, 1942.

Tracy, George A. *History of the Typographical Union*. Indianapolis: International Typographical Union, 1913.

Train, George Francis. *The Great Epigram Campaign of Kansas: Championship of Woman*. Leavenworth, Kans.: Prescott and Hume, 1867.

U.S. Commissioner of Labor. *Industrial Depressions, First Annual Report*. Washington, D.C.: Government Printing Office, 1910–1911.

U.S. Labor Bureau, *History of Women in Trade Unions*. Vol. 10 of Report of Bureau, ed. John B. Andrews and W.D.P. Bliss. Washington, D.C.: Government Printing Office, 1910–1911.

U.S. Labor Bureau. *History of Women in Industry in the United States*, Vol. 9 of Report of Bureau, ed. Helen L. Sumner. Washington, D.C.: Government Printing Office, 1910–1911.

Weitzman, Lenore J. *The Divorce Revolution: The Unexpected Social and Economic Consequences for Women and Children in America*. New York: Free Press, 1986.

Wertheimer, Barbara Mayer. *We Were There: The Story of Working Women in America*. New York: Pantheon Books, 1977.

Whitney, Sharon. *The Equal Rights Amendment: The History and the Movement*. New York: Franklin Watts, 1984.

Wolfson, Theresa. *The Woman Worker and the Trade Unions*. New York: International Publishers, 1927.

ARTICLES

Crowell, Mimi Grand-Jean. "Feminism and Modern Psychoanalysis: A Response to Feminist Critics of Psychoanalysis." *Modern Psychoanalysis*, 6, no. 2, (1981).

Dixon, Marlene. "Why Women's Liberation." *Ramparts*, 8 (December 1969).

Friedan, Betty. "How to Get the Women's Movement Moving Again." *New York Times Magazine*, November 3, 1985.

Hinton, Richard F. "Organization of Labor: Its Aggressive Phase." *Atlantic Monthly*, 27, no. 163 (May 1871).

Kirk, Elinor. "Woman and Labor." *Packard's Monthly*, 1 (September 1869).

Rogan, Helen. "Top Women Executives Find Path to Power Is Strewn with Hurdles." *Wall Street Journal*, October 25, 1984.

Welter, Barbara. "The Cult of True Womanhood, 1820–1860." *American Quarterly*, 18 (Summer 1966).

Women's Bureau, U.S. Department of Labor. *20 Facts on Women Workers*. 1984. *Facts on U.S. Working Women*. Fact Sheet No. 85–7. July, 1985.

SELECTED PERIODICALS

Cincinnati Daily Gazette. 1870, 1872.

Commercial and Financial Chronicle (New York). 1866, 1868, 1869, 1871, 1872.

Congressional Globe (Washington, D.C.) 1867, 1869.

Evening Express (New York). 1868.

Golden Age (New York). 1871, 1872, 1873.

Independent (New York). 1869, 1870, 1871.

New York Herald. 1868.

New York Star. 1870, 1871.

New York Sun. 1868.

New York Times. 1866, 1867, 1870, 1985.

New York Tribune. 1866, 1868.

New York World. 1866, 1867, 1868, 1869, 1870, 1871, 1873.

Revolution. 1868, 1869, 1870, 1871.
Woman's Journal. 1870, 1871, 1872.
Woodhull and Claflin's Weekly. 1870, 1871.
Workingman's Advocate. 1870, 1871.

INDEX

ABOUT THE AUTHOR

ISRAEL KUGLER is Professor Emeritus in Social Science at the City University of New York. His numerous articles have appeared in such journals as *Labor History*, *Midstream*, *Dissent*, and *The Journal of Educational Sociology*.